Wiltshire Record Society

(formerly the Records Branch of the Wiltshire
Archaeological and Natural History Society)

VOLUME 68

Oure most holy fadres the popes above specified, that is to say pope Innocent of blessed memory the [viij] And Alexandre the [vj] the pope that now is for the rest fulnes of this land have confermed decreed and ordeyned dyuers and many thynges as a lawe and ordinance specially to be observed, as by their bulles vnder leed more playnly appereth, the verray copies whereof bee above written. Of the which [ij] thynges here vnderwritten be to be had specially in remembraunce.

The first is, that the said most holy fadres certaynly knowyng and considryng that our souerayne lord kyng henry the [vij] is the treue and rightwous enheritour vnto the crown of England, of their owen mocion mere liberalite certayn knowlege And by the auctorite of the see apostolique. With the expres advise and consent of alle the holy college of Cardinalles, have declared decreed and establisshed, that alle such of the subiectes and inhabitauntz of reame of England as doo or wyll presume to moue or stirre, or cause or procure to be moued or stirred, any comocions or assemblees ayenst the kyng our said souerayne lord or his heyres, or any other colour or cause What so euer it be. Doo any thyng contrary to the peace tranquillite and restfulnes of our said souerayne lord his henryes or this his reame, falle in their so doyng into the feerful censures of the church and the dreadful peynes of the great curs. And not to be assoiled thereof by any other person than by the see apostolique, or by such as the kyng our said souerayne lord hath auctorite of the pope to depute in that behalue. Not withstondyng any other indulgence priuileges or grauntz to the contrary.

The second is that the forsaid most holy fadres by the said mocion knowlege and auctorite, haue geuen their blessyng to alle persons wheche prynces of other landes as the inhabitauntz within this land that serue help or socond our said souerayne lord kyng henry the [vij] and his heyres ayenst their rebelles or any other that wyll attempt any thyng ayenst hym or theom or their succession. And if it fortune any man to dye in the title or quarell of our said souerayne lord or any of his heyres, the said most holy fadres haue graunted vnto them plenary indulgence and remission of alle their synnes. The which promisses and dyuers other thynges them concernyng bee more atlarge conteyned in the above written copy of the said bulles autentiquely transsumed vnder the seale of the above said lord Cardinal Archbisshop of Canterbury And primate of Alle England.

Nos itaque Johannes Cardinalis et Archiepiscopus antedictus ex parte ipsius illustrissimi principis Domini viri regis instanter requisiti, vt omnia in prescriptis bullis apostolicis contenta per totam nostram prouinciam publicari faceremus, mature considerantes ipsam publicationem, huius domini regis subditis sublicam oportunam atque necessariam fore, ne in censuras ecclesiasticas in eisdem bullis contentas ignoranter incidant, venerabilibus confratri et cooperatori nostre ecclesie episcopis coprouincialibus omnibus et singulis, et absentium huiusmodi a personis sua fuerunt Auctoritate in sinodalibus generalibus ceteros et ecclesiarum prelatos tam seculares quam religiosos quibuslibet infra nostram prouinciam Cantuariensem constitutos, et supradictis plennius specificatos requirimus et auctoritate diocesana ipsorum monemus distincte precipiendo mandamus ipsis et eorum singulis oia prussia modo et forma superius in bullis constricta quater in Anno, viz in die cinerum in ramis palmarum Ac festis corporis popi omnis stori, et epiphanie in ecclesiis cathedralibus conuentualibus collegiatis et parrochialibus infra suas prouincias prouinciam Cantuariensem episcopi intra missarum et aliorum diuinorum solemnia cum maior in eisdem adest populi multitudo publicent Declarent et exponant.

English translation of the papal letter supporting the king's legitimacy, 1499.
(**309b** pp. 54–55)

THE REGISTER OF
JOHN BLYTH
BISHOP OF SALISBURY
1493–1499

edited by

DAVID WRIGHT

CHIPPENHAM

2015

ISBN 978-0-901333-45-2

*The Wiltshire Record Society gratefully acknowledges the continued
financial support of Wiltshire Council.*

Typeset by John Chandler
Produced for the Society by
Salisbury Printing Company Ltd, Salisbury
Printed in Great Britain

CONTENTS

PREFACE

I INITIALLY VENTURED from Cambridge to Salisbury to examine
the register of Thomas Langton, Blyth's predecessor as bishop of
Salisbury. The Diocesan Record Office was still housed in the cathedral
close in those days, and I struggled to concentrate on Langton's register
when through the open window, framed by climbing roses, I could
gaze uninterruptedly on the west front of Salisbury cathedral. Long
after the preparation of my edition of Langton's register, working
from microfilm, without distraction, and having retired from full-time
teaching, I turned to Blyth's register, which was on the same microfilm.
I am grateful to the late Miss Pamela Stewart, archivist of the former
Salisbury Diocesan Record Office, for the warmth of her welcome
and generosity of wisdom, and to her successors at the Wiltshire and
Swindon History Centre. Above all, I thank Steven Hobbs, General
Editor, for his inspired guidance and patient corrections, in supporting
this work and seeing it through to publication. For all imperfections
that remain, I am alone responsible.

David Wright

I wish to record my thanks to Jane Silcocks and Emily Naish for the
photographs, and to John Chandler for his invaluable assistance and
support.

General Editor

ABBREVIATIONS

ALibM	Master of Liberal Arts
archbp	archbishop
archdn	archdeacon
B	Archdeacon of Berkshire (inductor)
BA	Bachelor of Arts
BCL	Bachelor of Civil Law
BCnL	Bachelor of Canon Law
BC&CnL	Bachelor of Civil and Canon Law
BMus	Bachelor of Music
bp	bishop
BTh	Bachelor of Theology
BM, BVM	Blessed Mary, Blessed Virgin Mary
cath.	cathedral
ch.	parish church (rectory) unless otherwise indicated
chapl.	chaplain
cl.	clerk
coll.	college; collegiate
CPL	*Calendar of Papal Letters*
CPR	*Calendar of Patent Rolls*
D	Archdeacon of Dorset (inductor)
DCL	Doctor of Civil Law
DCnL	Doctor of Canon Law
DC&CnL	Doctor of Civil and Canon Law
dim.	having a letter dimissory
Dn	Dean of Salisbury (inductor)
dioc.	diocese
DTh	Doctor of Theology; *Sacrae Paginae Professor, Sacrae Theologiae Professor*
esq./esqs.	esquire/esquires, *armiger*
Fasti	Joyce Horn, *Fasti Ecclesiae Anglicanae 1300-1541 Salisbury Diocese* (University of London, 1962)
Fol./fol.	Folio
gent.	gentleman
ind.	inductor; induction
instal.	installed (in Salisbury cath.) by
kt/kts	knight/knights
LicCL	Licentiate in Civil Law
LicCnL	Licentiate in Canon Law
M.	Master
MA	Master of Arts

mand.	mandate
MD	Doctor of Medicine
Mon.	monastery
NP	Notary Public
OCarth	Carthusian order
OCist	Cistercian order
OClun	Cluniac order
OESA	Order of Augustinian Hermits
OFM	Franciscan order
OP	Dominican order
OPrem	Premonstratensian order
OSA	Augustinian order (canons)
OSB	Benedictine order
OTiron	Tiron order
OTrin	Trinitarian
p.a.	*per annum*
r.	rector/rector of
Reg. Langton	D.P. Wright, *The Register of Thomas Langton, Bishop of Salisbury, 1485-1493* (Canterbury and York Society, lxxiv, 1985)
res.	resignation
S	Archdeacon of Salisbury (inductor)
St/Sts	Saint/Saints
t.	title of sponsor of candidate for ordination
Tax. Eccl.	T. Astle, S. Ayscough, J. Caley, *Taxatio Ecclesiastica 1291* (The Record Commissioners, 1802)
TNA C 81, C 82	The National Archives, warrants for the Great Seal Series, Series II
v.	vicar/vicar of/vicarage
vac.	vacant
Valor Eccl.	J. Caley, *Valor Ecclesiasticus 1535*, vol 2 (The Record Commissioners, 1814)
VCH	*Victoria County History*
W	Archdeacon of Wiltshire (inductor)

Abbreviations appended to index numbers (ordination lists):

A	acolyte
D	deacon
E	exorcist
F	first tonsure
P	priest
S	subdeacon

INTRODUCTION

JOHN BLYTH

JOHN BLYTH (or Blith) was born c.1450.[1] His father was William Blyth of Norton, on the Derbyshire-Yorkshire border, and his mother was a sister of Thomas Rotherham, bishop of Rochester (1468-72), bishop of Lincoln (1472-80), and archbishop of York (1480-1500), from whom he received many preferments. A fellow of the King's Hall in the University of Cambridge 1476-7, subsequently pensioner 1478-80, and warden 1488-98, John Blyth was created DCL in 1485 and served as chancellor of the university 1494-96. He was ordained subdeacon in December 1479, and he was a deacon when, as archdeacon of Richmond, he received from archbishop Rotherham of York letters dimissory, dated 14 February 1486.[2] It may be assumed that he advanced to the priesthood soon afterwards.

Rotherham, while bishop of Lincoln, gave his nephew John Blyth the archdeaconry of Stow in 1477, and then the archdeaconry of Huntingdon in 1478, which he held until his promotion as bishop in 1494;[3] he also held a canonry in Lincoln cathedral with the prebend of Leighton Ecclesia 1482-5. Benefiting further from Rotherham's patronage after his uncle's translation to York, Blyth was a canon of York Minster, with the valuable prebend of Masham[4] 1484-94, and held the important office of archdeacon of Richmond 1485-94.[5] Henry VII promoted him to the bishopric of Salisbury by papal provision on 13 November 1493, and he was consecrated on 23 February 1494. He was installed in his cathedral church by proxy (**252**), and his first recorded presence in the diocese was on 8 July 1494 (**64**). He resided chiefly

---

1   Unless otherwise noted, all biographical detail is taken from the *New Oxford Dictionary of National Biography* or A.B. Emden's *A Biographical Register of the University of Cambridge to 1500*.

2   *Register of Thomas Rotherham, Archbishop of York 1480-1500*, Vol. I, No. 1686.

3   According to *Valor Eccl.* the archdeaconry of Stow was worth £28.2s.8½d., while that of Huntingdon was worth £57.14s.2d.

4   The *Valor Eccl.* return for Masham does not survive; however, in *Tax. Eccl.* it is valued at £166.13s.4d.

5   The *Valor Eccl.* return for the archdeaconry of Richmond does not survive; however, in *Tax. Eccl.* it is valued at £200. The combined income of the prebend of Masham and the archdeaconry of Richmond exceeded that of some bishoprics; most clerks were less fortunate in the accumulation of revenue from so few benefices.

at the episcopal manors at Ramsbury and Sonning. He advanced the fortunes of his younger brother Geoffrey, to whom he gave several benefices including – on the day before he died – the archdeaconry of Salisbury.[1] (Geoffrey Blyth became bishop of Coventry and Lichfield in 1503.) In 1496 the islands of Jersey and Guernsey were taken from the see of Coutances and added to that of Salisbury, but in 1499 they were incorporated in Winchester diocese.

On 5 May 1492 Blyth was appointed Master of the Rolls.[2] This was an office several times given to trained civilians who afterwards became bishops in the later middle ages, and like other such holders Blyth resigned it when he was consecrated to his see.[3] This appointment suggests involvement in government at this time, as does the fact that he was appointed to commissions of the peace for fifteen counties in the midlands in May 1493; however, from November 1494 he served only on the commissions for Berkshire, Dorset, and Wiltshire (counties in his diocese), and for the town of Cambridge. There is no evidence that he served the civil government of Henry VII in any capacity during his tenure of the bishopric of Salisbury.

He died on 23 August 1499, apparently suddenly or after a short illness,[4] and was buried behind the high altar of his cathedral church, beneath the confessional chair, being laid north and south, in a tomb which, according to Leland, was constructed for, but not used by, Bishop Richard Beauchamp.[5] Blyth was probably not yet fifty years

1   On 22 August 1499 he gave the archdeaconry of Salisbury and the prebend of
     Stratton to Geoffrey Blyth (**240, 241**), the prebend of Beminster Secunda to his
     registrar Robert Toneys (**242**), and the prebend of Axford, vacated by Toneys, to
     Hugo Peynthwyn (**243**). Peynthwyn was archdeacon of Canterbury and (probably)
     commissary general of the prerogative of Canterbury at the time; his presence
     suggests that Blyth's death was anticipated.
2   He was resident at the Domus Conversorum – of which the Master of the Rolls
     was *ex officio* Warden – when he was promoted to Salisbury.
3   Kathleen Edwards, in her chapter on the 'Cathedral of Salisbury' in *VCH Wilts*,
     Vol. 3, p. 14, writes: 'Right through the fifteenth century royal servants continued
     to find their way to Salisbury as bishops...John Blyth (1494-9) had also been a
     Chancery clerk....' However, Blyth can hardly be called a *career* civil servant, since
     this was his only known royal appointment, and he held it for a scant two years.
4   On 28 June 1499 he appointed proctors to visit Rome (**272**) – the obligatory *ad
     Limina* visit to which bishops had to commit themselves before their consecration;
     that he had apparently not visited Rome personally or by proxy during the first
     four years of his episcopate but now felt the need to take action just nine weeks
     before his death may suggest the onset of illness. However, he continued to preside
     over heresy trials during July and the first week of August.
5   'Bisshop Beauchamp had made afore a riche tumbe and a chapel over it at the
     west end of our Lady Chapelle, but one John Blith Bisshop of Sarum was after
     buried under it' (*Leland's Itinerary in England and Wales*, ed. Lucy Toulmin Smith,
     Vol. I, London, 1964, p. 264). This apparently refers not to Bishop Beauchamp's
     chantry chapel, which stood on the south flank of the Lady Chapel until swept

old and had not prepared a tomb for himself. Blyth's will, made on the day of his death and proved one month later, does not survive. Thus the tantalising insights into the testator's personality that a will often provides are unavailable for Blyth.

Ordination lists survive (**385-402**) for eighteen of the possible thirty-three canonical dates during Blyth's tenure of the see.[1] In all but two (**398-399**) Blyth's suffragan, Augustine Church, titular bishop of Lydda *in partibus infidelibus*, otherwise abbot of Thame, presided. In April 1496 he instructed the archdeacon of Salisbury to enforce residence of all clergy in his archdeaconry (**255**), but no deprivations subsequent to this mandate are recorded in his register.[2] His itinerary records his presence in monastic houses from time to time (Wilton, Cerne, Shaftesbury, Sherborne, Edington, Abingdon, Lacock, Reading), but there is no evidence of his conducting any formal visitations. From March to August 1499, on thirteen dates, Blyth presided over a series of heresy trials at Reading, Sonning, and Ramsbury (**319-347**),[3] but the proceedings afford no insight into Blyth's character. Six monastic heads changed during Blyth's episcopate, four by canonical election and two by collation, the patronage falling to the bishop by lapse of three months or more; however, even in the latter two cases there is no indication of positive episcopal initiative.[4] Otherwise he left little impression on his diocese, retaining the officials of his predecessor and leaving the day-to-day administration to those officials. Nothing out of the ordinary is to be found in his register, though one document is of seminal importance to the history of Henry VII's reign and has not heretofore been published elsewhere.

Having despatched the first Cornish uprising at Blackheath in

---

away by Wyatt during his 'restoration' (1789-92), because this observation *follows* Leland's account of Bishop Beauchamp's chantry and who, apart from Beauchamp himself, was buried therein. Blyth's body now reposes in a tomb chest, with a recumbent effigy, in the north transept.

1   It is not possible to conclude from internal evidence that ordinations took place on any of the other canonical dates but have not been registered.

2   In February 1495 he instituted to a benefice vacated by deprivation in the archdeaconry of Berkshire.

3   22 persons were prosecuted and abjured. Archbishop Morton's register of *sede vacante* administration records one other case, involving the rector of Letcombe Basset and the chaplain of Sparsholt, heard by the Official of the Consistory (Laurence Cockys), starting on 29 June (when the abjurations were made, and finishing with the imposition of sentences on 2 November 1499 (*The Register of John Morton, Archbishop of Canterbury, 1486-1500*, ed. Christopher Harper-Bill, Vol. II, Canterbury and York Society, 1991, pp. 158-160).

4   At Cerne the abbot died 22 April 1497, and the royal licence to elect was granted 11 May but not delivered until 4 July 1497; even given this inexplicable delay, there was still time for an election to be held. That this was not done raises suspicion that all was not well at Cerne.

June 1497, and swept aside the second – and captured Perkin Warbeck – in September 1497, Henry VII began to take steps to eliminate once and for all the threat to his kingship, culminating in the execution of Warbeck and the Earl of Warwick in 1499. Henry obtained from pope Alexander VI letters confirming letters of his predecessor Innocent VIII proclaiming *de facto* excommunication and greater anathema on anyone who questions the king's legitimacy. Henry had the text of these papal letters translated into English and reduced so that it could be sent to all parishes in the country and propounded by the clergy in the vulgar tongue. This process began in late November 1498 (**306-311**). The English text (**309b**) is an important source which has not appeared in print before. The campaign was meticulously detailed; for example, Blyth had to certify to Archbishop Morton that he had sent his registrar to London to collect the 150 copies of the English translation, duly transcribed and notarised, for the Salisbury diocese, and that they had been published throughout the diocese (**311**). Indeed, Morton ordered that they be published four times a year in perpetuity (**310**).

Just as Blyth had benefited from the patronage of his uncle Thomas Rotherham, likewise he proved a notable nepotist. He collated to his younger brother Geoffrey Blyth the Treasurership of Salisbury cathedral, and the prebend of Calne annexed thereto, in November 1494 (**81**).[1] In March 1495 Geoffrey exchanged the Treasurership for the prebend of Chisenbury and Chute, the rectory of Corfe Castle, and the Wardenship of St Nicholas Hospital, Salisbury (**97-99**). And in August 1499 the bishop gave his brother the Archdeaconry of Salisbury and the prebend of Stratton in Salisbury cathedral (**240-241**). The bishop collated to his namesake John Blyth the free chapel of Chisbury St Martin in 1497 (**152**); this John Blyth, who may or may not have been related to the bishop, was also presented to the free chapel of Haxton in 1498 (**194**).

THE REGISTER

BISHOP BLYTH's register[2] consists of 114 parchment folios, measuring 36x25cm., bound in hide-covered boards with paper flyleaves.[3]

---

1   Geoffrey Blyth had been a canon of Beverley and prebendary of St Michael's altar, which he resigned when he obtained the prebend of Strensall in York Minster in April 1493, and shortly thereafter the archdeaconry of Cleveland; he was also rector of Headon in Nottinghamshire. The first three of these benefices were in the gift of his uncle Thomas Rotherham, Archbishop of York; the patron of Headon was the Sub-Dean of York Minster.
2   The register is held at Wiltshire and Swindon History Centre (D1/2/13)
3   There are no folios 8-9 or 68 – fol. 67ᵛ is numbered 68; so the numbering of the

There are the usual three divisions: Institutions (fols 1-7 and 10-34);[1] Miscellaneous Memoranda (fols. 35-101); and Ordination lists (fols. 102-117).[2] The bishop's registrar was M. Robert Toneys BCL, NP; he identifies himself repeatedly (e.g., **320**, **322**, **324**), and his elaborate sign-manual occurs at **380** and **384**:

The accounts of the monastic elections at Abingdon (**352-355**), Abbotsbury (**356-364**), and Shaftesbury (**365-368**) are full of detail, some of it repetitive and some of it engaging. For example, at Abingdon the form of the citation of monks to attend the election suggests that one of their number had run away from the monastery, though it is not clear how long he had been gone (**352, 352n**). At Shaftesbury the election had to be delayed twice, the first time for an unspecified reason and the second because the nuns had misplaced the royal licence to elect (**365**). Also at Shaftesbury some of the proceedings were conducted in English, perhaps suggesting that not all of the nuns were literate in Latin (**365**). These are tantalisingly colourful glimpses of monastic life at the end of the fifteenth century. What happened at Cerne to result in the collation of the abbatial dignity by the bishop because of lapse remains a mystery: the old abbot died 22 April and was buried 24 April 1497, and one week later the prior and monks petitioned the king for licence to elect a successor. This was granted 11 May but curiously not delivered (under the Great Seal) until 4 July 1497. This is an unaccountable delay, but it still allowed enough time for the chapter to elect before the elapse of three months, after which the burden fell on the bishop (**372, 372n**). Clearly not all was well at Broomhall either (**375, 375n**), but precisely what the irregularity was is not revealed. Finally, these monastic elections indicate that numbers of vocations were holding up well in the greater houses such as Abingdon (where 26 monks took part in the election), Abbotsbury (12), and Shaftesbury (25), while some of the smaller houses such as Poughley were in trouble and ripe for dissolution – *not* the dissolution by the state but rather by the Church – the fruits often passing to academic institutions.

The heresy abjurations (**319-347**) follow on from those during the episcopate of Thomas Langton,[3] albeit after an interval of nearly

---

folios runs from 1 to 117.

1 Institutions by the vicar-general M. Laurence Cockys occupy fols. 1-7, those by the bishop fols. 10-34. A place index of institutions is to be found on fols 44^r-45^r.

2 Fol. 117^v is a list of benefices in the gift of Sir William Herbert.

3 *Reg. Langton*, **419-20, 459-60, 476, 484-504**.

eight years.[1] In 1499 heretics were detected at Reading, Hungerford, and mostly in the vicinity of Wantage and Faringdon. There is no evidence of the existence of a list of topics for the interrogation of the accused,[2] but most of the abjurations follow loosely the following pattern:

(1) keeping company with known heretics and welcoming them into their houses instead of detecting them; mention of heretical books;

(2) denial of Real Presence in the Sacrament of the Altar; reception of the sacrament without right belief;

(3) denial of efficacy of pilgrimages and offerings; money better spent on relief of the poor;

(4) against the worship of images, especially the crucifix, the Blessed Virgin Mary, and other saints, calling this idolatry; offerings ought not to be made;

(5) curses/indulgences of the pope and/or prelates/priests void; the pope is Antichrist and priests his disciples;

(6) against fasts, days of abstinence, against offerings/tithes.

Two of the accused mentioned 'our sect' and one other asserted the priesthood of all believers.

Perhaps the most interesting case is that which is not recorded in Blyth's register but in the *sede vacante* register of Archbishop Morton,[3] though it began in Blyth's lifetime, on 29 June 1499 before M. Laurence Cockys; however, the abjuration and imposition of penance did not take place until 2 November 1499, again before Cockys, whom Morton re-appointed as Official during the vacancy of the see.[4] John Whitehorne, rector of Letcombe Basset, and John Lydtister, chaplain of Sparsholt, admitted denial of Real Presence in the Sacrament of the Altar, Whitehorne going considerably further in his assertion that Christ's words of Institution referred not to the bread that he broke but to God's Word, as in the beginning of St John's Gospel. Whitehorne also denied the efficacy of confession to a priest, asserted that the crucifix and images of the Blessed Virgin Mary and other saints ought not to be worshipped or offerings made to them, denied the value of

---

1 Some continuity was perhaps provided by M. Laurence Cockys, Langton's chancellor (kept on in that post by Blyth) who was present or presided at many of the abjurations during Langton's episcopate (*Reg.* Langton, **460, 485, 487, 493, 494, 496, 500, 502**); however, the only case over which Cockys presided during Blyth's episcopate was recorded not in Blyth's register but in Morton's *sede vacante* register (*op. cit.*, **549**). Langton's registrar M. John Wely had also present, but he moved with bishop Langton to Winchester.

2 But there is some evidence that the registrar copied the formulaic beginning and ending of each abjuration from the preceding text (**342n**).

3 *Register of John Morton, op.cit.*, **549–551**.

4 *Register of John Morton, op.cit.*, **511**.

pilgrimages, asserted that the pope is Antichrist and other ministers of the Church his disciples, asserted the priesthood of all believers, and denied the effectiveness of the curses and sentences of the Church. Whitehorne also possessed prohibited books, certain of which were to be suspended around his neck while doing the penance imposed on him, at the end of which Whitehorne was to cast those books into the fire. Perhaps surprisingly, there is no notice of the de-frocking of either Whitehorne or Lydtister.[1]

The fact that Blyth chose not to preside over the abjurations of the two clergy is inexplicable from the evidence available. Perhaps he was already ill (he did not leave Ramsbury after 30 March 1499; but he could very well have summoned the clerics to Ramsbury where he presided over all the other abjurations). Blyth was assisted at the abjurations by two or three clergy recorded as witnesses. M. Edmund Crome DTh (**320, 324, 327, 339, 341, 343, 345, 347**) was a canon of Salisbury cathedral and previously a fellow of Caius College, Cambridge. M. John Pykeryng BCnL (**322, 324, 327, 329, 331, 333, 335, 343**), also a Cambridge man, was a canon of St Paul's, London. M. John Foted BTh (**324, 329, 331, 333, 339, 347**), Blyth's receiver-general (**245**), was Master of Michaelhouse, Cambridge.

During Blyth's episcopate, 248 institutions were made, some benefices figuring more than once in this total. 106 livings were vacant because of the death of the incumbent, and 129 because of resignation or exchange (including one deprivation); the cause of the vacancy in thirteen instances is unrecorded. Ten or eleven benefices were encumbered with the provision of a pension for the last holder, amounting to 7-8% of the benefices vacated by some cause other than death.[2] Using the *Valor Ecclesiasticus* (1535) valuations, we can see that in only one instance among the 10/11 benefices cumbered with pensions was the benefice impoverished by the granting of a pension to the resigned holder (see Table I: Pensions).

EDITORIAL PRACTICE

ALL ENTRIES in the register have been assigned consecutive numbers and are normally given in calendar form, apart from entries in English, chiefly the heresy abjurations, which are recorded in full.

1 Whitehorn came before Bishop Audley in 1508, accused of possessing Scriptures in English, and of exchanging heretical books with others. He admitted the charges and was degraded and handed over to the bailiff of Abingdon for burning (Anne Hudson, *The Premature Reformation*, Oxford, 1988, p. 468).
2 These statistics (recorded very slightly differently) are discussed in the introduction to *Reg. Langton*, where the point is made that such pensions were rather rare than 'extremely common' and hardly worsening the financial plight of the parish priest.

All dates between 1 January and 24 March have been altered to new style. Place names are given in their modern form, but variant forms occurring in the manuscript are preserved only in the index, except in the case of uncertainty of identification. Surnames are given as in the manuscript and variants brought together also in the index. Some Christian names of ambiguous modern forms, such as Hugo/Hugh or Johanna/Joanna/Joan, are recorded as in the manuscript. In literal transcripts all abbreviations have been expanded to the commonest occurring form; for example, the symbol for '-s', '-es', '-is', or '-ys' has always been rendered '-ys'. Academic degrees are given in the forms preferred by Emden.[1]

---

1   Emden, *Cambridge*, pp. xxviii–xxix.

ITINERARY OF JOHN BLYTH,
BISHOP OF SALISBURY 1493–1499

(All references are to his register as bp of Salisbury, unless otherwise stated.)

Petition from Edward Cheyne, dean, and the chapter of Salisbury cath, to elect a successor to Thomas Langton, translated to Winchester, dated Salisbury, 3 July 1493; bearers M. William Russell and M. John Bostok (TNA C 82/114/6). Licence to elect, 16 November 1493, signed by Purde; delivered 20 November 1493 (TNA C 82/114/5[145]; *CPR, Henry VII, 1485-1494*, p. 454). Petition (English) and grant to John Blythe, clerk and counsellor, Keeper of the Rolls, of the income from the farm of the temporalities of the bishopric of Salisbury by the dean and chapter of Salisbury cath., and of knights fees, advowsons, etc., from the vacation by the translation of Thomas Langton to Winchester, undated, by the king; delivered 18 November 1493 (TNA C 82/114/11(26); *CPR, Henry VII, 1485-1494*, p. 451). Papal provision of John Blyth to Salisbury, 13 November 1493 (TNA SC 7/37/21; *CPL, Vol. XVI, Alexander VI 1492-98*, 1092). Mandate (English) for restitution of temporalities of Salisbury, to M. John Blyth, counsellor, on receipt this day of the papal bull (enclosed) preferring him to that see in succession to Thomas Langton, translated to Winchester, 21 December 1493, signed by Bele; no delivery date (TNA C 82/115/23[111]; delivered 22 December 1493 (*CPR, Henry VII, 1485-1494*, p. 455). Royal grant (English) to John Kyte of the pension which the next bp of Salisbury is bound to give a clerk at the king's nomination until he be preferred by that bp. to a competent benefice, 13 December 1493, signed by Bele; delivered 29 April 1494 (TNA C 82/115/15[105]).[1] Consecration at Lambeth, 23 February 1494.

1493

31 Dec.	London: Domus Conversorum[2] 244

1494

19 Jan.	London: Domus Conversorum 55, 56
30 Jan.	London: Domus Conversorum 54

---

1   Kyte was collated to Boscombe ch. on 16 April 1499 (233).
2   The house, subsequently known as the Rolls, annexed to the office of Keeper or Master of the Rolls.

11 Feb.	London: Domus Conversorum	57
20 Feb.	London: St Bride's	253
23 Feb.	Lambeth	
28 Feb.	London: Domus Conversorum	249
7 Mar.	London: Fleet Street[1]	58
8 Mar.	London: Fleet Street	59, 251
14 Mar.	London: Fleet Street	60
20 Mar.		
23 Mar.	London: Fleet Street	252
12 May	London: Fleet Street	61
5 June	London: Fleet Street	62
13 June	London: Fleet Street	63
8 July	Ramsbury	64
9 July	Ramsbury	65
28 July	Ramsbury	66
22 Aug.	Ramsbury	67
2 Sep.	Salisbury: The Close	68
4 Sep.	Wilton Abbey	69, 70
8 Sep.	Cerne Abbey	71
14 Sep.	Sherborne Castle	72
15 Sep.	Sherborne Castle	73
17 Sep.	Shaftesbury Abbey	74, 75, 76
18 Sep.	Shaftesbury Abbey	77
22 Sep.	Edington	78
3 Oct.	Ramsbury	79
4 Oct.	Ramsbury	80
1 Nov.	London: Fleet Street	81
9 Nov.	London: Fleet Street	82
26 Nov.	London: Fleet Street	83
27 Nov.	London: Fleet Street	84
11 Dec.	Ramsbury	85
13 Dec.	Ramsbury	86
16 Dec.	Ramsbury	87
19 Dec.	Ramsbury	88
24 Dec.	Ramsbury	89
27 Dec.	Ramsbury	90

1495

16 Feb.	London: Fleet Street	91
21 Feb.	London: Fleet Street	92, 93
28 Feb.	Ramsbury	94
2 Mar.	Ramsbury	95
4 Mar.	Ramsbury	96
5 Mar.	Ramsbury	97, 98, 99

1   The bp. of Salisbury's London residence, where famously Prince Henry was betrothed to Catherine of Aragon in 1503, was on the south side of Fleet Street on the site today known as Salisbury Square.

13 Mar.	Ramsbury	100
18 Mar.	Ramsbury	101
21 Mar.	Ramsbury	102
30 Mar.	Ramsbury	103
2 Apr.	Ramsbury	104
25 Apr.	Ramsbury	105
6 June	Ramsbury	106
24 June	Ramsbury	270
30 July	Ramsbury	107
9 Aug.	Ramsbury	108
14 Aug.	Ramsbury	109, 254
20 Aug.	Ramsbury	110
26 Aug.	Ramsbury	111
2 Sep.	Ramsbury	112
15 Sep.	Sonning	113
18 Sep.	Sonning	115
24 Sep.	Sonning	114
5 Oct.	Sonning	348
6 Oct.	Sonning	116
10 Oct.	Sonning	256

Parliament met at Westminster 14 Oct.-22 Dec.
Convocation met at St Paul's 19 Oct.-21 Dec.

22 Oct.	London: Fleet Street	117
24 Oct.	London: Fleet Street	118
25 Oct.	London: Fleet Street	257
28 Oct.	London: Fleet Street	119
29 Oct.	London: Fleet Street	120, 121
7 Nov.	London: Fleet Street	122
17 Nov.	London: Fleet Street	123
23 Nov.	London: Fleet Street	124
12 Dec.	London: Fleet Street	125, 126

1496

8 Jan.	Sonning	349
24 Feb.	Sonning	127
7 Mar.	Sonning	128
10 Mar.	Sonning	129
20 Mar.	Ramsbury	265
24 Mar.	Sonning	130
28 Mar.	Sonning	131
19 Apr.	Ramsbury	132
20 Apr.	Ramsbury	133
21 Apr.	Ramsbury	134, 255, 281
15 May	Ramsbury	135
23 May	Ramsbury	TNA C 82/149/10
24 May	Ramsbury	136

4 June	Ramsbury	137
14 June	Ramsbury	138
21 June	London: Fleet Street	139
30 June	London: Fleet Street	141
7 July		
8 July	Ramsbury	360
12 July	Ramsbury	359
25 July	Corfe Castle	TNA C 82/151/5(87)
28 July	Wimborne Minster	142
3 Aug.	Salisbury: Palace	143
26 Aug.	Ramsbury	144
23 Sep.	Ramsbury	145
24 Sep.	Ramsbury	146, 147
12 Oct.	Ramsbury	261
30 Oct.	London: Fleet Street	148
18 Nov.	Sonning	149
4 Dec.	Sonning	260
7 Dec.	Sonning	259, 288
12 Dec.	Sonning	150

1497

4 Jan.	Sonning	151, 152
6 Jan.	Sonning	153

Parliament met at Westminster 16 Jan.-13 Mar.
Convocation met at St Paul's 23 Jan.-11 Mar.

26 Jan.	London	154[1], 155
8 Feb.	London (?)	156
18 Feb.	London (?)	157
22 Feb.	London (?)	158
27 Feb.	London (?)	159, 160
28 Feb.	London (?)	161
17 Mar.	Salisbury: Palace	266
18 Mar.	Sonning	262
20 Mar.	Sonning	162
22 Mar.	Sonning	163, 164
23 Mar.	Sonning	165
25 Mar.	Sonning	263
30 Mar.	Sonning	166
4 Apr.	Sonning	167
12 Apr.	Sonning	168
13 Apr.	Sonning	169, 292
17 Apr.	Sonning	295

1   London' interlined, presumably to correct 'in the same place'; the next few entries
    (155-161) 'in the same place' (*anno et loco praedictis*) are therefore ambiguous: they
    may refer to Sonning or London.

7 May	Sonning	170, 269
18 May	Sonning	298
3 June	Sonning	171
1 July	Sonning	172
4 July	Sonning	173
10 July	Sonning	174
18 July	Sonning	268
22 July	Sonning	175
5 Aug.	Woodstock: the king's manor	176
10 Aug.	Ramsbury	177
25 Aug.	Ramsbury	178
14 Sep.	Ramsbury	179
23 Sep.	Ramsbury	180
11 Oct.	Ramsbury	181
13 Oct.	Ramsbury	182
21 Nov.	Ramsbury	183
9 Dec.	Sonning	184
20 Dec.	Sonning	185

1498

20 Jan.	Sonning	186, 187
24 Jan.	Sonning	300
28 Jan.	Sonning	380
29 Jan.	London: Fleet Street	188
31 Jan.	London: Fleet Street	189
12 Feb.	London: Fleet Street	190
22 Feb.	Abingdon Abbey	191
23 Feb.	Newbury	192
27 Feb.	Sonning	193
3 Mar.	Sonning	194
4 Mar.	Sonning	195
5 Mar.	Sonning	196
9 Mar.	Sonning	384
13 Mar.	Sonning	197
20 Mar.	Sonning	198
31 Mar.	Sonning	
10 Apr.	Salisbury: Palace	199
21 Apr.	Salisbury: Palace	200
27 Apr.	Shaftesbury	201
15 May	Sherborne Castle	202
19 May	Sherborne Castle	203
29 May	Chardstock	204
8 June	Sherborne Castle	205
9 June	Sherborne ch.	
18 June	Lacock	206
5 July	Ramsbury	207
10 July	Ramsbury	208
26 July	Ramsbury	209

30 July	London: Fleet Street	210, 211
11 Aug.	Ramsbury	212
21 Aug.	Ramsbury	375
28 Aug.	Ramsbury	213
31 Aug.	Ramsbury	214
3 Sep.	Ramsbury	215
25 Sep.	Ramsbury	216
19 Oct.	Ramsbury	217
30 Oct.	Westminster	218
24 Nov.		
30 Nov.	Westminster	219
18 Dec.	Westminster	220
20 Dec.	Sonning	313, 315[1]

1499

7 Jan.	Westminster	221
18 Jan.	Westminster	222, 223
26 Jan.	Westminster	224
30 Jan.	Sonning	303
5 Feb.	Westminster	226
9 Feb.	Westminster	225
13 Feb.		
15 Feb.	Westminster	227, 228
2 Mar.	Sonning	306
6 Mar.	Westminster	229
11 Mar.	Westminster	230
15 Mar.	Westminster	231
16 Mar.	Westminster	232
22 Mar.	Reading Abbey	320
23 Mar.	Sonning	322
30 Mar.	Ramsbury	324
15 Apr.	Ramsbury	317
16 Apr.	Ramsbury	233
19 Apr.	Ramsbury	327
23 Apr.	Ramsbury	235
4 May	Ramsbury	236
18 May	Ramsbury	237, 329
27 May	Ramsbury	234
28 May	Ramsbury	331, 333
8 June	Ramsbury	335
10 June	Ramsbury	337
22 June	Ramsbury	339
28 June	Ramsbury	272
9 July	Ramsbury	238

---

1   313 is dated 20 December 1498 *et anno consecrationis quinto*; 315 is dated 20 December 1498 *et a.c. sexto*; this error is perhaps explained by the writing up of this part of the Register at the time of – or shortly after – the bp's unexpected death.

17 July	Ramsbury	239, 341[1]
19 July	Ramsbury	343
1 Aug.	Ramsbury	345
3 Aug.	Ramsbury	347
21 Aug.	Ramsbury	273
22 Aug.	Ramsbury	240, 241
23 Aug.	Ramsbury	242, 243

He died 23 August 1499 and is buried in Salisbury Cathedral. Leland says that 'Bisshop Beauchamp had made afore a riche tumbe and a chapel over it at the west end of our Lady Chapelle, but one John Blith Bisshop of Sarum was after buried under it.'[2] His monument (tomb chest with recumbent effigy) is now in the North Transept.

---

1   341 is dated *17 June*, an obvious error for *17 July*; *28 July* fell on Sunday in 1499.
2   *Leland's Itinerary in England and Wales*, Volume 1, ed. by Lucy Toulmin Smith (London, 1964), p. 264.

THE REGISTER OF JOHN BLYTH

INSTITUTIONS

A note on inductors:
Each institution is followed by a note of the addressee of the mandate for induction. In this calendar the usual inductors, the four archdeacons – Berkshire, Dorset, Salisbury, and Wiltshire – are abbreviated B, D, S, and W respectively. Thus 'Ind. S.' means 'Mandate for induction directed to the Archdeacon of Salisbury or his official.' In cases where the inductor is not named, this has been supplied by reference to the Valor Ecclesiasticus (1535) as the most authoritative list for that period. A few emendations have been made, also from that source. In the case of canonries and prebends in Salisbury cathedral, the norm was reception and installation by the dean and chapter; in this calendar this is abbreviated 'Instal. Dn.' This means: 'Mandate for reception etc. addressed to the dean or his locumtenens and chapter of Salisbury cath., and mandate for installation addressed to the dean or his locumtenens.' Inductors other than the four archdeacons, or the dean and chapter of the cathedral, have been noted in full.

1 [Fol. 1][1] Institution[2] of M. Robert Forster BCL to Gillingham (*Gyllyngham*) v., vac. by death of Studarde [*sic*]; patron, M. George Hardegyll, r. and prebendary of the same. 15 [January 1494]. Ind. D.

2 Institution of John Shephey, chapl. Worplesdon [*Wurpsden*] free chapel, Lincoln dioc., to Stockton (*Stokton*) ch., on an exchange of benefices with William Palmer; [Fol. 1ᵛ] patron, Thomas [Langton], bp of Winchester. 28 February [1494]. Ind. S.

3 Institution of Thomas Key to Ditteridge (*Dicheryche*; *Dycheryche*) ch., vac. by the death of Morgan Bekett; patron, Edward [Stafford], earl of Wiltshire. 11 April [1494]. Ind. S [*rectius* W].

4 Institution of Robert Goddysgrace to Dinton (*Donyngton*) v., on an exchange of benefices with Robert Dykons; patron, M. Thomas

---

1 Top half of fol. 1 blank; marginal: Institution to Iwerne Courtney (*Ewern Courtenay*) ch.
2 Institutions 1-53 conducted by M. Laurence Cockys, Vicar-General.

Holes BCL, r. Donnington; and institution of Robert Dykons to Teffont Evias (*Teffont Evyas*) ch.; patron, Walter Hungerford, kt. 12 April [1494]. Ind.

5 Institution of Roger Cervyngton, chapl., in the person of William Rondell, chapl., his proctor, to Odstock (*Odestoke*; *Odistok*) ch., vac. by the death of John Macy; patron, William Gereberd, esq. 22 April [1494]. Ind. S.

John [Blyth] was consecrated bishop of Salisbury at Lambeth on 23 February [1494], the vigil of St Mathias and the second Sunday in Lent.

6 Institution of John Best, chapl., to Tarrant Keyneston (*Kayneston*) ch., vac. by the res. of John Knyght; patrons, abbess and convent Tarrant (*loci Regine super Tarent*). 20 March [1494]. Ind. D.

7 Institution of George Reed, chapl., to Up Cerne (*Up Cern*) ch., vac. by the death of John Shepton; patron, John Cheyne, kt, in the right and name of Margaret his wife. 24 March [1494]. Ind. D.

On 25 March the year changes from 1493 to 1494.

8 Institution of John de Lahern, priest, to Winterborne Farringdon (*Wynterborn Germyn alias Faryngdon*; *Faringdon*) ch., vac. by the res. of Richard Hancockys; patron, William Martyn, esq. Salisbury, 20 May 1494. Ind. D.

9 Institution of John West, chapl., to Garsdon (*Garesden*) by Malmesbury ch., [Fol. 2ᵛ] vac. by the res. of M. John Haster; patrons, abbot and convent Malmesbury. Salisbury, 21 May 1494. Ind. W.

10 Institution of M. Mathew Dalamer, NP and priest, to Enford v., vac. by the death of M. John Westley; patron, M. Thomas Jane DCnL for this turn by a grant from prior and convent Winchester cath. Salisbury, 7 June 1494. Ind. S.[1]

11 Institution of M. William Spekynton BC&CnL to Nettleton (*Netelton*) ch., vac. by the death of M. William Reynoll; patrons, abbot and convent Glastonbury. Salisbury, 16 June 1494. Ind. W.

12 Institution of M. John Vaughan, chapl., to Longbridge Deverill

1   See below 238.

(*Deverell Langbrig, Langbrige*) v., vac. by res. of M. Richard Colyns BTh; patrons, abbot and convent Glastonbury. Salisbury, 19 June 1494. Ind. – [*sic; rectius* S.]

13 Institution of Roger Swan, chapl., to Fisherton Delamere (*Fyssherton Delamere; Fissherton de la mere*) v., vac. by the death of Philip Smyth; [Fol. 3] patrons, prior and convent Maiden Bradley (*Maydenbradley*). Salisbury, 21 June 1494. Ind. S.[1]

14 Institution of Humfry Hall, priest, to St Giles, Kellaways (Keyleweys) ch., vac. by the death of John Edwardys; patron, John Bagod, esq. Salisbury, 26 June 1494. Ind. W.

15 Institution of M. Ralph Hethcoot BCnL to Fugglestone (*Fouleston*) ch., vac. by the death of M. Richard Whitby; patrons, abbot and convent St Modwen, Burton upon Trent, and John Touke, esq., by a grant from the abbess and convent Wilton. Salisbury, 5 November 1494. Ind. S.

16 Institution of Thomas Dalyson, chapl., by his proctor George Dalyson, to Tisbury (*Tyssebury*) v., vac. by the death of John Kyngman; patrons, abbess and convent Shaftesbury. Salisbury, 5 November 1494. Ind. S.

17 Institution of John Yonge MA to [West] Overton v., vac. by the res. of M. Mathew Dalamer; patrons, prior and convent St Swithun, Winchester [cath.]. Salisbury, 4 December 1494. Ind. W.

18 [Fol. 3ᵛ] Institution of Hugh Short, priest, to Stanbridge (*Stanbrige; Stanbryge*) ch., vac. by the res. of John Herry[s]; patron, M. Thomas Bar[owe] DCL, on nomination by Richard Wyllybe, esq., Bath dioc. Salisbury, 9 February [1495]. Ind. D.

19 Institution of M. Thomas Mogworthy BC&CnL, priest, by his proctor John Mogworthy, to Bradpole (*Bradepole*) v., vac.; patrons, abbess and convent St Saviour and Sts Mary the Virgin and Brigit, Syon. Salisbury, 14 February [1495]. Ind. D.

20 Institution of Thomas Rooke, priest, to Pentridge (*Pentriche; Pentrych*) ch., vac. by the res. of John Belche; patrons, abbot and convent Tewkesbury. Salisbury, 25 February [1495]. Ind. S. [*rectius* D.]

---

1   See below 171.

21 Institution of Edward Newlond, cl., to Cheselbourne (*Cheselborn*) ch., vac. by the res. of M. John Osplete MA; patrons, abbess and convent Shaftesbury. Salisbury, 23 February [1495]. Ind. D.

22 [Fol. 4] Institution of M. John Osplete to Stour Provost (*Stourpriaux alias Stourpriaulx*) ch., vac. by the res. of Edward Newlond; patrons, Walter Field (*Feld*), provost, and scholars of King's coll., Cambridge. Salisbury, 23 February [1495]. Ind. D.

On 25 March the year changes from 1494 to 1495.

23 Institution of William Vutan, priest, to Wilsford (*Wyllesford*) v., vac. by the res. of M. Thomas Watere BCnL; patron, M. Geoffrey Blythe, keeper or master of St Nicholas hospital, Salisbury. Salisbury, 18 May 1495. Ind. S.

24 Institution of M. Thomas Bewshyn *alias* Hedley to Buckland (*Buckelond; Bucklond*) St Mary v., on an exchange of benefices with M. William Lane; patrons, r. and convent Edington (*Edyndon*);[1] and institution of M. William Lane to Orcheston St George ch., on the above exchange; patron, Thomas [Fitz Alan], earl of Arundel. Salisbury, 2 June 1495. Ind. S.

25 [Fol. 4ᵛ] Institution of Hugh Vaghan, priest, to Purse Caundle (*Caundelpurs*) ch., vac. by the death of Henry Pendrisse; patrons, abbess and convent Shaftesbury. Salisbury, 2 June 1495. Ind. D.

26 Institution of Walter Norreys, chapl., to Melbury Sampford (*Melbury Samford*) ch., vac. by the res. of William Hayward; patron, Katherine Brownyng, widow of William Brownyng, esq. Salisbury, 4 June 1495. Ind. D.[2]

27 Institution of M. Thomas Martyn DCnL, priest, to the v. of the prebendal ch. of Wilsford with Woodford chapel (*Wyvelesford cum Woodford*), vac. by the res. of John Kyrkby; patron, M. Richard Lychefeld DCL, prebendary of Wilsford and Woodford. Annual pension of £4.6s.8d. assigned to Kyrkby for life. Salisbury, 19 November 1495. Ind. Dn.

---

1   The original spelling of Edington is not hereafter noted.
2   See below 207.

28 Institution of William Thomson, chapl., to Melbury Abbas ch., vac. by the res. of John Aleyn; patrons, abbess and convent Shaftesbury. Annual pension of £4.16s.8d. assigned to Aleyn for life. Salisbury, 23 November 1495. Ind. D.

29 [Fol. 5] Institution of John Russhewe, chapl., to Padworth [*Padworthe*] ch., vac. by the res. of Thomas Clerk; patron, the king. Salisbury, 2 December 1495. Ind. B.

30 Institution of William Bayly, cl., to Dorchester All Saints ch., vac. by the death of Tristram More; patron, the king. Salisbury, 16 December 1495. Ind. D.[1]

31 Institution of M. Henry Rawlyns BCL to Maiden (*Mayden*) Newton ch., vac. by the res. of M. Thomas Morton; patron for this turn, Henry Rogers, esq. Salisbury, 14 January [1496]. Ind. D.

32 Institution of John Horn, deacon, to St Nicholas de Burglen free chapel, Porton, in Idmiston (*Idmoston*) parish, vac. by the res. of Christopher Lamberd, last keeper or r.; patron, John Chancy, gentleman. Salisbury, 14 February [1496]. Ind. S.

On 25 March the year changes from 1495 to 1496.

33 [Fol. 5ᵛ] Institution of M. Edmund Chaderton, by his proctor M. Ralph Derelove, to Wroughton (*Wroughton alias Elyndon*) ch., vac. by the res. of M. Ralph Hethcote; patron, Thomas [Langton], bp of Winchester. Salisbury, 21 July 1496. Ind. W.

34 Collation of Chitterne (*Chittern, Chyttern*) All Saints v., vac., to John Herryes, priest. Salisbury, 12 August 1496. Ind. S.[2]

35 Institution of John Belingeham, chapl., to the perpetual chantry at the altar of St Katherine [*Catherine*] the Virgin in Gillingham (*Gylyngham*) ch., vac. by the death of Richard Wheler; patron, John Brereton, esq., by the right and title of Katherine Barkeley, late his wife, *hac vice* patron. Salisbury, 20 October 1496. Ind. D.

36 Institution of John May, priest, to Stinsford (*Stynsford*) v., vac. by the res. of M. John Twyktwyn; patron, brother John Kendale, prior

1 See below 46.
2 See below 183.

of the Hospital of St John of Jerusalem in England. Annual pension of £3.19s.8d. assigned to Twyktwyn. Ind. D.

37 Institution of John Wadham, chapl., to Catherston [Leweston] (*Caturston*) ch., vac. by the res. of John Mabbe; patron, ~~hac vice~~ [*sic*] William Wadham, [Fol. 6] lord of Catherston. Salisbury, 21 February [1497]. Ind. − [*sic; rectius* D.]

38 Institution of M. John Newman BCnL, priest, to Charborough (*Wynterborn, Wynterborne Chirburgh*) ch., vac. by the res. of Thomas Keymer *etc.* [*sic*]; patron, Thomas Husee, esq. Salisbury, 1 February [1498]. Ind. S. [*rectius* D.]

39 Institution of John Odland, priest, to Upavon (*Uphaven*) v., vac. by res. of John Toker; patrons, prior and convent Ivychurch (*Ivechurch*). Salisbury, 3 February [1498]. Ind. S.

40 Institution of John Wannesleigh to Bettiscombe (*Bettiscomb*) ch., vac. by the res. of John Crokker; patrons, dean and chapter St Stephen free chapel, Westminster. Salisbury, 6 February [1498]. Ind. D.

41 Institution of William Penne, chapl., to Fifield Bavant (*Fyffyde Bavent*) St Martin ch., vac. by the res. of John Lyott; patrons, prioress and convent Dartford (*Dertford*) BVM and St Margaret the Virgin, Kent. Salisbury, 1 August 1498. Ind. S.

42 [Fol. 6ᵛ] Institution of John Elys, chapl., to Chirton (*Chyryton*) v., vac. by the death of John Brounsmyth; patrons, Henry [Dean], bp of Bangor, as prior of Llanthony, with the convent of the same. Salisbury, 12 August 1498. Ind. S.

43 Institution of Thomas Chyld, chapl., to Winterborne (*Wynterborn*) Came ch., vac. by the res. of John Roly; patrons, dean and chapter St Stephen free chapel, Westminster. Salisbury, 13 August 1498. Ind. D.

44 Institution of James Waryn, chapl., to Compton Abbas ch., vac. by the res. of John Stokfissh; patrons, abbot and convent Milton (*Middelton*). Salisbury, 3 November 1498. Ind. D.

45 Institution of Richard Chille, priest, to West Chelborough (*Westchelburgh*) ch., vac. by the res. of John Shepperd; patron, Richard Kymer. Salisbury, 17 November 1498. Ind. D.

46 Institution of John Ap Herry, cl., ~~by proctor Nicholas Gylle~~ [*sic*] to Dorchester All Saints ch., vac. by the res. of Denis (*Dionisius*) Solow; [Fol. 7] patron, the king. Salisbury, 30 November 1498. Ind. D.[1]

47 Institution of M. John Griffeth BCnL to Spettisbury (*Spettebury*) ch., vac. by the res. of M. Thomas Harper DTh; patrons, prior and convent Witham BM, OCarth, Bath dioc. Salisbury, 10 February [1499]. Ind. D.[2]

48 Institution of Ralph Clerk, priest, to West Parley (*Westperle*) ch., vac. by the death of Elias Bromefeld; patron, William Camell, esq. Salisbury: The Close, 25 March 1499. Ind. D.[3]

49 Institution of Thomas Asshwod, chapl., to Manston ch., vac. by the death of Christopher Faryngton; patron, John Well, esq. Salisbury, 5 April 1499. Ind. ~~Archdeacon of Salisbury~~ [*sic – corrected to* D.]

50 Institution of William Taylour, chapl., to East Lulworth (*Estlulworth*) v., vac. by the death of Stephen Mathew; patrons, prior and convent Merton, Winchester dioc. Salisbury, 17 May 1499. Ind. D.

51 Institution of John Launcy, chapl., to Tarrant Rushton (*Russheton alias Tarrant Russheton*) ch., vac. by the res. of Richard Bampton; patron, William, Lord Stourton, kt. Salisbury, 10 July 1499. Ind. D.

52 [Fol. 7ᵛ] Institution of John Bryan, abbot of Bindon (*Byndon*), dispensed by the Apostolic See [to hold a secular benefice], to Chaldon Herring (*Chaldon Heryng*) ch., vac. by the death of M. Edmund Martyn DC&CnL; patrons for this turn, Roger Newburgh, kt, and John Stourton, esq., by reason of a grant to them by abbot and convent Bindon. Salisbury, 11 August 1499. Ind. D.

53 Institution of William Rawle, priest, to West Parley (*Westperley*) ch., vac. by the res. of Ralph Clerk; patron, William Camell, esq. Salisbury, 23 August 1499. Ind. D.[4]

[Bottom half of fol. 7ᵛ and top half of next fol. (numbered 10) blank.]

1   See above 30.
2   See below 185 and 208.
3   See below 53.
4   See above 48.

54 [Fol. 10] Institution[1] of Robert Hewster, priest, to Cookham (*Cokeham*) v., vac. by the death of John Carter; patrons, abbot and convent Cirencester (*Cirencestre*), Worcester dioc. Domus Conversorum by London, 30 January [1494]. Ind. B.

55 Collation to M. Thomas Birchold BCnL, priest, by his proctor Thomas Wylcock[ys], of a canonry and the prebend of Torleton in Salisbury cath., vac. by the death of M. William Gyen. Domus Conversorum by London, 19 January [1494]. Mandate for installation addressed to the Dean or his *locumtenens* and Chapter of Salisbury cath.; mand. ind. addressed to the bp of Worcester.

56 Institution of M. Mathew Poole to Fyfield (*Fyffhyde, Fiffhyde*) ch., vac. by the death of M. William Browghton; patron, Richard Poole, kt, chamberlain to Prince Arthur. Domus Conversorum by London, 19 January [1494]. Ind. B.

57 [Fol. 10ᵛ] Institution of William Paynell, priest, to Sutton Courtenay ch., vac. by the death of M. Edmund Hamden; patrons, dean and chapter St George's royal free chapel, Windsor. Domus Conversorum by London, 11 February [1494]. Ind. B.

John [Blyth] was consecrated bishop of Salisbury at Lambeth on 23 February [1494], the vigil of St Mathias and the second Sunday in Lent.

58 Institution of Richard Randal, priest, to Cholsey v., vac. by − [*sic*], v.; patrons, abbot and convent Reading (*Radyng*). London: Fleet Street (*Fletestrete*),[2] 7 March [1494]. Ind. B.

59 Institution of William Adam, priest, by his proctor Thomas Whetley, literate, to the chantry in Clewer (*Clewar*) ch., vac. by the res. of John Everard, chapl.; patron, William Brocas, esq. London: Fleet Street, 8 March [1494]. Ind. B.

60 Institution of M. William Edyngdon BCL, priest, to Reading (*Radyng*) St Giles v., vac. by the death of M. Robert Gleyn; patrons, abbot and convent Reading. London: Fleet Street, 14 March [1494]. Ind. B.

[Fol. 11] *On 25 March the year changes from 1493 to 1494.*

1   Institutions 54ff. by the bp in person.
2   The original spelling of Fleet Street is not hereafter noted.

61 Collation to M. John Foted BTh of Poulshot (*Pawlesholt*) ch., vac. by the death of William Hulle, r. of the conventual ch. of Edingdon (*Edyndon*) and commendary of Poulshot. London: Fleet Street, 12 May 1494. Ind. S.[1] [Marginal: *Non soluit feoda*]

62 Institution or appointment of John Saynt John, priest and brother of Edington (*Edyndon*) ch. or convent, to the deanery there, vac. by the death of William Hulle, r. London: Fleet Street, 5 June 1494. Ind. S. Mandate for obedience addressed to *Correctori* and convent Edington. [Marginal: *Dominus recepit feoda*]

63 Institution of William Cumberton, priest, to Rushall (*Rusteshale*) ch., vac. by the death of M. John Westley; patron, Edward Hastyng[ys], kt, lord Hastyng[ys] and Hungerford. London: Fleet Street, 13 June 1494. Ind. S.

64 Institution of M. Gregory David BCL, priest, to Peasemore (*Pesemere*) ch., vac. by the res. of Robert Browghton; patron, the king. Ramsbury (*Remmesbury*),[2] 8 July 1494. Ind. B.

65 [Fol. 11ᵛ] Collation to Richard Norton, priest, of Little Chalfield (*West Chaldfelde*) free chapel, vac. by the death of Thomas Sqwier and in the bishop's collation by lapse.[3] Ramsbury, 9 July 1494. Ind. W. [*rectius* S.] [Marginal: *Non soluit feoda*]

66 Institution of M. Thomas Doyly *alias* Dayly, priest, to Marcham (*Mercham*) v., vac. by the res. of M. William Jane; patrons, abbot and convent Abingdon (*Abendon*) BVM. Ramsbury, 28 July 1494. Ind. B.

67 Collation to M. Simon Stalworth MA, by his proctor Henry Brynkhill, literate, of a canonry and the prebend of Warminster (*Warmynstre, Warmynster alias Warmystre Netherbury*) in Salisbury cath., vac. by the res. of M. Robert Shirborn. Ramsbury, 22 August 1494. Instal. Dn.[4] [Marginal: *Vacat.*]

68 Institution of Thomas Lowson, priest, to Woodsford (*Wirdeford*) ch., vac. by the res. of John de la Heron; patrons, abbot and convent

1   See below 86, 182, 190, 229.
2   The original spelling of Ramsbury is not hereafter noted.
3   The advowson of Little Chalfield descended with the manor; however, it had fallen to bp Langton's collation by lapse in 1488 (*Reg. Langton*, 179). For the somewhat confused descent of the manor, see *VCH Wilts*, Vol. VII, p. 63.
4   See below 79, 123, 155.

Cerne. Salisbury: The Close, 2 September 1494. Ind. D.[1]

69 Institution of M. William Ketylton MA to Wilton St Mary in Breadstreet (*Bredstrete*) ch., vac. by the res. of William Thomas; patrons, abbess and convent Wilton. Wilton Abbey, 4 September 1494. Ind. S.

70 [Fol. 12] Institution of William Kent, deacon, to the subdeaconry in Wilton (*Wylton*) abbey, vac. by the res. of George Rood; patrons, abbess and convent Wilton. Wilton Abbey, 4 September 1494. Ind. S.

71 Institution of Robert Boord, priest, to Whitchurch Canonicorum (*Whitechurch*) v., vac. by the res. of William Dawbys; patron, Richard [Foxe] bp of Bath [and Wells]. Cerne abbey, 8 September 1494. Ind. D. [Marginal: Assignment of pension of £9.19s.6d. to Dawbys.]

72 Institution of Edward Roberd[ys], priest, to Winterborne (*Wynterborne*) Abbas ch., vac. by the res. of Robert Boord; patrons, abbot and convent Cerne. Sherborne Castle, 14 September 1494. Ind. D.

73 Institution of Nicholas Hendlawe, priest, to Waltham St Lawrence v., vac. by the death of Otis Moreton; patrons, prior and convent Hurley. Sherborne Castle, 15 September 1494. Ind. B.

74 [Fol. 12ᵛ] Institution of John Hyde, chapl., to Tilehurst (*Tylehurst*) v., vac. by the res. of M. Henry Raynford; patrons, abbot and convent Reading (*Rading*). Shaftesbury Abbey, 17 September 1494. Ind. B.

75 Institution of William Thomas to Shaftesbury St Martin ch., vac. by res. of M. William Ketylton; patrons, abbess and convent Shaftesbury. Shaftesbury Abbey, 17 September 1494. Ind. D.

76 Institution of Andrew Kerver, priest, to Bradford Abbas v., vac. by the death of Thomas Laurence; patrons, abbot and convent Sherborne (*Shirborne*). Shaftesbury Abbey, 17 September 1494. Ind. D. [Marginal: He is to present himself to the bp for examination within the year.]

77 Institution of Richard Bampton, OSB of Monk Bretton (*Monkebreton*) BM Magdalene, York dioc., to Tarrant Rushton

---

1 See below 199.

(*Tarraunt Russheton*) ch., vac, by the death of Louis Panavenone;[1] patron, John Cheyne, kt, in the right of his wife Margaret, lady of the manor of Rushton, by reason of a jointure made and granted to her by Lord Stourton, lately her husband; Bampton has a dispensation from the pope [to hold a secular benefice]. Shaftesbury Abbey, 18 September 1494. Ind. D.

78 [Fol. 13] Institution of M. Edward Wiloughby MA, by his proctor Thomas Preston, literate, to Semley (*Semele*) ch., vac. by the death of M. Walter Hylle; patrons, abbess and convent Wilton. Edington, 22 September 1494. Ind. S.

79 Collation to M. Simon Stalworth MA, by his proctor Robert Gilbert MA, of a canonry and the prebend of Warminster (*Warmystre alias Warmynystre in laico feudo*) in Salisbury cath., vac. by the res. of M. Robert Sherborne. The oath of obedience was taken by Henry Brynkhyl, the said Simon's legally constituted proctor for that purpose. Instal. Dn. Ramsbury, 3 October 1494.[2]

80 Collation to M. Walter Brown BTh of v. of Potterne (*Potern*) prebendal ch., vac. by res. of M. [blank] Gubbe. Ramsbury, 4 October 1494. Mand. ind. directed to the priest there or his vice-gerent.

81 Collation to M. Geoffrey Blithe MA, deacon, by his proctor Richard Norton, priest, of the Treasurership and canonry and the prebend of Calne annexed to it in Salisbury cath., vac. by the death of M. Richard Whitby. London: Fleet Street, 1 November 1494. Instal. Dn.[3]

82 [Fol. 13ᵛ] Institution of Richard Mille, priest, to [East] Coulston (*Cowleston*) ch., vac. by the death of John Bynglee; patron, the king by right of the duchy of Lancaster. London: Fleet Street, 9 November 1494. Ind. S.

83 Institution of M. John Burton DTh to Stanford [in the Vale] ch., vac. by the res. of M. Thomas Ottley; patron, the king. London: Fleet Street, 26 November 1494. Ind. B. Assignment of annual pension of £20 for life to Ottley, on the petition of his proctor, Thomas Hersby.[4]

1   Claudius Panavilioni in *Reg. Langton*, 305.
2   See above 67 and below 123, 155.
3   See below 95.
4   See below 140, 141.

83a Copy of the bp's letters assigning the above pension. [Fol. 14] London: Fleet Street, 26 November 1494.

84 [Fol. 14ᵛ] Collation to M. Robert Toneys BCL, cl., of a canonry and the prebend of Axford in Salisbury cath., vac. by the death of M. Thomas Rope. London: Fleet Street, 27 November 1494. Instal. Dn.[1]

85 Institution of Richard Pemberton, priest, to Cholderton (*Chaldryngton*) ch., vac. by the res. of M. Thomas Thornburgh; patron, Thomas Lovell, kt of the king's body and king's counsellor, lord of the manor or lordship of Cholderton. Ramsbury, 11 December 1494. Ind. S.

86 Collation to M. Edmund Percy MA, priest, of Poulshot (*Pawlesholt*) ch., vac. by the res. of M. John Foted. Ramsbury, 13 December 1494. Ind. S.[2]

87 Institution of M. John Foted BTh, priest, to Symondsbury (*Symondesburgh*) ch., vac. by the death of M. Thomas Rope; patrons, abbot and convent Cerne. Ramsbury, 16 December 1494. Ind. D.

88 Institution of Nicholas Chauntrell, priest, to Hawkchurch (*Haukechurch, Hawkchurch*) ch., vac. by, the death of M. Thomas Rope; patrons, abbot and convent Cerne. Ramsbury, 19 December 1494. Ind. D.

89 [Fol 15] Collation to Thomas Philippes, priest, of a canonry and the prebend of Yatesbury in Salisbury cath., vac. by the res. of M. Henry Carnebull. Ramsbury, 24 December 1494. Instal. Dn.

90 Institution of John Lane, priest, by his proctor John Parker, to Loders (*Lodres*) v., vac. by the res. of M. John Rope; patrons, abbess and convent St Saviour and Sts Mary the Virgin and Brigit [Syon]. Ramsbury, 27 December 1494. Ind. D.

91 Institution of Thomas Clerk, chapl, to BVM chantry in Chippenham St Andrew ch., vac. by the death of John Salwey; patron, Walter Hungerford, kt. London: Fleet Street, 16 February [1495]. Ind. W.

---

1   See below 243.
2   See above 61 and below 182, 190, 229.

92 Institution of M. Richard Gotynden MA to Chilmark (*Chilmarke*) ch., vac. by the res. of M. Edward Willughby; patrons, abbess and convent Wilton. London: Fleet Street, 21 February [1495]. Ind. S.

93 [Fol. 15ᵛ] Institution of M. William Thornburgh BCL, by his proctor William Fairehere, chapl., to Codford St Mary ch., vac. by the death of Richard Gylquyte; patrons, John Huddleston, kt, and Joan (*Johanna*) his wife. London: Fleet Street, 21 February [1495]. Ind. S.

On 23 February the bp entered the second year of his episcopate.

94 Institution of M. Hugh Lyvesay BCnL, priest, to Yattendon (*Yatenden*) ch., vac. by the deprivation of William Garestange because of non-residence; patron, William Norreis, kt. Ramsbury, 28 February [1495]. Ind. B.

95 Collation to M. Henry Sutton MD, priest, of the treasurership and canonry and the prebend of Calne annexed to it in Salisbury cath., vac. by the res. of M. Geoffrey Blythe MA. Ramsbury, 2 March [1495]. Instal. Dn.[1] [2]

96 Institution of M. Peter le Penec DCL, by his proctor William Stodham, literate, to Christian Malford (*Cristian Malford*) ch., vac. by the death of M. William Sloughter; patron, the king by reason of the temporalities of Bath [and Wells] dioc. being in his hands *sede vacante*. Ramsbury, 4 March [1495]. Ind. W.

97 [Fol. 16] Institution of M. Geoffrey Blithe MA, by his proctor M. John Pykeryng, to Corfe Castle (*Corffe Castell*) ch., vac. by the res. of M. Henry Sutton MD; patrons, abbess and convent Shaftesbury. Ramsbury, 5 March [1495]. Ind. D.[3]

98 Collation to M. Geoffrey Blithe MA, by his proctor M. John Pykeryng, of a canonry and the prebend of Chisenbury and Chute (*Chesyngbury et Chute*) in Salisbury cath., vac. by the acceptance of the Treasurership and the prebend of Calne annexed to it by M. Henry Sutton MD. Ramsbury, 5 March [1495]. Instal. Dn.[4]

---

1   See above 81.
2   Nos. 95-99 constitute an intricate exchange of benefices.
3   See below 221.
4   See below 188, 219.

99 Collation to M. Geoffrey Blythe MA, by his proctor M. John Pykeryng, of St Nicholas hospital, Salisbury, vac. by the res. of M. Henry Sutton MD, last keeper. Ramsbury, 5 March [1495]. Mand. ind. directed to M. Richard Gyan BCL or Thomas Philyppes, canon and Subdean of Salisbury cath., together or singly.[1]

100 Collation to M. Edmund Percy MA, priest, of Winterborne (*Wynterborn, Wynterborne*) St Martin v., vac. by the death of William Hulverdale. Ramsbury, 13 March [1495]. Ind. D.[2]

101 [Fol. 16ᵛ] Institution of John Wyllughby, chapl., to Piddletrenthide (*Pydell Trenthyde*) v., vac. by the death of Nicholas Locke; patrons, abbot and convent Hyde by Winchester. Ramsbury, 18 March [1495]. Ind. D.[3]

102 Institution of John Peytrell, priest, to Chalbury (*Chellesbury alias Chaldebury*) ch., vac. by the death of John Brigges; patrons, abbess and convent Wilton. Ramsbury, 21 March [1495]. Ind. D.

On 25 March the year changes from 1494 to 1495.

103 Institution of William Crissall, chapl., to Pevesey ch., vac. by the res. of William Knyght; patrons, abbot and convent Hyde by Winchester. Ramsbury, 30 March 1495. Ind. W. Assignment of annual pension of £6.13s.4d. for life to Knyght.

104 Institution of Stephan Goldesburgh, chapl., to Chedington (*Chedyngton*) ch., vac. by the res. of Nicholas Chaunterell; [Fol. 17] patron *hac vice*, Peter Baunfeld, esq. Ramsbury, 2 April 1495. Ind. D.

105 Institution of Thomas Tame, deacon, to Castle Eaton (*Castell Eton*) ch., vac. by the death of M. John Mychell; patron *hac vice*, John Tame of Fairford (*Fayerford*), esq. Ramsbury, 25 April 1495. Ind. W.

106 Institution of M. Henry Sutton MD, by his proctor John Smyth, chapl., to Wyke Regis ch., vac. by the res. of M. Henry[4]; patron,

---

1   See below 201.
2   See below 119.
3   See below 232.
4   In the list of rectors in the ch. Henry Sutten occurs in 1480, succeeded by Henry Sutton MD in 1495; if two successive incumbents shared the same name, this may account for the scribe's confusion – resulting in his omitting the surname of the resigned r.

Thomas [Langton], bp of Winchester. Ramsbury, 6 June 1495. Ind. D.

107   Institution of William Birtport, priest, to Fifehead (*Fyffyde*) Magdalen v., vac. by the death of John Gylbert; patrons, abbot and convent St Augustine by Bristol, Worcester dioc. Ramsbury, 30 July 1495. Ind. D.

108   Institution of Robert Richardson, priest, to Marlborough (*Marleburgh*) v., vac. by the death of Robert Savery; patron, M. Edward Cheyne DC&CnL, dean of Salisbury cath. Ramsbury, 9 August 1495. Mand. ind. directed to M. William Jonys, official of the peculiar jurisdiction there.

109   [Fol. 17ᵛ] Institution of Robert Barre, priest, to Milton Lilbourne (*Milton Lilbon alias Milton Abbatis*) v., vac. by the res. of Robert Richardson; patrons, abbot and convent Cirencester (*Cirencestre*), Worcester dioc. Ramsbury, 14 August 1495. Ind. W. [Marginal: *Non dum soluit*]

110   Collation to M. Thomas Rewys BCnL, by his proctor Richard Norton, chapl., of [West] Lavington (*Lavyngton Episcopi*) v., on an exchange of benefices with John Weston, priest; and institution of John Weston to Ashley (*Assheley*) ch.; patron, Edward Hastyng[es], kt, lord Hastings (*Hastyng[es]*) and Hungerford. Ramsbury, 20 August 1495. Mand. ind. of Rewys directed to M. William Lane, v. of Steeple Ashton (*Stepull Assheton*), or Thomas Pope, r. of Orcheston (*Orston*) St George, together or singly; mand. ind. of Weston to W [*rectius* S?].

111   Institution of John Fawn, priest, to Hammoon (*Hammohon*) ch.,[1] patrons *hac vice*, Henry Strangwayse, William Filolle, and William Martyn, esqs, and Thomas Moleyns, by reason of their enfeoffment by John Trenchard, kt, with the assent of John Cheyne, kt, guardian of Thomas Trenchard, son and heir of John Trenchard, deceased, during his minority. Ramsbury, 26 August 1495. Ind. D.

112   [Fol. 18] Institution of William Okey BA, in priest's orders, to Tilshead (*Tydeleshed alias Tyledeshed*) v., vac. by the res. of M. John Holes BCL; patrons, prior and convent Ivychurch (*Ederose*). Ramsbury, 2 September 1495. Ind. S.

1   No indication of the cause of the vacancy; Roger Rostragyn, chapl., was instituted to this living in 1488 (*Reg. Langton*, 174).

113 Collation to M. William Mors DCL, by his proctor M. George Wood, of Sulhamstead Bannister (*Sulhampsted Banaster*) ch., vac. and falling to the bp's collation by lapse. Sonning (*Sonnyng[es]*),[1] 15 September 1495. Ind. B.

114 Collation to M. Hugh Oldham, priest, by his proctor William Chenaldys, of a canonry and the prebend of Alton Borealis (*Aulton Borialis*) in Salisbury cath., vac. by the death of M. John Coryngdon. Sonning, 24 September 1495. Instal. Dn. [Marginal (left): *.b.* ; marginal (right): *solutum*]

115 Collation to Robert Toneys BCL, cl., of Earley White Knights (*Arley Whight Knyghtys*) free chapel in Sonning parish, vac. and falling to the bp's collation by lapse. Sonning, 18 September 1495. Mand. ind. directed to M. John Hyde, v. Tilehurst (*Tylehurst*). [Marginal (left): *.a.*]

116 Institution of M. William Atwater DTh, by his proctor John Mason, chapl., to Cumnor (*Cumnour*) v., vac. by the death of M. William Parker; patrons, abbot and convent Abingdon BVM. Sonning, 6 October 1495. [Fol. 18^v] Ind. B.

117 Institution of Hervey Salmon, cl., to Frome Vauchurch (*Fromevawchurch*) ch., vac. by the death of John Lagwasshe; patron, Robert Willoughby (*Wylughby*), kt, lord Broke. London, Fleet Street, 22 October 1495. Ind. D.

118 Institution of Reginald Mutt, priest, to Sutton Courtenay (*Sutton Courteney*) v., then first vacant;[2] patrons, dean and canons of St George's royal free chapel, Windsor. London: Fleet Street, 24 October 1495. Ind. B.

119 Collation to Richard Jekyll, priest, of Winterborne (*Wynterborn*) St Martin v., vac. by the res. of M. Edmund Percy. London: Fleet Street, 28 October 1495. Ind. D.[3]

120 Institution of M. Reginald Swale BCL, priest, to Codford [St] Mary ch, vac. by the res. of M. William Thornborgh DCL; patrons, John Huddilston, kt at arms, and Joan (*Johanna*) his wife. London: Fleet Street, 29 October 1495. Ind. S.

1   The original spelling of Sonning is not hereafter noted.
2   See *Reg.Langton*, 467-9 for the appropriation of this ch. in February 1481.
3   See above 100.

121 Collation to John Taylour, cl., of the custody or wardenship of Shottesbrooke (*Shotesbroke*) coll. ch., vac. by the death of M. John Bayly, last keeper or warden, and falling to the bp's collation by lapse. London: Fleet Street, 29 October 1495. [No mand. ind.; *rectius* B?]

122 [Fol. 19] Collation to M. John Andrewe BTh of Broad Windsor (*Brodwyndesore*) v., vac. London: Fleet Street, 7 November 1495. Ind. D.

123 Collation to William Oldham, priest, of a canonry and the prebend of Warminster (*Warmynstre in laico feodo*) in Salisbury cath., vac. by the res. of M. Simon Stalworth MA. London: Fleet Street, 17 November 1495. Instal. Dn.[1]

124 Collation to Robert Frenssh, priest, of Compton Chamberlayne (*Compton Chamberlayn*) v., vac. by the res. of John Botell, and falling to the bp's collation by lapse. London: Fleet Street, 23 November 1495. Ind. S.

125 Institution of M. Henry Horneby BTh to Burton (*Brideton alias Birton*) [Bradstock] ch., vac. by the death of M. Robert Bukmoth; patrons, dean and chapter of the royal free chapel or coll. ch. of [St Stephen,] Westminster. London: Fleet Street, 12 December 1495. Ind. D.

126 Institution of Robert Pegge BC&CnL, cl., to Appleton (*Appulton*) ch., vac. by the death of M. William Parker; patron, John Denton, esq. London: Fleet Street, 12 December 1495. Ind. B.

[Fol. 19ᵛ] *On 23 February the bp entered the third year of his episcopate.*

127 Institution of Walter Samuell, cl., to Seacourt (*Sekworth*)[2] free chapel, vac. by the death of M. William Parker, last v. or keeper; patrons, Elizabeth Samuel, prioress, and convent Studley (*Stodeley*) BVM, Lincoln dioc. Sonning, 24 February [1496]. Ind. B.

128 Institution of M. Richard Trappe DTh, by his proctor Edward Fox, literate, to Chieveley (*Chyveley*) v., vac. by the death of M.

---

1   See above 67, 79 and below 155.
2   In Wytham parish. *The Place-Names of Berkshire, Part Two*, records 'Secourte' [*rectius* Secourte Hame] from the *Valor Ecclesiasticus* (1535), but ignores 'Sokeworth libera capella ex fundacionem domine Studeley.' The archaeological evidence is equivocal – see R.L.S. Bruce Mitford, 'The Excavations at Seacourt, Berks., 1939' in *Oxoniensia*, Vol. 5 (1940).

Philip Morgan; patrons, abbot and convent Abingdon (*Abendon*) BMV. Sonning, 7 March [1496]. Ind. B.

129 Institution of M. William Skynner MA, priest, to Buckland (*Buckelond*) v., vac. by the res. of M. Thomas Bewshyn *alias* Hedley; patrons, rector and convent Edington. Sonning, 10 March [1496]. Ind. B.

130 Institution of William Fauntleroy, priest, to [West] Overton v., vac. by the res. of M. John Yonge; patrons, prior and convent Winchester St Swithun [cath.]. Sonning, 24 March [1496]. Ind. W.

[Fol. 20] *On 25 March the year changes from 1495 to 1496.*

131 Institution of M. John Lichefeld DCL, by his proctor M. William Lichefeld DCL, to Childrey (*Chylray*) ch., vac. by the res. of M. Robert Shirborn; patron *hac vice*, Edward Darell, kt. Sonning, 28 March 1496. Ind. B.

132 Institution of John Stone, monk, OSB, prior of [Monkton] Farleigh (*Farlegh*), dispensed by the Apostolic See to obtain a benefice with or without the cure of souls, to Box (*Boxe*) v., vac. by the death of William Key; patron *hac vice*, Thomas Longe, esq. Ramsbury, 19 April 1496. Ind. W.

133 Collation to Thomas Clerk, priest, of John Brydde's chantry at the altar of St Katherine in Marlborough (*Marleburgh*) St Peter ch, vac. by the res. of Thomas Barett and falling to the bp's collation by a lapse of two months. Ramsbury, 20 April 1496. Mand. ind. directed to M. William Jonys, r. of Marlborough St Peter.

134 Collation to Richard Norton, priest, of Winfrith [Newburgh] (*Wynfrede*) ch., vac. by the death of Edward Godfryth. Ramsbury, 21 April 1496. Ind. D.[1] [Marginal: *soluit*]

135 [Fol. 20ᵛ] Institution of M. John Dale, chapl., to Tidpit (*Tutpytt*) ch., vac. by the death of Robert Elle; patrons, abbot and convent Glastonbury. Ramsbury, 15 May 1496. Ind. S.[2] [Marginal: by M. Whighthed]

---

1 See below 216
2 See below 204.

136 Institution of John Hylle, chapl., to Longbridge Deverill (*Deverell Langbrige, Deverel Langbrige*) v., vac. by the res. of M. John Vaughan; patrons, abbot and convent Glastonbury. Ramsbury, 24 May 1496. Ind. S.

137 Institution of M. John Jolyf MA to Belchalwell (*Bell sur lez downez*) ch., vac. by the res. of M. William Lacestre BCnL; patron, Alice, lady fitzhugh. Ramsbury, 4 June 1496. Ind. D.

138 Institution of John Garnett, priest, to Little Cheverell ch., vac. by the res. of Walter Joys *alias* Joy; patron, Walter Hungerford, kt. Ramsbury, 14 June 1496. Ind. S. [Marginal: by M. Whighthed]

139 Institution of M. Thomas Tymeot MA to Pulham ch., vac.; patrons, abbot and convent Cirencester (*Cirencestre*), Worcester dioc. London: Fleet Street, 21 June 1496. Ind. D.

140 [Fol. 21] Enrolment of royal letters: John Walssh, esq., appeared before William Danvers, one of the justices of the King's Bench, sitting at Abingdon (*Abendon*), Berkshire, on 22 March 1496, and successfully contested the patronage of Stanford [in the Vale] ch., by grant from the king, against John Burton, cl. Witness: William Danvers. Abingdon, 23 March 1496.[1]

141 Institution of M. Stephen Berworth MD, priest, to Stanford St Denys [Stanford in the Vale] ch., vac. by the res. and death of M. Thomas Otley; patron *hac vice*, John Walssh, esq., by grant from the king of the next only presentation to that ch., by letters patent dated Westminster, 1 December 1488.[2] London: Fleet Street, 30 June 1496. Ind. B.[3]

142 Institution of Henry Creche, priest, to Sutton Waldron (*Sutton Martyn*) ch., vac. by the death of M. Robert Beke; patron, Henry Rogers, esq. Wimborne Minster (*Wymborn Mynstre*), 28 July 1496. Ind. D.

143 Institution of M. Thomas Orchard BCnL, priest, to Fontmell [Magna] prebendal v., vac. by the death of M. Robert Beke; patron, Christopher Twynyho, cl., r. of Fontmell prebendal ch. Salisbury: The Palace, 3 August 1496. Ind. D.

1   See above 83 and below 141.
2   TNA C 82/45/32(110).
3   See above 83, 140.

144 [Fol. 21ᵛ] Institution of Cuthbert Baron, priest, to Cricklade (*Crickelaad*) BM ch., vac. by the death of John Brere; patrons, William May and Juliana his wife, widow of Richard George of Ampney (*Ameney*) St Peter, Worcester dioc. Ramsbury, 26 August 1496. Ind. W.

145 Institution of Christopher Hylle, priest, to West Hendred (*Westhenred*) St Mary v., vac. by the death of M. Thomas Hopkyns; patrons, prior and convent Wallingford (*Walyngford*). Ramsbury, 23 September 1496. Ind. B.

146 Institution of M. David Myles BCnL, priest, to Wareham (*Warham*) St Michael ch., vac. by the death of John Kewe; patrons, prior and convent Jesus of Bethlehem by Sheen, OCarth., Winchester dioc. Ramsbury, 24 September 1496. Ind. D.

147 Institution of M. Thomas Lane, Inceptor in Arts, to Wareham (*Warham*) St Peter ch., vac. by the res. of M. David Myles; patrons, prior and convent Jesus of Bethlehem by Sheen, OCarth., Winchester dioc. Ramsbury, 24 September 1496. Ind. D.

148 Institution of M. Thomas Whytamour, cl., by his proctor William Whitamour, to Chilton (*Chylton*) [Foliat] ch., vac. by the death of John Artur; [Fol. 22] patron, Edward Burgh, kt, not only as co-portioner but also as the heir of Thomas Burgh, kt, his father, by reason of an enfeoffment to use of the manor of Chilton [Foliat], next to Hungerford, Wiltshire, with the advowson there, and with the assent of the other co-portioners (feoffees). London: Fleet Street, 30 October 1496. Ind. W.[1]

149 Collation to M. Edmund Martyn DC&CnL, by his proctor Thomas Moleyns, literate, of a canonry and the prebend of Beminster (*Bemystre*) Secunda in Salisbury cath., vac. by the consecration of M. John Arundell as bp of Lichfield. Sonning, 18 November 1496. Instal. Dn.[2]

150 Institution of Richard Newson, priest, to Abbotsbury (*Abbotesbury*) v., vac. by the death of Peter Miller; patrons, abbot and convent Abbotsbury. Sonning, 12 December 1496. Ind. D.

---

1   See below 236.
2   See below 242.

151 Collation to M. William Warham DCL, cl., by his proctor William Portere, literate, of the custody or rectory of Bincknoll (*Benkenoll*) St Nicholas free chapel,[1] vac. and falling to the bp's collation by lapse. Sonning, 4 January [1497]. [No mand. ind. – *rectius* W?]

152 [Fol. 22[v]] Collation to John Blythe, cl., of the rectory or custody of the free chapel of [Chisbury] St Martin by Bedwyn,[2] vac. and falling to the bp's collation by lapse. Sonning, 4 January [1497]. [No mand. ind. – *rectius* W.]

153 Institution of Andrew Townyng, priest (*sacerdos*),[3] to Hazelbury (*Hasylbere, Hasilbere*) [Bryan] ch., vac. by the death of Vincent Veer; patrons, Eleanor (*Elianora*), countess of Wiltshire, and Robert Spencere, kt.[4] Sonning, 6 January [1497]. Ind. D.[5]

154 Institution of John Buclegh, chapl., to Sutton Mandeville (*Maundevyle*) ch., vac. by the death of Malachi Conyam; patron *hac vice*, Walter Hungerford, kt, by reason of a grant to him by Thomas West, kt, lord de la Ware. London,[6] 26 January [1497]. Ind. S. [*rectius* W.]

155 Collation to M. Christopher Randolf MA of a canonry and the prebend of Warminster (*Warmynstre in laico feodo*) in Salisbury cath., vac. by the res. of William Oldham. [London,] 26 January [1497]. Instal. Dn.[7]

156 Collation to M. Henry Babyngton BTh of a canonry and the prebend of Lyme [and Halstock] in Salisbury cath., vac. by the res. of Robert Husse. [London,] 8 February [1497]. Instal. Dn.

157 [Fol. 23] Institution of John Lawley, chapl., to Market Lavington (*Stepul Lavyngton alias Est Lavyngton*) v., vac. by the res. of Thomas Draper; patrons, r. and convent Edington. [London,] 18 February

---

1 In Broad Hinton, Wiltshire.
2 The ruined chapel of St Martin lies in the hamlet of Chisbury, ¾ m. west of Little Bedwyn.
3 The usual word is *presbyter*.
4 Eleanor was the widow of James Butler, earl of Wiltshire and Ormond (executed 1461); she married Sir Robert Spencer c.1470 and died 16 August 1501.
5 See *Register Langton*, 398.
6 'London' interlined, presumably to correct 'in the same place'; the next few entries (155-161) 'in the same place' (*anno et loco praedictis*) are therefore ambiguous: they may refer to Sonning or London.
7 See above 67, 79, 123, 155.

[1497]. Ind. S.

158 Institution of John Kynge, chapl., by his proctor M. Robert Laurence, to the chantry [of St John]¹ in Chippenham (*Chyppenham*) ch., vac. by the death of Richard Swan; patrons, prior and convent [Monkton] Farleigh (*Farlegh*). [London,] 22 February [1497]. Ind. W.

On 23 February the bp entered the fourth year of his episcopate.

159 Institution of Thomas Grevyle, cl., by his proctor John Mannyng, to Holwell (*Holwale*) ch., vac. by the death of Thomas Sterr, cl.; patrons, abbot and convent Cirencester (*Cirencestre*) BM. [London,] 27 February [1497]. Ind. D.

160 Collation to M. Edmund Crome DTh of a canonry and the prebend of Wilsford and Woodford (*Woodford alias Wyvelesford*) in Salisbury cath., vac. by the death of M. Richard Lichefeld DCL. [London,] 27 February [1497]. Instal. Dn.

161 [Fol. 23ᵛ] Collation to M. Thomas Hobbys MA of East Hendred (*Esthenreth*) ch., vac. by the res. of M. Roger Church DCnL. [London,] 28 February [1497].² Ind. B.³

162 Institution of M. David Knolles BCnL to Tollard St Peter [Tollard Royal] ch., vac. by the death [*sic*] of Thomas Hobbys; patron *hac vice*, John Savage, esq. Sonning, 20 March [1497]. Ind. S.

163 Institution of Laurence Joly, chapl., to Aldworth (*Aldeworth*) v., vac. by the death of Richard Hadyrson; patrons, prioress and convent Broomhall (*Bromhale*). Sonning, 22 March [1497]. Ind. B.

164 Institution of John Wyntryngham, chapl., to Pangbourne (*Pangborn*) ch., vac. by the death of John Huntyngdon; patrons, abbot and convent Reading (*Radyng*), Sonning, 22 March [1497]. Ind. B.

165 [Fol. 24] Institution of Ralph Eyre, chapl., to Sulhamstead (*Sulhampsted*) Abbots ch., vac. by the death of Richard Patte; patrons, abbot and convent Reading (*Radyng*) BM. Sonning, 23 March [1497].

1 There were two chantries in Chippenham; that dedicated to the BVM pertained to Stanley abbey.
2 *Ultimo die* = 29 February? See C.R. Cheney, *Handbook of Dates for Students of English History* for a discussion of dating.
3 See below 180.

Ind. B.

On 25 March the year changes from 1496 to 1497.

166 Collation to Edward Bray, cl., by his proctor M. John Foted, of a canonry and the prebend of Yetminster (*Yatemystre*) Prima in Salisbury cath., vac. by the res. of Richard Bray, cl. Sonning, 30 March 1497. Instal. Dn.

166a Enrolment of dispensation by Pope Alexander [VI] to Edward Bray, scholar, in his sixth year, to receive and retain after he has attained his eighth year, [Fol. 24ᵛ] any cath. and metropolitan canonries and prebends, otherwise requiring even priest's orders, and to resign or exchange them, and likewise any canonries or prebends in collegiate churches, notwithstanding the said defect. Rome: St Peter's, 15 (*idibus*) July 1496.[1] [Marginal at bottom of Fol. 24 (in English): In sixth year of his age.]

167 [Fol. 25] Institution of M. John Perkwyn, to Bray (*Braye*) v., on an exchange of benefices with Thomas Philips; patrons, abbot and convent Cirencester (*Cirencestre*) BM, Worcester dioc.; and institution of Thomas Philips, by his proctor John Esterby, to Winterslow (*Wynterslow*) ch.; patron, George Nevile, kt, lord Bergavenny (*Bergevenny*); John Perkwyn and Richard Norton, proctor [for Thomas Philips], swore the oath of canonical obedience. Sonning, 4 April 1497. Ind. B. (Perkwyn); ind. S. (Philips).

168 Institution of Thomas Everton, chapl., by his proctor Robert Laurence, NP, to [Long] Newnton (*Newenton*) ch., vac. by the res. of John Erton; patrons, abbot and convent Malmesbury. Sonning, 12 April 1497. Ind. W. Assignment to Erton of annual pension of 4 marks for life.

169 [Fol. 25ᵛ] Collation to John Sampson, priest, of the v. of Sutton [Benger] St Leonard[2] by Christian Malford (*Crystian Malford*), vac. by the res. of David Jonys. Sonning, 13 April 1497. Ind. W.[3]

170 Institution of M. Richard Bedyll MA to Little Shefford (*Shifford orientalis*) ch., vac. by the death of Ralph Whight; patron, Richard

---

1   See *CPL, Vol. XVI*, 539 – where the date is 9 July 1496.
2   The dedication of Sutton Benger today is All Saints.
3   See below 197, 202.

Feteplace, esq.[1] Sonning, 7 May 1497. Ind. B.

171 Institution of M. John Coydmore BCnL to Fisherton (*Fyssherton*) Delamere ch. [*rectius* v.], vac. by the death of Roger Swan; patrons, prior and convent Maiden Bradley (*Maydenbradley*). Sonning, 3 June 1497. Ind. S. [Marginal: *per W.*][2]

172 Institution of M. Benedict Dodyn MA to Wyke Regis ch., vac. by the res. of M. Henry Sutton MD; patron, Thomas [Langton], bp of Winchester. Sonning, 1 July 1497. Ind. D. [Marginal: *per W.*]

173 Institution of M. Robert Herryes BCnL to Milston (*Milleston*) ch., vac. by the death of John Ap Lethyn; patron, William Barkeley, kt. Sonning, 4 July 1497. Ind. S.

174 [Fol. 26] Institution of Thomas Warner, cl., to Little Wittenham (*Wytenham parva*) ch., vac. by the death of Richard Asshendon; patrons, abbot and convent Abingdon (*Abendon*) BVM. Sonning, 10 July 1497. Ind. B.

175 Institution of William Turnour, chapl., to the rectory of Beckhampton (*Bakhampton*) free chapel, vac. by the death of John Wilton; patron, William, lord Stourton. Sonning, 22 July 1497. Ind. W.

176 Collation to M. Thomas Jane DCnL of a canonry and the prebend of Fordington and Writhlington (*Fordyngton et Wrythelyngton, Fordington et Wrythelington*) in Salisbury cath., vac. by the res. of M. John de Gigliis DC&CnL. The king's manor of Woodstock, 5 August 1497. Instal. Dn.

177 Institution of M. John Hyslyngton DTh to Shaftesbury St Rumbold (*S. Rumwald juxta Shafton'*) ch., vac. by the death of Thomas Warwyk; patrons, abbess and convent Shaftesbury. Ramsbury, 10 August 1497. Ind. D.

178 Institution of Richard Chiltern BA, cl., to Winterborne Clenston (*Clenchton*) ch., vac. by the death of Robert Gryseby; patron, Thomas de la Lynde, kt. Ramsbury, 25 August 1497. Ind. D.

---

1   The Fettiplace family monuments are in Little Shefford ch.
2   See above 13, where Fisherton Delamere is correctly described as a v..

179 [Fol. 26ᵛ] Institution of M. David Knollys BCnL to custody of the hospital of St John the Baptist in Shaftesbury St Martin parish, vac. by the res. of George Twynyho, cl.; patrons, abbess and conv. of Shaftesbury. Ramsbury, 14 September 1497. Ind. D. [Marginal: *per W.*]

180 Collation to M. Richard Caute ALibM of East Hendred (*Easthenreth*) ch., vac. by the res. of M. Thomas Hobbys. Ramsbury, 23 September 1497. Ind. B.¹ [Marginal: *per W.*]

181 Institution of Thomas Skakylthorp, chapl., to Bishopstone (*Bysshopton, Bisshoppeston*) v. or prebendal ch., vac. by the death of Robert Ladyman; patron, M. William Eliott, canon and prebendary of Bishopstone in Salisbury cath. Ramsbury, 11 October 1497. Mand. ind. directed to the Dean of Salisbury cath.

182 Collation to M. James Whitstons DCnL, by his proctor James South, of Poulshot (*Paulesholt, Pawlesholt*) ch., vac. by the res. of M. Edward [*sic – rectius* Edmund] Peercy. Ramsbury, 13 October 1497. Ind. S.²

183 Collation to John Prysow, chapl., of Chitterne (*Chyttern*) All Saints v., vac. by the res. of John Herryes. Ramsbury, 21 November 1497. Ind. S.³

184 [Fol. 27] Institution of M. Richard Chaunceller BC&CnL, by his proctor Robert Laurence, NP, to Malmesbury St Paul v., vac. by the death of M. William Shirwood; patrons, abbot and convent Malmesbury. Sonning, 9 December 1497. Ind. W.

185 Institution of M. William Atwater DTh to Spettisbury (*Spectebury*) ch., vac. by the death of M. Robert Pester; patrons, prior and convent Witham BM, OCarth, Bath dioc. Sonning, 20 December 1497. Ind. D.⁴

186 Institution of M. John Bigges BC&CnL, cl., to Shaftesbury St Laurence ch., vac. by the death of M. Walter Strotinger; patrons, abbess and convent Shatesbury. Sonning, 20 January [1498]. Ind. D. [Marginal: *quarto* (?)]

1   See above 161.
2   See above 61, 86 and below 190, 229.
3   See above 34.
4   See above 47 and below 208.

187   Collation to M. Robert Pevesey MA, by his proctor Ralph Ryland, of West Ilsley (*Ildeslee, Ildesle*) ch., vac. by the death of [blank]. Sonning, 20 January [1498]. Ind. B.[1]

188   Collation to Silvester [Fol. 27^v] de Gigles, cl., by his proctor Peter Carmelianus, the king's Latin Secretary, of a canonry and the prebend of Chisenbury and Chute (*Chute et Chesyngbury, Chesingbury*) in Salisbury cath., vac. by the res. of M. Geoffrey Blythe BTh. London: Fleet Street, 29 January [1498]. Instal. Dn.[2]

189   Institution of Thomas Alderson, priest, to South Moreton (*Southmorton*) ch., vac. by the res. of M. Thomas Popeley; patron, Thomas Metham, kt, of Metham, Yorkshire. Annual pension of 33s.4d. assigned to Popeley for life. London: Fleet Street, 31 January [1498]. Ind. B.[3]

190   Collation to Thomas Cowley, chapl., of Poulshot (*Pawlesholt*) ch., vac. by the res. of M. James Whitstons. London: Fleet Street, 12 February [1498]. Ind. S.[4]

191   Institution of Thomas Jackson, chapl., to Besselsleigh (*Lighe alias Besillesliegh, Beseillesleghe*) ch., vac. by the res. of William Irelond MA; patron, William Besilles, esq. Abingdon (*Abendon*), 22 February [1498]. Ind. B. [Marginal: *per canc* (?)]

   On 23 February the bp entered the fifth year of his episcopate.

192   [Fol. 28] Institution of John Sutton, chapl., to Preshute (*Presshut*) v., vac. by the res. of M. Robert Pevesey; patron, master (*custos*) of the choristers of Salisbury cath., on nomination by the bp. Newbury, 23 February [1498].[5] Mand. ind. directed to the official of the peculiar of Marlborough (*Marleburgh*). [Marginal: per canc (?)]

193 Institution of M. John Estmond MA, chapl., to Locking (*Lokynge*) ch., vac. by the res. of M. ~~John~~ [*sic*] Robert Bassett; patrons, abbot and convent Abingdon (*Abendon*). Annual pension of £10.13s.4d. assigned to Bassett for life. Sonning, 27 February [1498]. Ind. B.

---

1   See below 203.
2   See above 98 and below 219.
3   See below 239.
4   See above 61, 86, 182 and below 229.
5   See below 202.

194 Institution of John Blithe, cl., to the free chapel or portion of Haxton (*Hacleston, Hakleston*) in Fittleton (*Fedylton*) parish, vac. by the res. of M. John Estmond; [Fol. 28ᵛ] *hac vice* patron, Edward Darell (*Derell*), kt, of Littlecote (*Lytelcote*). Sonning, 3 March [1498]. Ind. S.

195 Institution of M. Geoffrey Elyes BCL to Thatcham (*Thacham*) v., vac. by the death of John Skynner; patrons, abbot and convent Reading (*Rading*). Sonning, 4 March [1498]. Ind. B.

196 Institution of William Shepherd, chapl., to Poole Keynes (*Pole*) ch., vac. by the res. of John Clifford; patron, the king as Duke of Lancaster. Sonning, 5 March [1498]. Ind. W.

197 Collation to M. Richard Broughton BCL, priest, of Sutton Benger v., vac. by the death of John Sampson. Sonning, 13 March [1498]. Ind. W.[1]

198 Institution of M. Christopher Baynbrige DC&CnL, by his proctor M. John Wely, NP, to All Cannings (*Alcanynges*) prebendal ch., vac. by the death of John Wele [*sic*],[2] last prebendary; patrons, abbess and convent Nunnaminster, Winchester, Winchester dioc. Sonning, 20 March [1498]. Ind. W.

On 25 March the year changes from 1497 to 1498.

199 [Fol. 29] Institution of Walter Norreys, chapl., to Woodsford (*Wirdesford*) ch., vac. by the res, of Thomas Lawson; patrons, abbot and convent Cerne. Salisbury: the Palace, 10 April 1498. Ind. D.[3] [Marginal: *per canc* (?)]

200 Institution of John Burduax, chapl., to Robert Godmanston's chantry in Salisbury St Thomas the Martyr ch., vac. by the death of Nicholas Staysett; patrons, dean and chapter of Salisbury cath. Salisbury: the Palace, 21 April 1498. Mand. ind. directed to Dean and Chapter of Salisbury cath. [Marginal: *per canc*]

201 Collation to M. Henry Sutton MD, by his proctor Elisha Goold, literate, of St Nicholas hospital, Salisbury, vac. by the res. of M.

---

1 See above 169, and below 202.
2 Probably a scribal error for Richard Waren *or* Waryn, who was instituted in 1492 (*Reg. Langton*, 384). John Wely is the name of the proctor. There is a gap in the list of rectors in the church after Richard Waryn.
3 See above 68.

Geoffrey Blythe, last keeper. Shaftesbury, 27 April 1498. Mand. ind. directed to William Stokfyssh and John Otland, chapl.[1] [2] [Marginal: *per canc*]

202 Institution of M. Richard Broghton BCnL to Preshute (*Presshute*) v., on an exchange of benefices with John Sutton; patron, master (*custos*) of the choristers of Salisbury cath., on nomination by the bp; and collation to John Sutton of Sutton Benger v., on the above exchange with Broghton. Sherborne (*Shirborn*) castle, 15 May 1498.[3] Ind. (Sutton) W.; mand. ind. of Broghton directed to the official of the peculiar of Marlborough (*Marleburgh*).

203 [Fol. 29[v]] Collation to Richard Norton, chapl., of West Ilsley (*West Ildeslee*) ch., vac. by the death of M. Robert Pevesey. Sherborne (*Shirborn*) castle, 19 May 1498. Ind. B.[4]

204 Institution of M. Thomas Saye BCL to Tidpit (*Tuttpytte*) ch., vac. by the res. of John Dale; patrons, abbot and convent Glastonbury. Chardstock (*Chardstok*), 29 May 1498. Ind. S.[5]

205 Institution of William Tacy, chapl., to Ludgershall (*Ludgarsale*) ch., vac. by the res. of William Jokyns; patrons, prioress and convent Amesbury (*Ambresbury*). Sherborne (*Shirborn*) castle, 8 June 1498. Ind. S.

206 Collation to John Esterby, chapl., of Lord Beauchamp's chantry in Salisbury cath., vac. by the death of Robert Hunt. Lacock, 18 June 1498. Mand. ind. blank; *rectius* Dn?

207 Institution of John Bigge, chapl., to Melbury Sampford (*Melbury Samford*) ch., vac. by the res. of Walter Norreys; patron, Katherine Brownyng, widow, lady of the manor or lordship of Melbury Sampford (*Melbury Samford*). Ramsbury, 5 July 1498. Ind. D.[6]

208 [Fol. 30] Institution of M. Thomas Harper DTh, by his proctor Robert Stofford, literate, to Spettisbury (*Spectebury*) ch., vac. by the

---

1   William Stockfyssh was a vicar-choral of Salisbury cath. (*Reg. Langton*, 427); John Otland or Odlande was cantarist of Godmanston chantry in Salisbury St Thomas ch. (*Reg. Langton*, 286). Godmanstone's chantry supported two cantarists.
2   See above 99.
3   See above 169, 192, 197.
4   See above 187.
5   See above 135.
6   See above 26.

res. of M. William Atwater DTh, patrons, prior and convent Witham (*Wittham*), OCarth., Bath dioc. Ramsbury, 10 July 1498. Ind. D.[1]

209   Collation to M. Thomas Holes BCL of a canonry and the prebend of Bitton (*Bytton*) in Salisbury cath., vac. by the death of M. John Gunthorp. Ramsbury, 26 July 1498. Mand. ind., dated 26 August 1498, directed to the keeper of the spiritualities of Worcester dioc.[2]

210   Collation to M. Henry Hawtre, priest, of a canonry and the prebend of Ratfyn (*Rotfen*) in Salisbury cath., vac. by the acceptance of another prebend by M. Thomas Holes. London: Fleet Street, 30 July 1498. Instal. Dn.

211 Institution of M. Robert Burton MA to Wootton Bassett (*Wotton Bassett*) v., vac. by the death of M. William Wykewyke; patrons, abbot and convent Stanley, OCist. London: Fleet Street, 30 July 1498. Ind. W.

212   [Fol. 30ᵛ] Collation to Augustine Church, bp of Lydda,[3] sufficiently dispensed by the apostolic see, of Boscombe ch., vac. by the death of Robert Wulf. Ramsbury, 11 August 1498. Ind. S.[4]

213   Institution of M. Thomas Randolf LicCnL to Abingdon (*Abendon*) St Nicholas ch., vac. by the res. of M. William Atwater, DTh; patrons, abbot and convent Abingdon (*Abendon*). Ramsbury, 28 August 1498. Ind. B.

214   Institution of Nicholas Staunton, chapl., to Winterborne Monkton (*Wynterborn alias Monkynton*) v., vac. by the res. of Philip Asshe; patrons, abbot and convent Cirencester (*Cirencestre*) BVM, Worcester dioc. Ramsbury, 31 August 1498. Ind. W [*sic*]; *rectius* D?

215 Institution of M. Thomas Daude MA to Great Shefford (*West Shifford alias Shifford Magna*) ch., vac. by the death of John Bateman; *hac vice* patron, the devout woman lady Florence Cheyne. Ramsbury, 3 September 1498. Ind. B.

---

1   See above 47, 185.
2   Bp Giovanni de Gigliis of Worcester died 25 August 1498, but the direction of the mandate for induction is probably based on the knowledge that he was permanently resident in Rome.
3   Augustine Church was abbot of Thame, OCist.
4   See below 233.

216 Collation to M. John Brice, ALibM, by his proctor Christopher George, literate, of Winfrith Newburgh (*Wynfred*) ch., vac. by the res. of Richard Norton. Ramsbury, 25 September 1498. Ind. D.[1]

217 [Fol. 31] Enrolment of the bp's letters of collation to William Tofte, chapl., of the succentorship of Salisbury cath. with Ebbesborne Wake (*Ebbesborn*) ch. annexed thereto, vac. by the death of M. Robert Pevesey. Ramsbury, 19 October 1498.

217a Enrolment of the bp's mandate directed to the dean of Salisbury cath. to receive Tofte.

218 Institution of William Bragg[es], cl., to Aston [Tirrold] ch., vac. by the res. of M. Thomas Gybon; patrons, prior and convent Witham (*Wittham*) BM, OCarth. Westminster, 30 October 1498. Ind. B.

219 Collation to Peter Carmelianus, priest, the king's Latin Secretary, of a canonry and the prebend of Chisenbury and Chute (*Chute et Chesingbury*) in Salisbury cath., vac. by the res. of Silvester de Gigliis. Westminster, 30 November 1498. Instal. Dn.[2]

220 [Fol. 31ᵛ] Institution of Thomas Mower, cl., to Sunningwell (*Sonnyngwell*) ch., vac. by the death of Richard Joyse; patrons, abbot and convent Abingdon (*Abendon*) BMV. Westminster, 18 December 1498. Ind. B.

221 Institution of M. Richard Horton ALibM to Corfe (*Corffe*) [Castle] ch., vac. by the res. of M. Geoffrey Blithe; patrons, abbess and convent Shaftesbury. Westminster, 7 January [1499]. Ind. D.[3] [Marginal: *debet*]

222 Collation to John Stratton of Wilton (*Wylton*) St Michael in Southstreet (*Southstrete*) ch., vac. and falling to the bp's collation *hac vice* by lapse. Westminster, 18 January [1499]. No mandate for induction; *rectius* S. [Marginal: *per donat* (?)]

223 Institution of William Hygons, chapl., by his proctor Thomas Henbury, to Sherston v., vac. by the res. of M. Robert Burton; patrons, abbot and convent Tewkesbury BM. Annual pension of £3.19s.8d. previously assigned by bp Thomas [Langton] to Thomas

1 See above 134.
2 See above 98, 188.
3 See above 97.

Strobull former v. for life.[1] Westminster, 18 January [1499]. Ind. W.

224 Institution of Thomas Gogyon, chapl., to Easton Grey (*Eston Gray*) ch., vac. by the acceptance of another incompatible benefice by M. Andrew Patryk; [Fol. 32] patrons, abbot and convent Gloucester (*Gloucestre*) St Peter, Worcester dioc. Westminster, 26 January [1499]. Ind. W.

225 Institution of M. William Broke DCnL, by his proctor M. John Havyrfeld, to Wallingford (*Walingford*) St Peter ch., vac. by the death of William Berton; patron M. Stephen Berworth MD, dean of St Nicholas free chapel in Wallingford Castle. Westminster. 9 February [1499]. Ind. B. [Marginal: *per W*]

226 Institution of Thomas Blakked, chapl., by his proctor William Clerk, cl., to Wimborne (*Wymbourn*) St Giles ch., vac. by the death of Thomas Edwardys; *hac vice* patrons, Thomas Strangways and Elizabeth his wife, in the name and right of the wardship of Henry Asshley granted to Elizabeth by the king. Westminster, 5 February [1499]. Ind. D. [Marginal: *per W*]

227 Institution of William Huntrode, chapl., to [North] Tidworth (*Tudworth*) ch., vac. by the res. of Richard Crowe, cl.; patron, the king by reason of the earldom of Salisbury. Westminster, 15 February [1499]. Ind. S.

228 Institution of M. Robert Cowper BMus, chapl., by his proctor James Plough, to Lydiard Tregoze (*Legiarde Tregosse*) ch., vac. by the death of M. [blank] Bullok;[2] patron, Elizabeth Bygod, widow, former wife of Oliver Sainct John, esq., deceased. Westminster, 15 February [1499]. Ind. W.

[Fol. 32ᵛ] *On 23 February the bp entered the sixth year of his episcopate.*

229 Collation to Nicholas Inglesent ALibM, by his proctor William Genyng[es], of Poulshot (*Pawlesholt*) ch., vac. by the res. of Thomas Cowley, chapl. Westminster, 6 March [1499]. Ind. S.[3]

230 Institution of Richard Haliday, chapl., to Stratton St Margaret v.,

1 *Reg. Langton*, 320, dated 1 October 1491.
2 Richard Bullok was instituted to Lydiard Tregoze in 1486 (*Reg. Langton*, 94).
3 See above 61, 86, 182, 190.

vac. by the death of Gilbert Lancastre; patrons, warden and scholars of Merton [coll.], Oxford, at the bp's nomination. Westminster, 11 March [1499]. Ind. W.

231 Institution of Henry Seffton [Sesston?], chapl., by his proctor M. William Jonys, to Teffont Evias ch., vac. by the death of John Haton; patron, Walter Hungerford, kt. Westminster, 15 March [1499]. Ind. S.[1]

232 Institution of M. John Holt ALibM, priest, by his proctor M. Richard Holte, to Piddletrenthide (*Pudel Trenthyde*) v., vac. by the death of John Willughby; patron, abbot of Hyde by Winchester St Peter. Westminster, 16 March [1499]. Ind. D.[2]

[Fol. 33] *On 25 March the year changes from 1498 to 1499.*

233 Collation to M. John Kyte BCnL of Boscombe (*Borscombe*) ch., vac. by the res. of Augustine [Church], bp of Lydda. Ramsbury, 16 April 1499. Ind. S.[3]

234 Collation to John Whitehedd BA, cl., of Brimpton (*Brympton*) free chapel, vac. and falling to the bp's collation by lapse. Ramsbury, 27 May 1499. Mandate for induction addressed to archd. of ~~Salisbury~~ [*sic*] Berkshire; no notice of oath of obedience.

235 Institution of Charles (*Karolus*) Carleton, chapl., to Aldermaston (*Aldermanston*) v., vac. by the death of Jerome Sparkforth; patrons, M. Christopher Baynbrigge DC&CnL, warden, and brothers and sisters of the hospital of St Julian, commonly called God's House, Southampton. Ramsbury, 23 April 1499. Ind. B.

236 Institution of M. William Stokes, v. of Hungerford in the jurisdiction of the dean of Salisbury, to Chilton [Foliat] ch., on an exchange of benefices with M. Thomas Whitamour; *hac vice* patron, Margaret [Beaufort], mother of the king, [Fol. 33ᵛ] countess of Richmond and Derby, by reason of a grant of the next presentation by Edward Burgh, kt, patron, not only as co-portioner but also as the heir of Thomas Burgh, kt, his father, by reason of an enfeoffment etc.

---

1   See above 4. Robert Goddysgrace was instituted to Teffont Evias ch. on the death of John Hatton on 13 June 1489 (*Reg. Langton*, 221); we may assume that the news of Hatton's death was premature.
2   See above 101.
3   See above 212.

[*sic*]; the case of the exchange committed by the bp on 4 May 1499 to be heard by Edward Cheyne, dean of Salisbury, reserving the bp's right to induct and receive the canonical oath of obedience, rendered by Stokes's proctor, Thomas Estoft. Ramsbury, 4 May 1499. Ind. W.[1]

237 Institution of William Rawlyns, cl., by his proctor Thomas Moleyns, literate, to the chaplaincy of Whitechurch [Canonicorum], vac. by the death of Thomas Ousteby; patron, Oliver [King], bp of Bath [and Wells]. Ramsbury, 18 May 1499. Ind. D.

238 Institution of M. Elisha (*Heliseus*) Ruthyn BC&CnL, by his proctor M. Richard Wodson BCL, to Enford v., vac. by the death of Mathew Dalamer; patrons, prior and convent Winchester cath. Ramsbury, 9 July 1499. Ind. S.[2]

239 [Fol. 34] Determination, with full powers *in hac parte* as ordinary granted by Thomas [Rotherham], archbp of York, of an exchange of benefices; and institution of Thomas Alderson, by his proctor John Dykson, to the mastership or custody of the ch. or chapel of St James, Sutton in Holderness, York dioc., on an exchange of benefices with M. Robert Ferries BCnL; patrons, William Bulmer and John Everingham, kts, and Ralph Salvan, Brian Stapilton, Henry Ughtrede, and William Bukton, esqs; the induction and canonical oath of obedience of Alderson being reserved to the archbp of York; and institution of Ferries to South Moreton (*Southmorton*) ch., on the above exchange with Alderson; patron, Thomas Metham, lord of Metham, York dioc., esq. Annual pension of 33s.4d. previously assigned to M. Thomas Popeley, former r. of South Moreton (*Southmoorton*). Ramsbury, 17 July 1499. Ind. (Ferries) B.[3]

240 [Fol. 34ᵛ] Collation to M. Geoffrey Blithe DTh of the archdeaconry of Salisbury, vac. by the death of M. Edmund Chaderton. Ramsbury, 22 August 1499. Instal. Dn.

241 Collation to M. Geoffrey Blithe DTh of a canonry and the prebend of Stratton in Salisbury cath., vac. by the death of M. Edmund Chaderton. Ramsbury, 22 August 1499. Instal. Dn.

1 See above 148.
2 See above 10.
3 See above 189; *cf. Register of Thomas Rotherham, Archbishop of York 1480-1500*, Vol. I, No. 1218, where the names of Alderson and Ferries are rendered 'Aderson' and 'Fereys'.

242 Collation to M. Robert Toneys BCL, cl., of a canonry and the prebend of Beminster (*Bemystre*) Secunda in Salisbury cath., vac. by the death of M. Edmund Martyn DC&CnL. Ramsbury, 23 August 1499. Instal. Dn.[1]

243 Collation to M. Hugo Peynthwyn DCL, priest, of a canonry and the prebend of Axford in Salisbury cath., vac. by the acceptance of another prebend by M. Robert Toneys. Ramsbury, 23 August 1499. Instal. Dn.[2]

MISCELLANEOUS MEMORANDA

244 [Fol. 35][3] Commission to M. Laurence Cock[ys] DCnL to be v. or commissary general in spiritualities and to be official principal of the bp's consistory court. [Fol. 35ᵛ] Not having at hand the seal of the bishopric of Salisbury, sealed with the seal of the archdeaconry of Richmond. London: Domus Conversorum, 31 December 1493.

245 Letters patent appointing M. John Foted BTh, bp's chapl., to be receiver general for Salisbury dioc. [No date]

246 [Fol. 36] Commission to M. George Wood BCnL to be commissary or sequestrator general in the archdeaconries of Berkshire and Wiltshire, for correction of the bp's subjects both clerical and lay, for imposing canonical penalties, for proving wills etc., for receiving oaths of canonical obedience, for levying and receiving profits and pensions, for making quittances, and for collecting fruits and profits pertaining to the bp from vacant benefices. Dated = [*sic*].

247 Note of a similar commission to M. John Westley BCnL for the archdeaconries of Dorset and Salisbury. On the same date and in the same place [*sic*].

248 Copy of a letter [from the dean and chapter of Salisbury cath.?] to John [Morton], cardinal priest of St Anastasia, archbp of Canterbury and primate of All England, legate of the Apostolic See, requesting that John [Blyth] DCL, priest, archdn Richmond, whom pope

1   See above 149.
2   See above 84.
3   Top half of this fol. blank, perhaps originally intended to be first fol. in register. As bound, this begins part 2a of the register.

Alexander VI has provided to the see of Salisbury, may be consecrated to that see. [No date.]

249   Commission to Augustine [Church], bp of Lydda, to reconcile the churchyard of Salisbury St Thomas, desecrated by the shedding of human blood; to confirm boys; to consecrate chalices, corporals, and altars; [Fol. 36ᵛ] to consecrate and bless crosses, images, bells, priests' vestments, etc.; to confer minor and major orders on both the bp's subjects and those from other dioceses sufficiently dimissed by their ordinary; during pleasure. London: Domus Conversorum, 28 February [1494].

250   Licence to M. William Cadihe MA, to preach. Date as above [*sic*].

251   Grant to Robert Balgey of the office of keeper or governor of Salisbury gaol and the convict clerks in it, during pleasure, with customary fees. London: Fleet Street, 8 March [1494].

252   Letters patent appointing M. Henry Sutton MD, M. Henry Carnebull, archdn East Riding (*Estredyng*), and M. Ralph Hethcote BCnL, canons of Salisbury cath.,[1] [Fol. 37] to be proctors for his installation as bp of Salisbury. London: Fleet Street, 23 March [1494].

253   The bp's instrument testimonial of his oath of obedience to the Apostolic See. [Fol. 37ᵛ] London: St Bride's, 20 February [1494].

254   Licence to John Atkynson, proctor or nuncio for St John the Baptist hospital, Devizes (*Devises*), to collect alms for that hospital, with the grant of 40 days' indulgence to those who contribute, for a period of one year from the grant. Ramsbury, 14 August 1495.

255   [Fol. 38] Mand. to archdn Salisbury or his official to call all beneficed clergy in his archdeaconry to residence in their benefice within two months of his monition to them, and to certify the results to the bp before St Peter ad Vincula next (1 August 1496). Ramsbury, 21 April 1496.

256   [Fol. 38ᵛ] Letters patent granting to John Chevely, monk and cellarer of Reading (*Radyng*) abbey, OSB, for the building of the altar

---

1   Sutton, Carnebull, and Hethcote were prebendaries of Chisenbury and Chute, Yatesbury, and Ramsbury respectively.

of the Transfiguration and Sts Katherine and Margaret, virgins, in Reading convent, an indulgence of 40 days for all those who give. Sonning, 10 October 1495.

257 Letters patent granting to William Sandes, gent., the office of bailiff of the lordship of Godalming (*Godalmyng*), Surrey, with customary fees, during pleasure. London: Fleet Street, 25 October 1495.

258 [Fol. 39] Letters patent granting an indulgence of 40 days to any and all who give to Marlborough (*Marleburgh*) Carmelite friary, on the occasion of their chapter, called a general chapter of the order, celebrated on the feast of the Assumption and seven days thereafter, during one continuous year from the grant. [No date]

259 Licence to John Edgecombe of Swineshill (*Swynyshyll*)[1] and Joan his wife that they may employ a chapl. to celebrate and that they may hear masses and other divine offices in the chapel or oratory in honour of St Katherine, virgin and martyr, in a tower on the south bridge from Oxford, provided this is not to the detriment of parish churches etc., during pleasure. Sonning, 7 December 1496.

260 [Fol. 39ᵛ] Commission to M. William Jonys BCnL to be official and sequestrator general in the peculiar jurisdiction of Devizes (*Devises*), Marlborough (*Marleburgh*), Potterne (*Potern*), and [West] Lavington (*Lavyngton*). Sonning, 4 December 1496.

261 [English] I John Yorke bycome your man from this day forth wardes and faith to you shal bere and worldly honour for londys and tenementys which I claym to hold of you in Remmesbury in the hundred of the same in the County of Wiltes saving the faith which I owe to oure soverayn lord the kyng and to myn other lordys of the which I hold by priorite.

Homage done by John Yorke for lands and tenements held of the bp in Ramsbury (*Remmesbury*), Ramsbury hundred, Wiltshire, saving the king, at Ramsbury on 12 October 1496. Present: M. John Pykeryng, cl., John Byrley, Thomas Copcot, and many others. [*Marginal:* form for doing homage]

---

1   Almost certainly 'immediately S. of Oxford, close to Folly Bridge, with its fields lying on either side of the causeway of Grandpont' (*The Place-names of Berkshire, Part 2*, ed. by Margaret Gelling, English Place-name Society vol. L, 1974).

261a [English] I Thomas Barow bycome your man from this day forth wardes and faith to you shal bere and worldy honour for londys and tenementys which I hold of you in Bemystre in the county of [blank] Saving the faith which I owe unto oure soverayn lord the kyng and to myn other lordys of the which I hold by prioritee.

Homage done by Thomas Barow for lands and tenements held of the bp in Beaminster (*Bemystre*), county — [*sic – rectius* Dorset], saving the king, at Sonning, — [*sic*] December 1496. Present: M. Geoffrey Blythe, Edmund Crome, and John Foted, clerks, James Hyde, Thomas Garard, and many others.

262 [Fol. 40] Memorandum that on 18 March [1497 (?)], at Sonning, the bp appointed M. Thomas Martyn DCnL his commissary and sequestrator general in the archdeaconries of Salisbury and Dorset, under the form of letters as above.[1]

263 Nomination, to the abbess and convent Shaftesbury, of Elianora Eliott to be damsel [*domicella*] in the convent, and Agnes Asshe, nun of that convent, to be Elianora's instructress in the monastic life; this nomination pertains to the bp by reason of his promotion to the see of Salisbury. Sonning, 25 March 1497.

264 Licence to Christopher Belyngeham and Margaret his wife that in their chapel or oratory in Lea (*Legh*) manor in [St Nicholas] Hurst parish they and their household may attend masses and other divine offices celebrated by priests, provided this is not to the prejudice of the parish ch., during pleasure. Sonning, etc. [*sic*]

265 Letters testimonial that Richard Pury received the habit of a hermit before Augustine [Church], bp of Lydda, on 26 February [1496], in Abingdon (*Abendon*) St Nicholas ch. [Fol. 40ᵛ] Ramsbury, 20 March [1496].

266 Letters patent introducing M. John Dogett DCnL, priest, chancellor of Salisbury cath., while on pilgrimage to Jerusalem to pray for the remission of his sins. Salisbury: The Palace, 17 March [1497].

267 Presentation to the dean and chapter of Salisbury cath. of John Tanner, chapl., who was nominated by the said dean and chapter along with two others, [Fol. 41] namely John Kent and

1   See above 246, 247.

John Nytyngale, vicars choral of Salisbury cath., in accordance with the ordinance of Robert, formerly lord of Hungerford, founder of the chantry in his memory in Salisbury cath., to be chapl. of that chantry, vac. by the death of Robert Phelps, last cantarist. Ramsbury, — [*sic*] June 1496.

268   Letters patent granting a licence to Lady Margaret, countess of Richmond, who has the king's licence by letters patent dated Westminster, 1 March 1497,[1] to found a perpetual chantry for four chaplains to the laud and honour of Jesus and the Annunciation of BVM and to pray for the souls of the countess and her parents and ancestors and all the faithful departed, in the coll. or royal free chapel [of St George] in Windsor (*Windesor*) [Castle]. [Fol. 41ᵛ] Sonning, 18 July 1497.

269   Letters patent granting a house in the close of Salisbury cath., commonly called Leadenhall (*Ledenhalle*), and the tenements and gardens adjacent, to M. William Elyott, canon and prebendary of Bishopstone (*Bisshoppeston*) in Salisbury cath., so that he may reside in his canonry. Sonning, 7 May 1497.

270   Letters patent granting to John Alston, the bp's servant, custody or the office of keeper of the episcopal palace in Salisbury and an annuity of 2d. per day to be taken from the manor of Milford, Wiltshire, for life. [Fol. 42] Ramsbury, 24 June 1495.

271   Confirmation by M. Edward Cheyne DC&CnL, dean of Salisbury BM cath., and by the whole chapter there, of the customs, liberties, and privileges of Salisbury cath. Sealed with the common seal: Salisbury: Chapter House, 27 August 1499.[2] [The bottom three inches of this fol. have been cut away directly below this entry; fol. 42ᵛ is blank.]

272   [Fol. 43] Letters patent appointing William Marshall, priest, prior of Easton [Royal] (*Eston*), OTrin., and Hugh Spaldyng and Edward Scott, clerks, or any of them, to be proctors etc. for visiting the see of Rome, in accordance with the oath at the bp's consecration, etc. [Fol. 43ᵛ] Ramsbury, 28 June 1499

273   Letters patent granting to Giles Daubeney, kt, the king's

1   *CPR.Henry VII 1494-1509*, p. 79.
2   The context of this unusual instrument is the bp's death on 23 August 1499 and the ensuing *sede vacante* period.

chamberlain, the office of constable of Sherborne (*Shirborn*) Castle, Dorset, with the customary fees, etc. Ramsbury, 21 August 1499.

274 [Fols. 44-45] Index to the above institutions (Fols. 1-34ᵛ).

275 [Fol. 45ᵛ] Concordat made by Thomas [Langton], bp of Salisbury, on 22 June 1487, between M. John Person on the part of the abbot and convent Beaulieu (*Bello Loco*), Winchester dioc., and M. Henry Stanfeld, v. [Great] Coxwell (*Cockeswell*), regarding tithes. First, M. Henry has, in augmentation of his portion, the tithes of the fruits and issues of a certain close called 'Pigges crofte' and the tithes of the lands that the tenants have had or have there, from the farm of the lord by the hand of Thomas Drewett, for the said close called 'Pigges crofte' and five measures[1] of fuel (wood) annually, and from the farm of the rectory from the tenants to be paid annually 20s. as it has long stood. Item, that the said M. Henry will not claim nor make a claim for any further augmentation against the said abbot and convent as long as he is in the v. Item, he will have this by indentures drawn up between the aforesaid parties and sealed with the common seal of the said abbot and convent for the part of M. Henry. Item, the said M. Henry will have the tithes of sheaves from the lands and meadows abandoned by tenants and the farms there as it has long stood in the said v. Indenture sealed with the seals of the two parties; dated as above.

275a [Half folio attached to top of fol. 45ᵛ; handwriting of c.1800; effectively an index to appropriations]

Coxwell (*Cokeswell*)	Concord and composition between abbot and convent Beaulieu (*Bello Loco*) and v. Coxwell	45
Shrivenham (*Shryvenham*)	Concord and composition between abbot and convent Cirencester (*Cirencestre*) and v. Shrivenham	68
Sutton Courtenay (*Courtney*)	Appropriation of Sutton Courtenay ch.	80
Sutton Courtenay	Assignment of vicar's portion in Sutton Courtenay	84

276 Final concord made in the Curia Regis at Westminster, three weeks from St Hilary's day [*i.e., 3 February*], 44 Henry III [1260], before Roger de Turkeby, Gilbert de Preston, John de Wyvill, and

---

1   The word is indecipherable, but the sense is clear.

John de Cane [*Cave* ?], justices, between Robert, dean, and the chapter of Salisbury cath., represented by Henry Sytob, and Giles [of Bridport], bp of Salisbury, regarding the advowson and custody of the hospital of St Nicholas, Salisbury: the dean and chapter concede for themselves and their successors, to the bp and his successors, that he and they shall have lifelong custody of the said hospital; for his part the bp grants for himself and his successors that the dean and chapter shall always have in that hospital one brother received by the bp and his successors; that one dying they shall present another to be received; that during vacancies of the see the custody of the hospital falls to the dean and chapter and their successors until the election of the next bp has been confirmed; that the dean and chapter shall receive no brother into that hospital during vacancies of the see unless another brother dies; and if the prior of that hospital dies during a vacancy of the see, the dean and chapter and their successors may institute a new prior.

277   [Fol. 46] Richard [Hill], bp of London, to John [Blyth], bp of Salisbury, rehearsing letters from John [Morton], cardinal priest of St Anastasia, archbp of Canterbury, primate of all England, legate, under his oblong seal in red wax, rehearsing letters from the king, dated Westminster, 12 August [1495], summoning a convocation of clergy to meet at London St Paul's, or elsewhere, for the security and defence of the English ch., the peace, tranquillity, public good, and defence of the realm and subjects. The convocation is to meet at London St Paul's, on Monday 19 October [1495]; the names of those cited to attend to be certified to the archbp. [Fol. 46ᵛ] Morton's letter dated Lambeth (*Lamehithe*) manor, 22 August 1495. Hill's letter dated Fulham manor, 24 August 1495.

278   [Fol. 47] Letters to archdn of Salisbury or his official, rehearsing the above letters from the bp of London, received 7 September 1495, directing him to convene the clergy of his archdeaconry before the bp or his commissary in Salisbury cath. on 1 October 1495, to choose proctors for the said convocation. Dated etc. [*sic*]

279   Letters to John [Morton], archbp of Canterbury, certifying the names, in the schedule annexed, of the persons cited to attend Convocation. Dated etc. [*sic*]

279a   [Fol. 47ᵛ] Names of persons cited to attend convocation:
     M. Edward Cheyne DC&CnL, dean of Salisbury, for the chapter of Salisbury cath.;

In the archdeaconry of Salisbury: M. Edward Chaderton, archdn Salisbury; John Saynt John, r. Edington; William Westbury, prior Maiden Bradley (*Maydenbradley*); Richard Page, prior Ivychurch (*Ederose*); — [*sic, rectius* John Stone], prior Monkton Farley (*Farlegh monachorum*);[1]

In the archdeaconry of Dorset: M. Robert Langton, archdn Dorset; Peter [Rampsham], abbot Sherborne (*Shirborn*); William [Middleton], abbot Milton (*Middelton*); Hugh [Dorchestre], abbot Abbotsbury (*Abbotesbury*); Roger [Bemyster], abbot Cerne; John [Bryan], abbot Bindon (*Byndon*);

In the archdeaconry of Wiltshire: M. Christopher Urswyk, archdn Wiltshire; Thomas [Olveston], abbot Malmesbury; Thomas, abbot Stanley; Thomas [Walshe], prior Bradenstoke;

In the archdeaconry of Berkshire: M. Stephen Berworth, archdn Berkshire; John [Santt], abbot of Abingdon (*Abendon*); John [Thorne], abbot of Reading (*Radyng*); Richard [Sewy], prior of Bisham (*Bustlesham*);[2] John [Hilston], prior of Hurley; Thomas [Ware], prior of Poughley;

Proctors for the whole clergy of the diocese: M. Laurence Cockys DCnL, canon of Salisbury cath.; M. Edmund Crome DTh.

280   [Fol. 48] Royal writ ordering collection of the clerical tenth granted to the king by the convocation which met in London St Paul's cath. from 19 October 1495 to 21 December 1495, the first moiety to be levied and collected at the feast of the Nativity of St John the Baptist next [24 June 1496], and the second at Martinmas [11 November 1496]; with the usual exemptions for poverty, lists of which are to be supplied to the Treasurer and Barons of the Exchequer; excepting also all benefices of the value of 12 marks *p.a.* or less, in which the incumbent personally resides, lists of these too to be supplied as above. Exempt also all the possessions of Oxford and Cambridge colleges; Winchester Coll., founded by William Wykeham, once bp. of Winchester; and Eton BM Coll. by Windsor. Exempt also, [Fol. 48ᵛ] as certified to the king or the Treasurer and Barons of the Exchequer, those who have been indicted by laymen or the lay power between the last day of the last convocation, 8 November 1491, and the last day for payment of the tenth. Exempt also Syon St Saviour, BVM, and St Bridget (*Brigit*) house or mon., OSA [*sic*], Sheen (*Shene*) Jesus of

1   Here as elsewhere surnames and/or forenames supplied from *The Heads of Religious Houses: England and Wales, III, 1377-1540*, ed. by David M. Smith (CUP, 2008).

2   Marginal: *William*. Richard Sewy resigned as prior and William Greve was elected to succeed him in February 1492 (*Reg. Langton*, 556).

Bethlehem (*Bethleem*) house or mon., Salutation of BMV house in the suburbs of the city of London, OCarth, and all other OCarth houses. Exempt also the mon. or priory churches as follows: Boxley mon., Canterbury dioc.; Milton (*Middilton*) mon., Salisbury dioc.; Bath priory, Bath and Wells dioc.; Earls Colne priory, London dioc.; Tarrant (*Terrant*) nunnery, Salisbury dioc., OCist. Exempt also Gate Burton (*Gateborton*) parish ch., Lincoln dioc.; Warboys (*alias Wardeboys*) parish ch., Lincoln dioc.; Orby (*Ourby*) parish ch., Lincoln dioc.; Sutterby (*Suthursby*) parish ch., Lincoln dioc.; London St John Zachary parish ch., London dioc.; provostship of Cotterstock (*Cotherstoke*) [coll.], Lincoln dioc.; Carlton-cum-Dalby (*Carleton cum Dalby*) prebend in Lincoln cath.; Corringham (*Coryngham*) prebend in Lincoln cath.; Langford Ecclesia prebend in Lincoln cath.; Nassington (*Nassyngton*) prebend in Lincoln cath., Melton Ross-cum-Scamblesby (*Scamellysby et Melton Roos*) in Lincoln cath.; Shoreham parish ch. in the immediate jurisdiction of Canterbury Christ Ch.; supposing that Corringham (*Coryngham*) prebend is worth £26.13s.4d. and not more, Langford Ecclesia prebend £16 and not more, Nassington (*Nassyngton*) prebend £40 and not more, Melton Ross-cum-Scamblesby (*Scamellesby et Melton Roos*) 15 marks and not more, and Shoreham parish ch. 45 marks and not more. Exempt also the master and fellows of Thompson (*Thomsun*) St Martin coll., Norwich dioc., Arundel (*Arundell*) Holy Trinity coll. [*sic – rectius* hospital], Chichester dioc. [Fol. 49] Proviso that the ordinary appoint collectors and certify their names to the Treasurer and Barons of the Exchequer by Pentecost next [22 May 1496]. For expenses the collectors are to take 8d. for every £1 collected. [Fol. 49ᵛ] Westminster, 30 January 1496.

281 Commission to the abbot and convent Milton (*Myddelton*) for collection of the above clerical tenth in the archdeaconry of Dorset. Exempt Bindon (*Byndon*) monastery (OCist) in Dorset archdeaconry; the poor nuns of Lacock monastery; the poor nuns of Kington St Michael (*Estkyngton*) priory; the poor religious of Easton (*Eston*) priory in Wiltshire archdeaconry; the poor religious of Poughley priory; the poor nuns of Broomhall (*Bromeholem*) in Berkshire archdeaconry; and the usual exemptions of the goods, benefices, and ecclesiastical possessions of any persons listed in the following schedule [284-286] not to be taxed except as directed in that schedule. Ramsbury, 25 April 1496.

282 [Fol. 50] Memorandum that similar mandates were sent to the abbot and convent Malmesbury for the archdeaconries of Salisbury and Wiltshire, and to the abbot and convent Reading for the archdeaconry of Berkshire.

283 Certification to the Treasurer and Barons of the Exchequer, rehearsing the king's writ received on 28 April [*sic*] [1496], of the names of the deputy collectors [as above, 281-282]. Ramsbury, etc. [*sic*]. Schedules attached:

284 The names of all the cures customarily assessed, not appropriated, of a modern value of 12 marks *p.a.* or less, [Fol. 50ᵛ] exempt from the said tenth, in which benefices the rectors or vicars reside, or if absent are licenced to study:

ARCHDEACONRY OF BERKSHIRE

Abingdon deanery: Sparsholt (*Spersholt*) v.; Letcombe (*Ledcombe*) Bassett ch.; Compton Beauchamp ch.; Kingston Bagpuize (*Kyngton Bagpuys*) ch.; East Hendred (*Esthenreth*) chapel *alias* portion of the chancellor of Salisbury in East Hendred ch.;

Reading (*Rading*) deanery: Padworth ch.; Sulham ch.; Woolhampton (*Wollavyngton*) ch.; Purley ch.; Aldermaston (*Aldermanston*) v.; Sulhamstead (*Sulhamsted*) Abbots ch.; Arborfield (*Herberghfeld*) chapel; Reading: St Giles's v.;

Wallingford (*Walyngford*) deanery: Wallingford, St Peter's ch.; Wallingford, St Mary Major ch.; Wallingford, St Leonard's ch.; Streatley (*Stretley*) v.;

Newbury deanery: Inkpen (*Ynkepenne*) ch.; Frilsham (*Frydlesham*) ch.; Brightwalton ch.; Avington (*Avyngton*) ch.; Enborne (*Enborn*) ch.; Hamstead (*Hampsted*) Marshall ch.; Kintbury (*Kenetbury*) v.;

ARCHDEACONRY OF SALISBURY

Chalke deanery: Tidpit (*Tudpytt*) ch.; Tollard [Royal] ch., one part; Tollard [Royal] ch., another part;[1] Bishopstone (*Bysshoppeston*) *alias* Ebbesborne (*Ebbesborn*) Episcopi v.;

Wyly deanery: Rollestone (*Rolveston*) ch.; Sherrington (*Sheryngton*)

---

1   In 1291 the ch. was held in medieties by two rectors; however, from some point in the mid- to late-fifteenth century the two medieties were held as one rectory (*VCH Wilts.*, Vol. XIII, p.86) – perhaps because of impoverishment.

alias Sherston ch.; Winterbourne (*Wynterborn*) Stoke v.; Compton Chamberlayne (*Chamburlayn*) ch.;[1] Baverstock (*Babestoke*) ch.;[2]

Amesbury (*Ambresbury*) deanery: Landford (*Laneford*) ch.; Idmiston (*Idmeston*) v.; Boscombe ch.; Alton (*Aleton*) ch. or chapel; [West] Dean (*Deane*) ch.;

Potterne (*Pottern*) deanery: [East] Coulston (*Cowleston*) ch.; [Monkton] Farleigh (*Farlegh*) ch.; Upavon (*Uphaven*) v.;

ARCHDEACONRY OF WILTSHIRE

Cricklade (*Cryklade*) deanery: Cricklade St Sampson's v.; Latton v.; Somerford Keynes v.; Eysey (*Eysy*) v.; Inglesham v.; Hannington (*Hanendon*) v.;

Marlborough (*Marleburgh*) deanery: Manningford Bruce (*Mannyngford Brewys*) ch.; Manningford (*Mannyngford*) Abbots ch.; Huish (*Huwyssh alias Hewes*) ch.; Wootton Rivers (*Wotton Ryvers*) ch.; Chisledon (*Chuselden*) ch.; Preshute (*Presshute alias Presshute cum capella*) v.;

[Fol. 51] Malmesbury deanery: Yatton [Keynell] ch.; Leigh (*Legh*) [Delamere] ch.; Malmesbury St Mary [Westport] vic.; Poole [Keynes] ch.; Sopworth ch.; Hullavington (*Hunilavyngton*) v.; [Long] Newnton (*Newenton*) ch.;

Avebury deanery: Beechingstoke (*Bechyngstoke*) ch.; Woodborough (*Woodburgh*) ch.; Alton [Barnes] ch.; Avebury v.; Corton (*Crofton*) ch.;

ARCHDEACONRY OF DORSET

Pimperne (*Pympern*) deanery: Ashmore (*Asshemere*) ch.; Pentridge (*Pentrych alias Petetrynch*) ch.; Stanbridge (*Stambrige*) ch.; Chettle (*Chetyll*) ch.; Chalbury (*Chetylbury*) ch.; Wimborne Up Monkton (*Wynterborn alias Wyhorn Carentham*) ch.; Wimborne (*Wynterborn*) St Giles chapel; Tarrant Rushton (*Tarrant Villers*) ch.;

Dorchester (*Dorchestre*) deanery: Frome Belett ch.; Woodsford (*Wyrdesford*) ch.; [West] Stafford ch.;[3] Frome Vauchurch (*From*

---

1   Marginal note assigns this ch. and the following to Chalke deanery.
2   See previous note.
3   In the lists in *Register Langton*, Upwey ch. appears here.

Vowchurch alias Negchurch) ch.; Kimmeridge (*Camberge alias Kemerych*) ch.; Bettiscombe (*Bettescombe alias Bestcombe*) ch.;

Shaftesbury deanery: Melbury Osmond ch.; Shaftesbury, St Rumbold's (*Rumwald*) ch.; Shaftesbury, St James's ch.; [Buckhorn] Weston ch.;

Whitchurch deanery: Wareham (*Warham*) St Martin's ch.; Winterborne Stickland (*Wynterborn Styklane*) ch.; Winterborne Zelston (*Wynterborn Malward alias Malford*) ch.;

Bridport (*Birtport*) deanery: Puncknowle (*Ponknolle*) ch.; [West] Bexington (*Bexynton*) ch.; Compton Abbas ch.; Wraxall (*Wrokesale alias Wroxale*) ch.

285   The names of the benefices exempt from the above clerical tenth because of their impoverishment:

ARCHDEACONRY OF BERKSHIRE: Faringdon (*Faryngdon*) v. in Abingdon deanery; Speen (*Spene*) v. in Newbury deanery; Chieveley (*Cheveley*) v. in Newbury deanery; Ufton Nervet (*Ufton Richere*) ch. in Reading (*Rading*) deanery;

ARCHDEACONRY OF SALISBURY: Alderbury (*Alwardbury*) v. in Amesbury (*Ambresbury*) deanery;

ARCHDEACONRY OF DORSET: Thornford ch. or chapel in Shaftesbury deanery; Longburton (*Burton*) v. in Shaftesbury deanery; Batcombe ch. in Shaftesbury deanery; Crofton chapel in Bridport (*Birtport*) deanery;

ARCHDEACONRY OF WILTSHIRE: [West] Overton v. in Avebury deanery.

286   The names of benefices not assessed, the true annual value of which in the common estimation exceeds 12 marks, as is clear below, out of which the tenth should be paid:

[Fol. 51ᵛ] ARCHDEACONRY OF BERKSHIRE: [New] Windsor (*Wyndesor*) ch. in Reading (*Rading*) deanery, estimated at £20; Bisham (*Bustlesham*) ch. in Reading deanery, estimated at £10;

ARCHDEACONRY OF DORSET: Durweston (*Knyghton*

alias Doresweston) ch. in Whitchurch deanery, estimated at £10; Winterborne Clenston (*Wynterborn Clynston*) ch. in Whitchurch deanery, estimated at £8.6s.8d.; Winterborne Came (*Wynterborn Cayme*) ch. in Dorchester deanery, estimated at 13 marks; Bincombe (*Byncombe*) ch. in Dorchester (*Dorchestre*) deanery, estimated at £8.6s.8d.; Shaftesbury, St Laurence's ch., in Shaftesbury deanery, estimated at £9;

ARCHDEACONRY OF SALISBURY: Imber (*Ymmer*) ch. or chapel in Potterne (*Pottern*) deanery, estimated at 8 marks;

ARCHDEACONRY OF WILTSHIRE: Kington (*Kyngton*) [St Michael] v. in Malmesbury deanery, estimated at 13 marks; [Broad] Hinton (*Henton*) ch. in Avebury deanery, estimated at 20 marks; Liddington (*Ludyngton*) v. in Cricklade (*Crickelaad*) deanery, estimated at 13 marks.

287 Thomas [Savage], bp of London to John [Blyth], bp of Salisbury, rehearsing letters from John [Morton], cardinal priest of St Anastasia, archbp of Canterbury, primate of all England, legate, received 26 November [1496] rehearsing letters from the king, dated Westminster, 19 November [1496], summoning a convocation of clergy to meet at London St Paul's, or elsewhere, for the security and defence of the English ch., the peace, tranquillity, public good, and defence of the realm and subjects. The convocation is to meet at London St Paul's, on Monday 23 January [1497]; the names of those cited to attend to be certified to the archbp. [Fol. 52] Morton's letters dated Lambeth (*Lamehith*) manor, 20 November 1496. Savage's letters dated London, 27 November 1496.

288 [Fol. 52ᵛ] Letters to the archdn of Salisbury or his official, rehearsing the above letters from the bp of London, received 4 December [1496], directing him to convene the clergy of his archdeaconry before the bp or his commissary in Salisbury cath. on 20 December [1496], to choose proctors for the said convocation. Sonning, 7 December 1496.

288a Memorandum that similar mandates were sent to the other archdns.

289 Mandate to the dean and chapter of Salisbury cath., rehearsing letters as above [288], to appear personally and the chapter by one proctor before the bp or his commissary on 16 January [1497] to take counsel of one another before the meeting of convocation. Dated etc. [*sic*].

289a Certification that the above was done.

290 [Fol. 53] Names of persons cited to attend convocation (list is nearly identical to that in 279a, with changes indicated in *italics*):

M. Edward Cheyne DC&CnL, dean of Salisbury, for the chapter of Salisbury cath.;

In the archdeaconry of Salisbury: M. Edward Chaderton, archdn Salisbury; John Saynt John, r. Edington; William Westbury, prior Maiden Bradley (*Maydenbradley*); Richard Page, prior Ivychurch (*Ederose*); John[1] [Stone], prior Monkton Farley (*Farlegh monachorum*);

In the archdeaconry of Dorset: M. Robert Langton, archdn Dorset; Peter [Rampsham], abbot Sherborne (*Shirborn*); William [Middleton], abbot Milton (*Middelton*); *John [Abbotesbury], abbot Abbotsbury (Abbotesbury)*; Roger [Bemyster], abbot Cerne; John [Bryan], abbot Bindon (*Byndon*);

In the archdeaconry of Wiltshire: M. Christopher Urswyk, archdn Wiltshire; Thomas [Olveston], abbot Malmesbury; Thomas, abbot Stanley; Thomas [Walshe], prior Bradenstoke;

In the archdeaconry of Berkshire: M. Stephen Berworth, archdn Berkshire; *Thomas[2] [Rowland], abbot of Abingdon (Abendon)*; John [Thorne], abbot of Reading (*Radyng*); *William [Greve], prior of Bisham (Bustlesham); John [Thornton], prior of Wallingford (Walyngford)*; John [Hilston], prior of Hurley; Thomas [Ware], prior of Poughley;

Proctors for the whole clergy of the diocese: M. Laurence Cockys DCnL, and M. Geoffrey Blythe BTh, canons of Salisbury cath.

291 [53ᵛ] Thomas [Savage], bp of London, to John [Blyth], bp of Salisbury, rehearsing letters from John [Morton], cardinal priest of St. Anastasia, archbp of Canterbury, primate of all England, legate, received by the bp of London on 18 March [1497], for levying the great subsidy of £40,000 granted to the king by the convocation that met in St Paul's cath., 23 January 149[7] to 11 March [1497], in two small subsidies, one due between 1 May [1497] and 1 June [1497], and the second due between 20 October [1497] and 21 November [1497]. All chaplains of Canterbury province, regular or secular, exempt or non-exempt, even mendicants, of whatsoever status, grade, or condition, who receive a stipend of 40s. *p.a.* with food and drink are

1 *John* apparently added later, as it does not fill the space left.
2 *Thomas* is written over *John*.

to pay 3s.4d. in both terms. All chaplains who receive a stipend of 4 marks with food and drink, or 7 marks [without], up to 10 marks *p.a.* are to pay 6s.8d. in both terms. All chaplains who receive between 10 marks and £10 *p.a.* [Fol. 54] are to pay 13s.4d. in both terms. All chaplains who receive more than £10 *p.a.* are to pay 20s. in both terms; and thus it is to rise to the maximum of a tenth in both terms. Exempt from the subsidy all poor chaplains actually studying in the universities of Oxford and Cambridge. Exempt also all chaplains and other ecclesiastical persons named by the cardinal archbp in his dioc. of Canterbury or by his suffragans within their dioc. All chaplains and other persons, regular and secular, of both sexes, exempt and non-exempt, of whatsoever status, grade, order, or condition, having annuities, pensions, portions, corrodies, or assignments from religious houses, in perpetuity or for a fixed term, or pensions etc. resigned or renounced, if they extend to 40s. *p.a.* the recipients are to pay 3s.4d. in both terms. If the value of the pensions etc. is between 7 marks and 10 marks *p.a.*, the recipients are to pay 6s.8d. in both terms. If the value of the pensions etc. is between 10 marks and £10 *p.a.*, the recipients are to pay 13s.4d. in both terms. If the value extends to £10 *p.a.* they are to pay 20s and thus it is to rise to the maximum of a tenth in both terms. All persons, regular and secular, exempt and non exempt, holding chantries, hospitals, free chapels, and parish churches not having portions within the parish churches, worth 4 marks *p.a.*, are to pay 3s.4d. in both terms. If the fruits of the chantries etc. is between 7 marks and 10 marks *p.a.*, they are to pay 6s.8d. in both terms. [Fol. 54ᵛ] If the fruits of the chantries etc. is between 10 marks and £10 *p.a.*, they are to pay 13s.4d. in both terms. If the fruits of the chantries etc. extend to £10 *p.a.*, they are to pay 20s. and thus it is to rise to a tenth in both terms. All chaplains holding benefices with cures, not taxed not paying the tenth, of an annual value between 10 marks and 12 marks, are to pay 13s.4d. in both terms. Each bp to appoint collectors for the subsidy in their dioc., the collectors taking 12d. for every pound collected; [Fol. 55] with certification of their names within two months of the first collection day. Morton's letters dated Lambeth (*Lamehith*), 16 March 149[7]. Savage's letters dated London, 18 March 149[7].

292 [Fol. 55ᵛ] Commission to M. George Wood BCnL, commissary general in the archdeaconry of Berkshire, for collection of the above two minor subsidies in that archdeaconry, ordering that he receive the first subsidy by 24 May 1497 and the second by 13 November 1497. Sonning, 13 April 1497.

293 Memorandum that similar commissions were sent to M. William Jonys, commissary general in the archdeaconry of Wiltshire; and M. Thomas Martyn DCnL, commissary general in the archdeaconries of Salisbury and Dorset.

294 [Fol. 56] Royal writ ordering collection of the great subsidy of £40,000 granted to the king by the convocation which met in London St Paul's cath. from 23 January to 11 March [1497], in two instalments, the first between 1 May and 1 June 1497, and the other between 1 November and 21 November 1497, the part of the great subsidy for which the dioc. of Salisbury is liable being £3,560, and to appoint collectors for the same who will answer to the Treasurer and Barons of the Exchequer; with certification of their names to the Exchequer for the first part by 20 May 1497 and for the second part by 20 October 1497. Westminster, 15 March 1497. By Skypton.[1]

295 Commission to the prior and convent Hurley (*Hurle*) for collection of the [Fol. 56ᵛ] first instalment of the great subsidy in the archdeaconry of Berkshire. Exempt: the goods, benefices, and ecclesiastical possessions of the colleges of Oxford and Cambridge, Winchester BM Coll. founded by William Wykeham, BM Eton by Windsor (*Wyndesore*) Coll., and of any persons listed in the following schedule [297] not to be taxed except as directed in that schedule. They are to certify to the bp by 12 May [Fol. 57] that they have collected and paid the first instalment into the Exchequer. Sonning, 17 April 1497.

296 Memorandum that similar mandates were sent to the abbot and convent Abbotsbury (*Abbotesbury*) for the archdeaconry of Dorset, and to the prior and convent Maiden Bradley (*Maydenbradlegh*) for the archdeaconries of Salisbury and Wiltshire.

297 Schedule of sums to be taken by collectors of the first part of the great subsidy from the churches specified herein:

ARCHDEACONRY OF BERKSHIRE: Windsor (*Wyndesore*) ch. in Reading (*Rading*) deanery, valued at £20, to pay £3; Bisham (*Bustlesham*) ch. in the same deanery, valued at £10, to pay 30s.; from the spiritual and temporal possessions of Poughley priory, £3; from the spiritual and temporal possessions of the prioress and convent Broomhall (*Bromehale*) priory, nil; from the spiritual and temporal possessions of Shottesbrooke (*Shotesbroke*) collegiate ch., nil;

---

1   Master Richard Skypton, a senior chancery clerk.

ARCHDEACONRIES OF SALISBURY AND WILTSHIRE: [Long] Newnton (*Newenton*) ch. in Malmesbury deanery, 16s.; v. of Potterne (*Potern*) prebendal ch. in Potterne deanery, nil; Axford (*Axeford*) prebend, 5s.; [Fol. 57ᵛ] Compton Chamberlayne (*Chamburlayn*) ch. in Chalke (*Chalk*) deanery, 26s.8d.; from the spiritual and temporal possessions of Easton (*Eston*) [Royal] priory, nil; from the spiritual and temporal possessions of Kington (*Kyngton*) priory, nil; from the spiritual and temporal possessions of the abbess and convent Lacock, £7;

ARCHDEACONRY OF DORSET: Winfrith (*Wenefred*) [Newburgh] ch. in [*blank* – *rectius* Dorchester] deanery, 13s.4d.; Shatesbury, St Rumbold's (*Rowald*) ch., nil; from the spiritual and temporal possessions of the abbess and convent Tarrant (*Tarent*), £10; from the spiritual and temporal possessions of the abbot and convent Bindon (*Byndon*) in Winfrith (*Wynfrede*) [Newburgh] ch. aforementioned, £11.

298 Certification to the Treasurer and Barons of the Exchequer, rehearsing the king's writ [Fol. 58] dated Westminster, 15 March 149[7], of the names of the collectors of the first instalment of the great subsidy granted to the king by convocation: abbot and convent Abbotsbury (*Abbotesbury*) in the archdeaconry of Dorset; prior and convent Maiden Bradley (*Maydenbradlegh*) in the archdeaconries of Salisbury and Wiltshire; and prior and convent Hurley (*Hurlegh*) in the archdeaconry of Berkshire. Of the total £3,560 to be collected in the diocese of Salisbury, abbot and convent Abbotsbury are to render £480 for the archdeaconry of Dorset; prior and convent Maiden Bradley are to render £900 for the archdeaconries of Salisbury and Wiltshire; and prior and convent Hurley are to render £400 for the archdeaconry of Berkshire; total for the first instalment: £1,780. Sonning, 18 May 1497.

299 [Fol. 58ᵛ] letters to John [Morton], archbp of Canterbury, rehearsing letters from Thomas [Savage], bp of London… [*unfinished; rest of fol. blank*]

300 [Fol. 59] Commission to the prior and convent Hurley (*Hurlegh*) for collection of the second instalment of the great subsidy in the archdeaconry of Berkshire, [Fol. 59ᵛ] and that they certify to the bp that this has been done before 4 March [1498]. Sonning, 24 January [1498].

301 Memorandum that similar mandates were sent to the abbot and convent Abbotsbury (*Abbotesbury*) for the archdeaconry of Dorset, and to the prior and convent Maiden Bradley (*Maydenbradlegh*) for the archdeaconries of Salisbury and Wiltshire.

302 Certification to the Treasurer and Barons of the Exchequer, rehearsing the king's writ dated Westminster, 15 March 1497, of the names of the collectors of the residue of the great subsidy granted to the king by convocation, [Fol. 60] the amount to be collected in the diocese of Salisbury having been reduced by the king from £1,780 to £890: the abbot and convent Abbotsbury (*Abbotesbury*) in the archdeaconry of Dorset; the prior and convent Maiden Bradley (*Maydenbradlegh*) in the archdeaconries of Salisbury and Wiltshire; and the prior and convent Hurley (*Hurlegh*) in the archdeaconry of Berkshire. Of the total £890 to be collected in the diocese of Salisbury, the abbot and convent Abbotsbury are to render £249.14s. for the archdeaconry of Dorset; the prior and convent Maiden Bradley are to render £392.3s.6d. for the archdeaconries of Salisbury and Wiltshire; and the prior and convent Hurley are to render £248.2s.6d. Dated etc. [*sic*].

303 [Fol. 60ᵛ] Mandate to M. George Wood BCnL, commissary general in the archdeaconry of Berkshire, to publish the letters testimonial annexed [305 *below*], carried by M. Robert Castellani, prothonotary and commissary of the Apostolic See, and to do whatever Castellani and M. John Esterfeld, king's chapl., or either of them, tell him to do. Sonning, 30 January [1499].

304 Memorandum that similar mandates were directed to M. Thomas Martyn DCnL, for the archdeaconry of Dorset, M. William Jonys for the archdeaconry of Wiltshire, and M. Laurence Cockys for the city and archdeaconry of Salisbury.

305 [Fol. 61] Tenor of the letters annexed, rehearsing a bull of Pope Alexander VI granting plenary indulgence to all the faithful upon condition that each parish ch. render at least one noble or more as [M. Robert] Castellani, the bearer, or his deputies should compose, within eight months of the publication of these letters. Rome: St Peter's, Kal. July [1 July] 1498, the 6ᵗʰ year of his pontificate. [Fol. 61ᵛ] Instrument of Robert Castellani, cl., prothonotary of the Apostolic See, dated at his residence near London St Paul's, 21 October 1498, Indiction the 2ⁿᵈ, the 7ᵗʰ year of Pope Alexander VI's pontificate, in the presence of dns William Haryngton DC&CnL and M. Francisco

Saxella DTh, witnesses. Notarial instrument by John Haus, Llandaff (*Landuvens.*) dioc., day and place etc. [*sic*].

306 Letters directed to archdn Dorset. The bp has received letters from Thomas [Savage], bp of London, dated Fulham (*Fulham*), 27 November 1498, rehearsing letters to him from John [Morton], cardinal priest of St Anastasia, archbp of Canterbury, and legate, dated Lambeth (*Lamhith*), 25 November 1498:[1] Recently [Fol. 62] the popes Innocent VIII of happy memory and Alexander [VI] that now is, together with the whole sacred coll. of cardinals, decreed and declared that that most illustrious prince Henry VII, king of England, rightly and justly obtained his kingdom, and that any of his subjects of whatsoever status, degree, or condition who question or disturb for any reason the title and succession of that king or the peace and tranquillity of his realm, shall automatically incur the penalty of excommunication and greater anathema, and this penalty cannot be lifted except by the Roman see or one specially commissioned by the Roman see, unless on the point of death, notwithstanding any indulgence or other faculty for that see. Mandate to all bps and other prelates, secular and regular, in Canterbury province to have published in accessible and prominent public places, in cath., conventual, coll., and parish churches, to all inhabitants of England and subjects of the king, a translation of those apostolic letters. All bps in the Southern Province, or in their absence their vicars general in spiritualities, to go or send to London St Paul's, before 1 March [1499], to obtain copies of the translation authenticated by NP and sealed with the archbp's seal; so that all bps or in their absence their vicars general in spiritualities may publish the instrument in English to the inhabitants of England and to the king's subjects, and so that other clergy may do the same in cath., conventual, coll., and parish churches, [Fol. 62ᵛ] and post the translation where it may be seen and read. The bp is to certify, under his seal, to the archbp the form and manner of the execution of this mandate, before Pentecost next [19 May 1499]. The archdn of Dorset is to send to Sonning parish ch., before Passion Sunday next, *viz.* 17 March 149[9], to receive a copy for him to publish to all the churches of his archdeaconry, [Fol. 63] and to certify that he has done so to the bp before St George next [23 April 1499]. Sonning, 2 March 149[9].

307 Memorandum that similar letters were directed to the archdns of Berkshire, Salisbury, and Wiltshire.

---

1   The dating clauses occur on Fol. 62v.

308 [Patent letters] To all to whom these letters or the enclosed instrument of translation should come, from John [Morton], Cardinal priest of St Anastasia, archbp of Canterbury, and legate, giving notice that on 8 March [1498],[1] the First Indiction, the sixth year of Pope Alexander VI, in a certain high chamber in the archbp's manor of Lambeth (*Lamehith*), of the immediate jurisdiction of Christ Church Canterbury, there appeared personally M. Hugo Payntwyn DCL, archdn Canterbury, and presented on behalf of the king and Elizabeth his consort certain papal bulls, the tenor which is as follows: Alexander [VI], for the peace and tranquillity of catholic kings and princes, and preservation from the scandal of wars and dissensions, [Fol. 63ᵛ] rehearsing letters from Innocent [VIII] to this effect: To end the dissensions which have prevailed between the houses of Lancaster and York, King Henry VII and Elizabeth, daughter of the late King Edward IV, desired to contract marriage, but as they are related in the fourth and fourth degrees, they needed apostolic dispensation to marry. The pope therefore dispensed them, notwithstanding the said impediments, to marry. The pope now confirms the said dispensation and the marriage to be contracted in virtue thereof, or already contracted in virtue of any other dispensation obtained from the apostolic see or its penitentiary, or from legates or nuncios having faculty from the said see for this purpose, [Fol. 64] and also the lawful succession of children, and the declaration of parliament concerning both the title of the said king and the succession of his children and heirs; with inhibition to all the inhabitants of the realm and subjects of the said king to stir up fresh disturbances in the matter of the right of succession, under pain of excommunication and greater anathema against any who is rebellious and be he of whatsoever status he must seek remission of that penalty from Rome unless on the point of death, there being none exempt from this sentence, [Fol. 64ᵛ] and not withstanding indults to the contrary. The pope further decrees that should the said Elizabeth die before the said king without offspring by him, or without offspring surviving, in that case his offspring by any other lawful wife shall succeed. Rome: St Peter's, 6 Kal. April [27 March] 1486, the 2ⁿᵈ year of his pontificate.[2] These letters Pope Alexander [VI] ratifies by his own. Rome: St Peter's, 4 Non. October [4 October] 1494, the 3ʳᵈ year of his pontificate. These bulls John [Morton], archbp of Canterbury, has examined and found them authentic and subscribed by his scribe M. John Barett, NP, [Fol. 65]

---

1   1497 *anno domini secundum cursum et computationem ecclesiae Anglicanae.*
2   Printed in *Calendar of Entries in the Papal Registers, Vol. XIV, Papal Letters, 1484-1492*, ed. by J.A. Twemlow (HMSO, 1960), pp. 1-2.

in the presence of M. Thomas Routhale DCnL, prothonotary of the Apostolic See, and Thomas Madeys DTh, witnesses.

309 Notice by M. John Barett (*see above* 308) of his adaptation of the bulls for publication in the form following:

309a Latin text, setting out the context of the bulls under two headings: (1) that King Henry VII is true king etc. and the penalties for those who rebel against him; and (2) that any man who dies in defence of King Henry VII against rebels gains thereby plenary remission of all sins.

309b [Fol. 65ᵛ] [English text:] Oure most holy faders the poopes above specified · that is to say poop Innocent of blessed memory the viij · and Alexandre the vj the poop that now is for the rest fulnes of this land have confermed decreed and ordeyned dyvers and many thynges as a lawe and ordinaunce perpetually to be observed · as by ther bullys under ledd more playnly appeereth · the veray copies wherof bee above wryten · Of the which ij thynges here underwryten be to behad specially in remembraunce · The first is howh that the said most holy fadres certaynly knowyng and consydryng that our soveraign lord king henry the vijᵗʰ is the trewe and rightwous enheritour unto the crown of England · of their owen moc[i]on mere liberalite certayn knowlege and by the auctorite of the see apostolique with the express advyse and consent of alle the holy college of Cardinallys · have declared decreed and establesshed · that alle such of the subiectes and inhabitauntes of reame of Englond as doo or wyl presume to move or stirre or cause or procure to be moved or styrred any commocions or assemblees ayenst the kyng our said soverayn lord or his heyres · or any other colour of cause whatsoevyr it be · doo any thyng contrary to the peace tranquillite and restfulnes of our said soverayn lord his heyrys or this his reame · falle in their soo doyng into the feerful censures of the church and the dredful paynes of the great curs · and not to be assoiled therof by any other person than by the see apostolique · or by such as the kyng our said soverayn lord hath auctorite of the poop to depute in that byhalve · Not withstandyng any other indulgences privilegys or grauntys to the contrary.

The second is that the forsaid most holy fadres by the said motyon knowlege and auctorite · have yeven ther blyssing to alle persones aswele pryncys of other landys as the Inhabitauntys within this land that serve help or socour our said soverayn lord kyng henry the vijᵗʰ and his heyres ayenst their rebellys or any other that wyl attempt any thyng ayenst hym or theym or ther succession · and if it fortune any man to dye in the tytle or quarell of our said soverayn lord or any of his heyres · the said most holy fadres have graunted unto them plenary indulgence and remission of alle their synnes. The which premisses and dyvers other thynges them concernyng be moreatlarge conteyned in the above wryten copy of the said bullys autentiquely transsumed under the seale of the above lord Cardinal Archbisshopp of Canturbury and primate of all England.

310   Memorandum that these bulls John [Morton], archbp of Canterbury, ordered published in English in all churches in his province four times each year, *viz.* on Palm Sunday, Corpus Christi, All Saints, and Epiphany.

311   [Fol. 66] Letter to John [Morton], archbp of Canterbury, certifying that on 30 January [1499] the bp sent his proctor M. Robert Toneys BCL to St Paul's to receive from Thomas [Savage], bp of London, 150 copies of the above bulls, signed by M. John Barett, NP, transcribed by M. Richard Spencer, NP and registrar to Thomas [Savage], bp of London, which have been published throughout the diocese of Salisbury. Ramsbury, etc. [*sic*].

312   [Fol. 66ᵛ] Letters from the king directing the bp to certify to the Barons of the Exchequer if the Provost and coll. of Eton BM hold, and how long they have held, to their use, Stratfield (*Stratfeld*) [Mortimer] ch., with titheable v., in Reading deanery in the archdeaconry of Berkshire; and if any v. was founded in that ch. at the time of appropriation, and at what sums; and what is the portion of the Provost and coll. and what of the v., for rendering the Tenth to the king? *Teste* W. Hody, kt. Westminster, 24 November [1498]. *Per Barones*.

313   Certification to the Treasurer and Barons of the Exchequer, replying to the above [312] writ of the king, which the bp received on 25 December [*sic*][1] [1498], having searched the registers, that the Provost and coll. of Eton BM hold, and have held from 1444, to their use Stratfield Mortimer (*Stratfeld Mortymer*) ch. in Reading deanery in the archdeaconry of Berkshire, taxed at 13 marks, of which a tenth is 17s.4d.; the v. has existed from the time aforesaid and before; and the v. is not taxed nor liable for tenths, but the Provost and coll. of

1   Probably an error for *November*.

Eton render the whole tenth to the king. Sonning, 20 December 1498.

314 Letters from the king directing the bp to certify to the Barons of the Exchequer if the Provost and coll. of Eton BM hold, and how long they have held, to their use, Hullavington (*Hundlavyngton*) ch., in the archdeaconry of Wiltshire, and Sturminster Marshall (*Stourmynstre Mareschall*) ch., in the archdeaconry of Dorset, and if any v. was founded in either ch. at the time of appropriation, and at what sums; and how much is the portion of the Provost and coll. and how much of the v., for rendering the Tenth to the king? *Teste* W. Hody, kt. Westminster, 28 November [1498]. *By FitzHerbert.*

315   [Fol. 67] Certification to the Treasurer and Barons of the Exchequer, replying to the above [314] writ of the king, which the bp received on 5 December [1498], having searched the registers, that the Provost and fellows of the coll. of Eton BM hold, and have held, to their use Hullavington (*Hundlavyngton*) ch. in the archdeaconry of Wiltshire from 1444, and Sturminster Marshall (*Sturmynstre Marschall*) in the archdeaconry of Dorset from 1457; the Provost and fellows of the coll. of Eton BM are bound to render to the king 32s. for their tenth of Hullavington ch.; but how much they should render for Sturminster Marshall ch. does not appear in the registers; there has been a v. in Hullavington ch. from 1444 and before, taxed at £4.6s.8d., of which a tenth is 8s.8d.; and there has been a v. in Sturminster Marshall ch. from 1457, taxed at £20, of which a tenth is 40s. Sonning, 20 December 1498.

316 Letters from the king, similar to the above two royal writs (312, 314), concerning Uffington (*Offington*) ch. and Chieveley (*Cheveley*) ch. with chapel in the archdeaconry of Berkshire, appropriated to the abbot and convent Abingdon. *Teste* W. Hody, kt. Westminster, 13 February 1499. *By FitzHerbert.*

317 Certification to the Treasurer and Barons of the Exchequer, replying to the above [316] writ of the king, having searched the registers, that the abbot and convent Abingdon hold, and have held from 1344, to their use Uffington (*Offington*) ch. in the archdeaconry of Berkshire, taxed at £20, of which a tenth is 40s.; the v. has existed from the time aforesaid; the abbot and conv. render 30s. and the vicar of Uffington renders 10s; [Fol. 68][1] and the abbot and convent

1   Fol. 67v is numbered 68, and the following fol. is numbered 69.

Abingdon hold, and have held from 1313, to their use Chieveley (*Cheveley*) ch. with chapel in the archdeaconry of Berkshire, taxed at 80 marks., of which a tenth is 106s.8d.; the v. has existed from 1314 and is not taxed nor liable for tenths, but the abbot and convent Abingdon render the whole tenth to the king. Ramsbury, 15 April 1499.

318 Concord and composition made by John de Maydenhith, canon of Salisbury cath.,[1] and vicar-general in spiritualities to John bp of Salisbury,[2] between the abbot and convent of Cirencester (OSA), Worcester dioc., appropriators of Shrivenham (*Shryvenham*) ch., and William Solito, v. of Shrivenham,[3] touching tithes of the hamlet of Beckett (*Becotte*) notoriously withheld by John Beckett, lord of that place; while the case was pending, the original party the second, M. David Candelan, v. of Shrivenham,[4] deceased (*fuit et est ab hac luce subtractus*), but his successor Solito reopened the case. [Fol. 69] The said vicar and his successors are to have the whole v. manse for their habitation with the close and garden adjacent, and the said vicar and his successors are to repair and maintain the manse and close and garden at their expense; they are also to have all the arable land in Shrivenham anciently pertaining to the said vicar; they are also to have a house for the habitation of the chaplain in Longcot (*Langcote*) together with the arable land and pasture for sixteen cows and three hundred or more sheep adjacent and pertaining thereto from antiquity, and the oblations and mortuaries in the hamlet of Fernham; they are also to have all the tithes both greater and lesser of the demesne of the abbot and convent in Shrivenham, the tithe of hay excepted, and the second tithe in Bourton (*Burton*), Bourton [*sic*] and Watchfield (*Wachinfeld*), the tithe of hay excepted as above. The tithe of the whole parish pertains to the abbot and convent and has done so from antiquity. The vicars are to have have from the mill of Acorn (*Ackorne*) in Bourton one quarter of the tolls; from the two mills in Watchfield each year for two quarters £4 from tolls; and from the tenants of Watchfield for three quarters a half of wheat and other grain (barley); they are to have three acres of corn of the demesne of the abbot and convent of Abingdon, if they want it; they are to have and take the lesser tithes, *viz.* the increase of foals, calves, oxen, horses in the curtilage, of the mills, markets, curtilages, with the stipendiaries'

1   M. John Maydenhyth BCL was prebendary of Alton Australis 1386-1407 (*Fasti Salisbury* p.21).
2   Probably John de Waltham (1388-95).
3   The list of vicars in Shrivenham ch. records William Sollite 1394-1418.
4   The list of vicars in Shrivenham ch. records David Candeler 1389-92.

sheaves of corn, with the sheaves and tithes of the gardens, eggs, doves, geese, apples, pears, garlic, leeks, arising from Shrivenham village and the whole parish; they are to have the full tithe of piglets, milk and milk products (*lactis et lacticinii*) from the whole parish as they are accustomed to taking; and they are to take all the oblations within the parish, from the inhabitants there and the hamlets, *viz.* in wax on the feast of the Purification of Blessed Mary, and for confessions, and on anniversaries and in all other services for the dead, and all other oblations of any sort in Shrivenham ch. The vicars may take no other oblations nor other fruits or produce arising pertaining to the said ch. And because it has been found before the said M. John, vicar general, that the lands, men, and tenancies in Beckett remain vacant because of the mortality in divers plagues in England and amalgamated with the demesne of Beckett, wherefore a true and just tithe of animals grazing there is not possible to determine, it is agreed that, because of the difficulty in separating the tithes there, the abbot and convent are to have in perpetuity all the greater and lesser tithes, real, personal, and mixed, of the demesne manor of Beckett and the demesne lands and the lands of the men and tenants therein. In compensation for the tithes sought by the vicars, the annual payment of 40s., part of the annual pension of 60s. that the vicars customarily paid to the abbot and convent, shall cease. [Fol. 69ᵛ] The vicars are to pay the remaining 20s. of the pension of 60s. to the abbot and convent of Cirencester annually at Easter. The vicars are to support and uphold the incumbent's work both in exercising the cure of souls and in the celebration of divine service and the provision of lights, books, and vestments and indeed the burden of the archidiaconal Whitsun dues. The vicars are liable for extraordinary charges that arise for the king. The vicars are liable for the maintenance and repair of the chancel of the said ch., just as all of the vicars of the said ch. have been since the foundation of the v., except that Nicholas [Ampney], formerly abbot of the said monastery,[1] inclined to the prayers and supplications of the parishioners of the said parish ch., and out of his affection for the ch. and parishioners, repaired the ruined chancel, in the time of David Candelan, a Welshman, v. of the said ch., who throughout the entire time of his incumbency absented himself and plundered and consumed the goods pertaining to the said v., and allowed the houses and other buildings to collapse. And subsequently, after the aforesaid parties mutually agreed and promised for themselves and their successors, should either of the parties contravene this concord by non-observance or in particular infringement, then they will

---

1   Nicholas Ampney was abbot of Cirencester 1363-93.

pay to Salisbury cath. a fine of 20s. for each offence, on pain of sequestration by the official of the bp of Salisbury or the official of the archdn of Berks. I William [Solito], v. of Shrivenham, affix my seal to these presents in Shrivenham ch. on 7 Kal. June [26 May] 1395; and we the abbot and convent aforesaid affix our common seal in our chapter house on 5 Kal. June [28 May 1395]. We John de Maydenhith, aforesaid vicar general in spiritualities, having inspected and examined these present letters, confirm this concord in each and every particular that the law requires. We [John de Maydenhith] affix our seal to these presents, at Shrivenham, 1 July [1395].

[In a later hand (conjectural reading):]
Tithe at the beginning of May 1567
was collected
by general agreement

[Notarial device:]
Hugo Powell
Notary Public

319 [Fol. 70] In the name of god Amen. We John Bisshopp Tanner[1] · Alice Bisshopp wyfe of the said John & John Roye Cowper of the paryssh of Saynt Laurence in Rading · Thomas Scochyn Taylour and John Stanwey Wevar of the paryssh of Saynt Gyles of the same town Noted diffamed and to you Reverend Fader in Cryste John by goddys grace Bisshopp of Sar' our Juge and ordinary denounced and detect for victous bylevyng persones knowlege and confesse of our free willes unconstreyned that divers and many tymes we and every of us have receyved willingly into our howses in the parisshes of Saynt Laurence and Saynt Gyles aforesaid : certayn mysbylevyng and evyl techying persones ayenst the veray feyth and true byleves of holy church · And with theym we and every of us hath wittingly kept company and comunicacion beyng content and glad to have theym uttre and tech their wrong opinions and fals heresies · And thorgh their evyl techyng and informacion we the sayd John Bisshopp · Alice · and Thomas Scochyn have thought said and byleved that in the blessyd sacrament of the aulter is not the veray body of cryste that was born of a mayde · that was putt upon the crosse and dyed to redeme mankynde · that aroos from deth to lyfe · and ascended in to hevens but that it is veray pure bredd and nought ellys · Thynkyng and bylevyng that sith Criste in his veray body ascended into hevyns he commeth not ner shal comme agayn hyder into the erth afor the day

---

1   Described in the marginal index as *John Bisshopp alias Tanner.*

of dome when he shal juge all the world · And more over we confesse and knowlege that we have receyved the said holy sacrament not for any devocion or byleve that we had therin but oonly for dreed of the people and to eschewe the Juberdye and daunger that we dredd to falle in if we had not doon as other crysten people dyd ·

Also we the said John Bisshopp · Alice Bisshopp · Thomas Scochyn · John Roye · and John Stanwey have holden byleved and said that pilgrimages which have been used of good Crysten people unto the corpsys or reliques of Sayntys be not lawfull and owght not to be doon · ner non offrynges shuld be maad unto theym · for the sayntys be in heven · and [have no] need to such thynges · wherfor the money spent on such pilgrimages is but wasted and lost and moch better it were to depart that money among poore people ·

Also that the said John Bisshopp · Alice Bisshopp · Thomas Scochyn · John Roye · and John Stanwey have byleved and sayd that no man ner woman shuld wurshipp the Images or pictures of the crucifixe · of oure blessed lady or of any other sayntys No make unto them any offrynges of lightes · wax · money · or other thynges · for somoch as they be but stockys and stonys and that they that otherwise doo : commytt Idolatrye · And I the said Thomas Scochyn used to say that such offrynges and giftes shuld rather be doon unto poore men than to such Images · for we shuld rather wurshipp the Image that god hath maad that is to say the poore man than the Image that man hath maad and peynted · the which standeth in the church ·

Also we the said Alice Bisshopp and Thomas S[1] Scochyn have holden and byleved that that [sic] the curses of the poop · or other prelates of the church arun not to be sett by as voyde and of no strengthe · For we have said that there is no cursyng to be dredd but the curs of Almyghty god · the which curs Neyther the poop · bisshoppes ner priestys have in there power ·

Also I the said Thomas Scochyn have byleved and said that the poop is Antycryste · and that priestys and other men of the church be his disciples ·

[Fol. 70ᵛ] Also we the said Alice Bisshopp and John Roye have holden and byleved that the evyns of thapposles and of other saynts commanded to be fasted by the church : are not of necessite to

1   Blotted.

be fasted · but that the people may eate flessh [at alle such seasons except] the Imbryng dayes · the Frydayes · and the tyme of lent · And hereupon I the said Alice confesse that upon thre yeres passed upon A sayntys eve that was a fast commanded by the church : I eete bacon in myn owen hows havyng no regard unto the sayd fast

Also we the said John Bisshopp and John Roye have holden and bileved that no man ner woman is bound unto soch offrynges as be customably maad in the church · unto the priestys hondys sayyng that thay [serve] of non other thyng but to make the preistys rych ·

Also I the said John Bisshopp have holden and byleved that it nedeth not any person to be confessed of his synnes unto a preist or any other mynystre of the church · For I have sayd It is Inow to aske forgifnes of all myghty god and to be sory for the synne · Not willying to retorne therunto · without any more confession ·

Also · I the said John Stanwey have been waveryng in my myde and greatly doubtyng upon the sacrament of the aultere · wheyther it were the veray body of our saviour Cryste or noo · Not havyng stedfast and herty byleve therin as a good and true crysten man shuld have.

Theis articles aforerehersed and to us John Bisshopp Tanner · Alice Bisshopp · John Roye · Thomas Scochyn · and John Stanwey by you reverend Fader in Cryste Judicially obiected : We knowlege and confesse that we have holden and byleved in such maner and forme as is afore expressed · The which articles as they concern us severally We under stand and knowe to <u>be fals heresies</u> and wrong opinions <u>contrary to the techyng and</u> <u>determination of the church</u> · And that we and every of us holdyng and bylevyng the said articles and opinions were <u>heretikes</u> and mysbelevyng persons · <u>out of the true feyth and</u> <u>right beleve of Cryste</u> · But for asmoch [of] as the lawes of holy church be grounded in mercy : rememberyng that god wyl not the deth of a synner · but rather that he be converted and lyve : And also that the church of god here in erth closeth not hir bosom to hym or theym that wyl turn agayn therunto we therfor and every of us willing to be partyners of the said mercy : forsake and abiure alle the said articles and every of theym for evermore And not oonly theym but alle other articles of heresy and wrong opinions contrary to the determination of the universal church of Cryste · so help us god and theys holy Gospells · promyttyng by a said othe that we and every of us from hensforth shal nevyr be favourers · concealors maynteynirs

nor receyvers of any persones to our knowlege openly ner pryvely ·
But if we or any of us know any such hereafter : we shal de[nounce]
and show theym to their ordinaries or to their officers · Submyttyng
us and every of us of our free willes unconstreyned unto the payn
Rigour and sharpnes of the lawe that a man fallen agayn to heresy
oweth to suffer in such caas : if we or any of us evyr doo or hold
from this day forth contrary to this our abiuracion or any part therof
In witnes wherof we and every of us severally subscribe with our
handys makyng a crosse ✚ and require all crysten people here present
to record and wytnes ayenst us and every of us of this our confession
and abiuracion · if we or any of us hereafter doo or hold contrary to
the same or any part therof.

320 [Fol. 71] This abjuration was read and made by John Bisshopp,
tanner, Alice Bisshopp his wife, and John Roye, cooper, before the
bp sitting in tribunal in the chapel of BVM in Reading abbey, on 22
March 149[9],[1] in the presence of John [Thorne], abbot of Reading,
M. Edmund Crome DTh,[2] John Hyde, v. Sonning, Christopher
Belingeham, esq., *et me* Robert Toneys BCL, NP, bp's registrar and
scribe, and many others. The abjuration of Thomas Sochyn [*sic*] and
John Stanwey was read and made before the bp sitting in tribunal in
the chapel in Sonning manor, on 23 March [1499], in the presence of
M. Edmund Crome DTh,[3] M. John Pykeryng, cl., Richard Norton,
r. of West Ilsley (*West Ildeslegh*), *ac me* the above NP, and many others.
The bp imposed the following penance: John Bisshopp, John Roye,
Thomas Scochyn, and John Stanwey, barefoot and bare headed, and
Alice Bisshopp barefoot, in the manner of penitents, each bearing
a faggot on the shoulder and a torch in the hands, on Saturday 23
March, the vigil of Palm Sunday [1499], to walk around in Reading
market when the greatest multitude of people are present, there each
of them to recite in a loud and clear voice, at the priest's lectern set
up there, the articles and opinions concerning each of them and their
abjuration. Then, the next day, Palm Sunday, John Bisshopp, Alice
his wife, and John Roye, in the manner above, are to walk publicly
in the procession of their parish ch. of St Laurence and Thomas
Scochyn and John Stanwey, in the same way in the procession in
their parish ch. of Reading St Giles, each of them bearing faggots on
their shoulders and a torch in the hands. And in the afternoon each
of the abjured are to hear the public sermon in Reading conventual
ch., where with faggots and torches as above they are to stand on a

1   Marginal [English]: 22 March 1498.
2   *Sacre pagine professor.*
3   *Sacre theologie professor.*

platform set up before the pulpit there from the beginning to the end of the sermon.

321   In the name of god Amen · we Cecely Letcomb and Annes Redhood of the parysshe of Saynt Gyles in Rading within the diocise of Sar' · Noted · diffamed and to you Reverend Fader in Criste John by goddys grace bisshopp of Sar' our Juge and ordinary denounced and detect for victous and mysbelevyng women knowlege and confesse that we have receyved wittingly in to our howses certayn persones mysbelevyng and evyl techyng ageynst the trewe byleve of holy church · And with theym we and eyther of us hath holden company beyng present with them sundry tymes at the techyng and redyng of their erroneous opinions and bokys · And not discoverd theym but favoured them · byleved them folowed them · and kept their counseylls in the same ·

And by their evyl techyng and informacion we and ech of us hath holden and byleved that Images of Saynctes owght not to be wurshipped and that non offrynges shuld be maad unto theyn for they be but stokkys and stonys

[Fol. 71ᵛ] Also we have holden and byleved that pilgrimages shuld not be doon unto any saynctes or to their reliques · Ner offrynges shuld not be maad unto them · for they have no nede of our money · And therfor the money that is spent aboute such cause : is but wasted and lost ·

Also we have thought and byleved that in the sacrament of the aulter is not the veray body of our lord Jesu Criste · but that it is oonly material bredd · and non other thyng ·

Theis articles afor rehersed and to us Cecyly Letcombe and Annes Redhood by you Reverend Fadre in Criste in jugement severally obiected : we knowlege and confesse that we have holden and bylevyd · The which articles we know and understand to be fals heresies and wrong opinions ayenst the determinacion of holy church · And that we holdyng and bylevyng the said articles and opinions were heretykes and mysbelevyng persones out of the true feyth of Cryste · But forasmoch as the lawes of holy church be grounded in mercy · remembryng that god wyl not the deth of a synnar but rather that he be converted and lyve · And also that the Church of god here in erth closeth not bir boson from such persones as wyl turn ageyn therunto · we therfor and eyther of us wyllyng to be partyners of the sayd mercy forsake and abiure alle the said articles and every of them upon theis holy gospells · And not oonly theym but also alle other articles of heresy and wrong opinions contrary to the determination of holy church promyttyng by our said oth that we and ech of us from hensforth shal nevyr be favourers councellers[1] maynteyners nor receyvers of any such persons openly ner pryvyly · But as sone as we or any of us shal have knowlege of theym : we shal shew and disclose them to their ordinaries or to their officers · Submyttyng us and ech of us unto the payn and sharpnes of the lawe that persones abiured and fallen agayn to heresy owe to suffre in such caas : If we or any of us evyr doo or hold from this day forth · contrary to this our abiuracion or any part therof · In witnes wherof : we and ech of us subscribe with our owen handys makyng a crosse [blank] And require alle crysten people here present to record and wytnes ayenst us and ech of us of this our confession and abiuracion : if we or any of us here after doo or hold contrary to the same in any poynt ·

322   This abjuration was read and made by the aforesaid Cecilia Letcombe and Agnes Redhood before the bp in the chapel of Sonning manor on 23 March [1499] at 2 p.m. in the presence of: M. John Pykeryng, canon and prebendary London St Paul's; John Hyde, v. Sonning; and Richard Norton, r. West Ilsley (*West Ildeslegh*); Thomas Barker, literate; *et me* Robert Toneys, NP; and many others. The bp then imposed the following on Cecilia and Agnes: that on the next day, namely Palm Sunday, they are to go barefoot in the manner of a penitent in and for the whole procession on that day in St Giles's parish, each of them bearing a faggot on the shoulder and a torch in the hand. And in the afternoon they are to go to the conventual ch. of Reading and from the beginning of the sermon until the end, barefoot and carrying a faggot on the shoulder and a torch in the hand, publicly stand and remain in a prominent place prepared for this purpose in the full view of the congregation there.

323   [Fol. 72] In the name of god Amen · I Annes Scochyn wife of Thomas Scochyn Taylor of the parissh of Saynct Gyles In Rading · of the diocise of Sar' · Noted · diffamed and to you Reverend Fadre in Cryste John by goddes[2] Bisshopp of Sar' my Juge and ordinary denounced and detect for a mysbelevyng woman : knowlege and confesse that dyvers tymes I have bee drawyng and leanyng unto certayn evyl techyng and mysbelevyng persones : Receyvyng them

---

1   *Read* concealers.
2   the next word *grace* is omitted.

wittingly in to myn hows And theyr I have herd them speke and shew their fals errours and wrong opinions ageynst the true byleve of holy church · And not discoverd theym · but favoured theym byleved theym · and kept their counseyl in the same

And by their evyl techyng and informacion I have holden and byleved that in the sacrament of the Aulter is not the veray flessh and blood of our lord Jesu cryste : And soo not the veray body of hym · but oonly material bredd ·

Also I have holden and byleved · that the Images of the crucifixe · of our blessyd Lady and of other saynctes shuld not be wurshipped · for they bee but stockys and stonys ·

Also I have holden and byleved that the curses and other sentences of the church be not to be dradd ner sett by · for ther is no cursyng to be fearyd but the curs of almyghty god the which curs the bisshoppes and the preestys have not in their power ·

Theis articles and every of theym to me Annes Scochyn by you Reverend Fadre in cryste here in Jugement obiected · I confesse that I have holden and byleved · The which articles I now understond and know to be fals opinions and heresies ayenst the techyng and determinacion of holy church And also I knowlege and confesse that I holdyng and bylevyng wilfully the said articles was an heretyke and a mysbelevyng woman · out of the true feith of Cristes church · But forasmoch as god wyl not the deth of a synner · but rather that he be converted and lyve · And also that the church of god here in erth closeth not hyr bosom to theym that wyl retorne therunto I therfor beyng sory and repentaunt of my sayd mys byleve : with an hool mynde and a pure hert of my good wyl and not constreyned forsake and forswere alle the said articles and every of theym for evermore upon their holy gospells And not oonly theym but alle other errours heresies and wrong opinions that be damned and reproved by our modre holy church · And moreover I make a fulle promys by my said oth that from hensforth I shal nevyr wittingly be favourer concealer maynteyner ne receyvor of any such mystechyng or mysbelevyng persons or person but as sone as I shal have knowlege of theym : I shal do that in me is that they shal be detect and doscoverd unto their ordinaryes or to their officers · Submyttyng myself unto the payn and sharnes of the lawe that a persone abiured : and fallen agayn to heresy oweth to suffre in such caas · If evyr I doo or hold contrary to this my confession and abiuracion or to any part therof In witnes wherof : I subscribe with myn owen hand makyng a crosse · ✝ And requir alle crysten people here present : to record and wytnes ayenst me of this myn open confession and abiuracion · if I from this forthward offend or doo contrary to the same ·

324   This abjuration was read and made by the aforesaid Agnes Scochyn before the bp in the chapel of BM in Ramsbury manor on 30 March 1499, the vigil of Easter, in the presence of: M. Edmund Crome DTh; M. John Foted BTh; John Pykeryng, cl.; Richard Norton, chapl.; *et me* Robert Toneys, NP; and many others. [Fol. 72ᵛ] The bp then imposed the following on Agnes then and there: that on the next day, Easter Sunday, Agnes is to go barefoot in the manner of a penitent, bearing a faggot on the shoulder and a torch in the hand, in the procession in St Giles's parish, and at the priest's lectern provided for this purpose in the nave of the church before the entrance to the choir the articles and abjuration aforesaid are to be publicly recited.

325   In the name of god Amen · I Richard Herford Miller of Netherledcomb · otherwise called Ledcombe Regis in the county of Berks of the diocise of Sar' · Noted diffamed and to you Reverend Fadre in Criste John by goddys grace Bisshopp of Sar' my Juge and ordinary denounced and detect for a mysbelevyng man : knowlege and confesse that I have mysspoken & mysbelevyd ayenst the techyng determinacion and laudable use and custome of all holy church · That is to wytt I have holden and byleved that Images of the crucifix · of our blessyd lady and of other saynets be but dedd stockys and stonys · And therfor they owght not to be wurshipped · ner any offrynges to be maad unto theym · And that it is wrongfully doon to punyssh any man as a theef for takyng awey of such offrynges · Inso moch that not long agon I was in company in Ledcombe aforsayd wher it was spoken that an evyl disposed man the which had robbed an Image of our lady at Allesford in hamshire was sone after hanged therfor at Winchestre · wherunto I answerd ther openly that he has the more wrong · for if it so were : than was he hanged for robbyng of a ded stocke ·

326   In the name of god Amen · I Richard Hughlott labourer of Hanney in the County of Berks · of the diocise of Sar' · Noted diffamed and to you Reverend Fadre in Criste John by goddys grace bisshopp of Sar' my Juge and ordinary denounced and detect for a mysbelevyng man · knowlege and confesse that I have holden and byleved certayn fals errours and wrong opinions agayn the veray feyth

of cryste · and ayenst the techyng and deteminacion of holy church ·
That is to wyt that noman nedeth to be shryven of his synnes to his
Curate or any other preest · but I have thought and byleved that such
shryft was of no strengthe ner profight to mannys soule ·

Also I have holden and byleved that in the sacrament of the aulter is
non other thyng but oonly bredd and wyne · And that therin is not
the veray body of our lord Jesu cryste and hereupon I am aknowen
that of alle this yere last passed I was nevyr confessed unto my curate
ner to any other preest · And at this holy tyme of Ester last passed I
receyved not the holy sacrament of the aulter as every good and true
cristen man is bound to doo ·

Theis articles afor reherced and us Richard Herford and Richard
Hughlot by you Reverend Fadre in cryste iudicially obiected we
knowlege and confesse that we have holden and byleved in such
maner and forme as is afore expressed · The which articles as they
concerne ech of us we understond and know to be wrong opinions
· and heresies ayenst the determinacion of the church · and ageyn
the feyth of cryste · But forasmoch as the lawys of holy church be
grounded in mercy : remembryng that god wyll not the deth of
a synner but rather that he converted and lyve : and also that the
church of god here in erth : closeth not hir bosum to hym that
wyl turn agayn therunto : we therfor and eyther of us willing to be
partyners of the said mercy forsake and abiure the said articles and
heresies upon theis holy gospells · And not oonly theym but also
other articles of heresy and wrong [Fol. 73] opinions contrary to
the determinacion of holy church · Promyttyng by the oth that we
have maad that from hensforth we ner non of us shalbe favourers
concealers maynteyners nor receyvers of any such persones or person
· but if we or eyther of us shal know any such hereafter we shal do
asmoch as is in us that they shal be shewed and discoverd to their
ordinaryes or to their officers · Submyttyng us and ech of us unto the
peyn and sharpnes of the lawe that men abiured and fallen agayn unto
heresy owe to suffre in such caas : if we or any of us hold or doo from
hensforth : contrary to this our abiuracion or any part of the same ·
In wytnes wherof we and ech of us subscribe with our owen handys
makyng ech of us a crosse [*space for two crosses*] And requir alle cristen
people here present to record and wytnes ayenst us if we or any of us
hereafter doo or hold ayenst this our abiuracion or any part therof ·

327 This abjuration was read and made by the aforesaid Richard
Herford and Richard Hughlott before the bp sitting in tribunal in

the BMV chapel in Ramsbury manor on 19 April 1499, there being present then: M. Edmund Crome DTh; M. John Pykeryng, canon and prebendary of St Paul's; M. Thomas Whighthed, NP; and Richard Norton, chapl.; *et me* Robert Toneys, registrar and scribe *etc.* [*sic*]; and many others. The bp imposed penance on Richard Herford and Richard Hughlott in this form: both Richard and Richard are to go barefoot and bare-headed in the manner of a penitent, some (*aliquo*) Saturday at Wantage market when the greatest number of people are there, each of them carrying a faggot on the shoulder and a torch in the hand, and there publicly recite and profess the said articles and opinions concerning both of them and the above abjuration in a loud and intelligible voice at the priest's lectern set up for them. Item, on the following Sunday each of them is to go, barefoot and bare-headed and carrying a faggot on the shoulder and a torch in the hand, in the procession in his parish, and in the nave of the church before the entry to the choir, to recite and profess publicly and intelligibly the articles that apply to him and the aforesaid abjuration at the priest's lectern as above.

328 In the name of god Amen. We Roger Parker of Netherletcombe otherwise called Letcombe regis And Thomas Loryng Of Chippyng Faringdon Taylor in the Countye of Berks · of the diocise of Saresbury · Noted diffamed and to you Reverend Fadre in Cryst John by goddys grace bisshopp of Sar' our juge and ordinary denounced and detect for mysbelevyng men · knowlege and confesse that dyvers and many seasons and of long tyme passed we have been drawyng and leanyng unto certayn mysbelevyng persones which have holden and taught errors fals opinions and heresies ayenst the veray feyth and true byleve of holy church · And with the said mysbelevyng persones we and ech of us wittingly have kept company and felashipp · Beyng present with theym many tymes at the spekyng uttryng and commounyng of their erroneous opinions and heresies · Not shewyng nor descoveryng theym but favouryng theym folowyng theym belevyng them and kepyng their counseyl in the same · And I the said Roger Parker divers and many tymes have receyved them knowyngly into myn owen hows · Aswele at Ledcombe regis aforsayd · As in the forsaid Chippyng Faringdon wher I sumtyme dwelled ·

[Fol 73ᵛ] And thorgh their evyl informacion we the said Roger and Thomas have holden byleved and taught that Images of Criste · of our lady and of other sayncts owght not to be wurshipped Ner non offrynges shuld be maad unto theym · And that to doo wurshipp or to make offringes unto any Images was Idolatrye ·

Also we the said Roger and Thomas have byleved and sayd that pilgrimages which good cristen people use unto the Corpsis or reliques of holy sainctes or to their Images bee of no profight and that they owght not to be doon · And I the sayd Roger said precisely and held opinion that the money so spent : shuld rather be departed among the poore people · Inso moch that upon xvj or xvij yeres past whan I was dwellyng in Bampton in Oxenfordshir · seyng men and women to goo barefote and offer Images of wax or money to the reliques of Sainct Bernold[1] ther : I scorned theym and called theym foolys in their soo doyng ·

Theis articles afor reherced and to us Roger Parker and Thomas Loryng by you Reverend Fadre in Criste iudicially obiected : we confesse that we have holden and byleved in such maner and forme as is afore expressed The which articles we now understond and know to be fals errors and wrong opinions Ayenst the determinacion and laudable custome of holy church · But forasmoch as the lawys of holy church be grounded in mercy · Remembryng that god wyl not the deth of A synnar but rather that he be converted and lyve : And also that the church of god here in erth closeth not hir bosom to hym that wyl retorne therunto : we therfor and ech of us willing to be partyners of the said mercy : forsake and abiure the said articles and opinions and every of theym upon theis holy gospels · And not oonly them · but alle other errours heresies and wrong opinions that be damned and reproved of holy church · Promyttyng by our said othe · that we and ech of us here after shal nevyr wittingly be favourer concealar maynteyner ner receyver of any such mysbelevyng or mystechyng persones or person · but so sone as we shal have knowlege of any such : we shal do asmoch as in us is to disclose and detecte them to their ordinaries or to their officers · Submyttyng our self · and ech of us to the payn and rigour of the lawe that men abiured and falled agayn to heresy owe to suffre in such caas · if ever we doo or hold contrary to this our confession and abiuracion or to any part of the same · In witnes wherof ech of us severally subscribeth with his owen hand makyng a crosse ✝ ✝ And require alle cristen people here present : to record and witnes ayenst us of this our abiuracion If we or any of us hereafter doo or hold contrary to the same ·

329   This abjuration was read and made by the said Roger Parker and Thomas Loryng before the bp sitting in tribunal in the chapel

---

1   St Bernwald or Beornwald, 8th-century priest in Bampton.

of BMV in Ramsbury manor on 18 May 1499, there being present then and there: M. John Foted BTh; M. John Pykeryng, canon and prebendary of St Paul's, London; M. Thomas Whighthed, NP; Richard Norton, chapl.; John Byrley, literate; *et me* Robert Toneys BCL, NP, bp's registrar; and many others.

[Fol. 74] The bp imposed on the said Roger Parker and Thomas Loring penance as follows: that the aforesaid Roger, barefoot and bare-headed in the manner of a penitent, is to go before the procession on Pentecost Day in Letcombe Regis parish, carrying a faggot on his shoulder, and after the procession has entered the nave of the church, there Roger, before the entrance to the choir at the curate's lectern set up there for him, is to publicly recite and state the said articles and opinions and abjuration of them. Item, that on the following day, Monday in Pentecost week, both Roger Parker and Thomas Loryng are to go in the place frequented by the multitude at Great Faringdon (*Chipping Faringdon*), barefoot and bare-headed, carrying faggots on their shoulders, and each of them is to recite and state, saying after the priest, both the articles and abjurations above insofar as they apply to either of them, loud and intelligibly when the greatest multitude of people are there. Item, that Thomas Loryng likewise (*pariformiter*) barefoot and bare-headed, carrying a faggot, is to go publicly before the procession in Great Faringdon (*Chipping Faringdon*) on the next Sunday, *viz.* Trinity Sunday, and after the clergy and people have entered the church before the entry to the choir, to recite publicly, saying after the priest, the aforesaid opinions and his abjuration, as before. Item, the bp ordered Roger Parker to dwell at Letcombe Regis, and Thomas Loryng to dwell at Great Faringdon (*Chippyng Faringdon*), and not to move unless with the knowledge of the bp and having asked for his licence.

330 In the name of god Amen · I Thomas Boughton of Hungerford Shomaker and wullewynder of the diocise of Sar' Noted diffamed and to you Reverend Fadre in Criste John by goddys grace bisshopp of Saresbury my juge and ordinary[1] for a mysbeleving man : knowlege and confesse that I have bee moch drawyng unto dyvers and many mysbeleving and mystechyng persones and heretikes the which have holden and tawght fals errours wrong opinions and great heresies ayenst the veray feyth and true byleve of holy church and with the said mysbelevyng persones I have wittingly kept company and felashipp beyng with them present many seasons at the spekyng

---

1   The words *denounced and detect* are omitted.

uttryng and techyng of their said opinions and heresies · Not shewyng ne discoveryng theym : but folowyng theym favouryng them kepyng their conseyls and bylevyng theym in the same ·

First I have holden and byleved by the space of theis xxv yern passed or therupon · that in the sacrament of the Aulter is not the veray body of cryste our savyor · but that it is oonly material bredd · For I have thought it not possible that the preest which is but A man and the handwerk of god · shuld have power to make god his maker · And moreover I have said and holden that the said bredd was better whan it cam from the bakers handys than whan it come from the preestys handys after the consecracion · forsomoch as the preest mysused it otherwyse than to the pleasur of god · and soo dyd not the baker · Of the which wrong opinion and heresy : of alle this long season of xxv yeris I was nevyr confessed to any gostly fadre · And nevertheles I have every yere receyved the said holy sacrament · Not for that I had any stedfast byleve therin : but that I shuld not be noted and knowen of the people · And beyng in the church or ellyswher · whan the said holy sacrament was present I feyned with myn handys to honour it as cristen men use to doo · but my mynd and entent was nothyng therto · but to god almyghty above in heven · thinkyng that he has not ther present in the blessid sacrament ·

[Fol. 74ᵛ] Also I have holden and byleved that pilgrimages to the corpsis of holy sainctes of to their reliques bee not profightable to mannys sowle and that they owght not to be doon · Insomoch : that wher in my youthe byfor that I was acqueynted with the said heretikes I had avowed and promysed to doo A pilgrimage to Saynct James in Compostella : by their evyl informacion I have not yett doon it ne nevyr purposed to doo ·

Also I have holden and byleved that the Images of the crucifixe · of our blessed lady and of other holy sainctes shuld not be wurshipped · For nothyng wrought or graven with mannys hand owght to be honoured or lowted too · as I have herd redd dyvers tymes in An englissh booke that we calle the commaundment boke ·

Also I have byleved and sayd that the Poop is Antycryste · And that men of the church bee his disciples · And the church is but Sinagog · A denne of thevys and an hows of merchaundyse · For I have sayd that nothyng can be hadd ther without money · As Crystenyng buryyng · matrimony · And such other ·

Also I have holden and bylevyd that the pardons and indulgencys graunted by the Poop · and other prelatys of the church : be not profightable to mannys sowle and of noneffect · for <u>I have thought that non may grount pardon and forgifnes of synne but god Aloone</u> ·

Also I have holden and bylevyd that the cursyng of the poop is not to be sett by · For if a man have doone forwhy to be accursed : he is cursed by godd · and soo shal he be althowgh the poop blysse hym · And if A man be not cursed or god for his synne : the curs of the poop : is of non effect ·

Also I confesse and knowlege that sith the tyme of my first acqueyntance with the said heretikes : I have had a great mynde to here sermouns and prechynges of doctours and lerned men of the church · And as long as they spack the veray woordys of the gospels and the epistles such as I had herd afore in our englissh bookys : I herkned wele unto them and had great delight to here them but assone as they began to declare scripture after their doctourys and brought in other maters and spack of tythes and offrynges I was sone wery to here them and had no savour in their wordys · thynkyng that it was of their owen makyng for their profight and avauntage ·

Theis articles afore rehersed and every of theym · to me by you Reverend Fadre in god iudicially obiected : I confess and knowlege that I have holden and bileved · the which articles I now understond and know to be fals errors and heresies ayenst the determinacion and true byleve of holy church · And also I confesse that I holdyng and bylevyng the said articles was an heretyke And A mysbelevyng man out of the right feyth of Cryste · But forasmoch as the lawys of holy church be grounded in mercy Remembryng that god wyl not the deth of A synner but rather that he be converted and lyve · And also that the church of god here in erth closeth not hir bosom to hymn that wyl turn agayn therunto : I therfor willing to be partyner of the said mercy forsake and abiure alle the said articles and every of theym upon theis holy gospels · And not oonly them but alle other errours damnable opinions and heresies ayenst the determination of the holy church · And here I promys by the oth afor maad that from hensforth · I shal nevyr be favourer · concealer · maynteyner · ne receyver of any such persones of person · openly [Fol. 75] ner pryvyly · but as sone as I shal have understondyng of any of theym I shal doo asmoch as in me is that they shal be detect unto their ordinaries or to their officers · Submyttyng myself unto the payn and sharpnes of the lawe that A man fallen abiurate and fallen ageyn to heresy oweth to suffre in such caas · if evyr I doo or hold contrary to this myn abiuracyon or to any part of the same · In witnes wherof I subscribe & with myn owen hand makyng a crosse ✝ And requir alle cristen people here present : to record and wytnes ayenst me of this my confession and abiuracion · If I from this day forthward offend or doo contrary therunto ·

331 This abjuration was made by the aforesaid Thomas Boughton before the bp sitting in tribunal in BMV chapel in Ramsbury manor on 28 May 1499, there being present then and there: M. John Foted BTh; M. John Pykeryng, canon and prebendary of St Paul's, London; M. Thomas Whitehed, NP; *et me* Robert Toneys, registrar and scribe; and many others.

On that day and in that place the bp imposed public penance on Thomas Boughton, *viz.* that Thomas, barefoot and bare-headed in the manner of a penitent, carrying a faggot on the shoulder, is to go to the villages of Hungerford, Wantage, and Abingdon, to the market in each, when the greatest multitude of people are in the market, and once and again (*singulis vicibus*), repeating after the priest, in a loud and intelligible voice, to recite and state each word of his confession and abjuration, just as in the paper schedule drawn up for this purpose. And moreover on a Sunday Thomas is to go in the procession in Hungerford parish in the same manner (*pariformiter*) and after the entrance to the church before entering the choir, and after the offertory in the parish mass, repeating after the priest, he is to recite his abjuration and confession.

332 In the name of god Amen. I John Clerk of Burwardscot · otherwise called Burscot · in the County of Berks · husbondman of the diocise of Sar' · Noted diffamed And to you Reverend Father in Criste John by goddys grace bisshopp of Sar' my Juge and ordinary No denounced and detect for a mysbelevyng man : knowlege and confesse that I have be drawyng and leanyng to dyvers mysbelevyng persones and heretikes the which have holden and taught fals heresies and errours ageyn the veray feith and true byleve of holy church And with the said heretikes I have wittingly kept company and felashipp and have bee with theym present dyvers tymes at the spekyng uttryng and techyng of their fals opinions and heresies · Not shewyng ner discoveryng theym · but favouryng them · folowyng them bylevyng them and kepyng their counseyl in the same

And by their evyl techyng and informacion I have holden and bylevyd that in the sacrament of the Aulter is not the veray body of our savior cryst · but oonly material bredd ·

[Fol. 75ᵛ] Also I have holden and bileved that Images of Sainctys be not to be wurshipped ner that offringes shuld be maad unto theym · for they by maad with mannys hand and be but stokkys and stonys[1]

Also that men shuld doo no pilgrimages unto the corpsys of holy sainctys nor to their Images for they be not profightable to mannys sowle And the money and labour spent in such maner : is but wasted and lost ·

Theis Articles afor rehersed and every of them · to me John Clerk by you Reverend Father in criste iudicially obiected I confesse that I have holden and byleved · The which articles I now understond and know to be heresies and wrong opinions ayenst the true feyth and determinacion of holy church · And that I holdyng and belevyng the said articles was a mysbelevyng man and an heretyke · But forasmoch as the lawys of holy church be grounded in mercy Remembryng that god wyl not the deth of A synnar but rather that he be converted and lyve : And also that the church of god here in erth closeth not hir bosom to hym that wyl turn agayn therunto : I therfor willing to be partyner of the said mercy and beyng contryte and repentant of myn offens in the premisses · forsake renounce and abiure alle the said articles and every of theym for evyr more upon this holy gospels · And not oonly theym but also alle other errors heresies and damnable opinions contrary to the determinacyon of holy church · Makyng a fulle promys by my said oth that from hensforth I shal nevyr bee favourer councealer · maynteyner · ner receyver of any such persons or person openly ner pryvyly · but as sone as I shal have knowlege of any of theym I shal endever me unto my power that they shal be detect and shewed unto their ordinaries or to their officers · submytting myself unto the peyn and rigour of the lawe that a man abiured and fallen ageyn to heresy oweth to suffer in such caas : If evyr I doo or hold contrary to this myn abiuracion or to any part of the same · In witnes wherof I subscribe with myn owen hand makyng A crosse · ✝ And require alle cristen men here present · to record and wytnes ageynst me of this my confession and abiuracion · if I hereafter offend or doo contrary to the same · in any poynt ·

---

1   *and stonys* interlined, having been originally omitted.

333 The present abjuration was made by the said John Clerk before the said bp sitting in tribunal in BMV chapel in Ramsbury manor on 28 May 1499, there being present then and there: M. John Foted BTh; M. John Pykeryng, canon and prebendary of St Paul's, London; M. Thomas Whitehed, NP; *et Me* Robert Toneys, registrar and scribe; and many others. The bp imposed public penance then and there on the said John Clerk, in the following form, *viz.* that John Clerk, barefoot and bare-headed, bearing a faggot on the shoulder, is to go humbly in the manner of a penitent before the procession on some Sunday or feast day in Buscot (*Burwardscot*) parish; and in that procession, after the entrance to the ch. and before the entrance to the choir, he is to recite publicly and intelligibly, repeating after the priest, the aforesaid articles and abjuration; and also he is to go in the same manner in the villages of Wantage and Faringdon in the markets there, and when the greatest multitude of people is there he is to recite and state, in the same way repeating after the priest, the aforesaid articles and abjuration – in each of the markets of the aforesaid villages.

334 [Fol. 76] In the name of god Amen · We Thomas Seward of Chipping Faringdon in the County of Berks · husbondman of the diocise of Sar' · And Elizabeth Seward wyfe of the said Thomas · Noted diffamed and to you reverend Father in Criste John by goddys grace bisshopp of Sar' our Juge and ordinary denounced and detect for mysbelevyng persones : knowlege and confesse that we have drawyng unto divers persones mysbelevyng and evyl techyng ayenst the veray feyth and true byleve of holy church · And with them we have wittingly kept company and felashipp within our owen hows At Faringdon Aforsaid and in other placys · Beyng present with theym At the spekyng uttryng and commounyng of their heresies and fals opinions And not shewed ner discoverd them · but favoured theym folowed theym byleved them · And kept their counseyls in the same ·

And thorgh their evyl techyng we have holden and byleved that Images of cryste of our blessyd lady and of other saynctys owght not to be wurshipped Ner non offrynges shuld be maad unto theym forsomoch as they bee but stockes and stoonys ·

Also that folkes should not goo in pilgrymagys unto the corpsys or reliques of saynctes ner offre their money ner other thynges unto theym · For alle such offrynges goo unto preestys avayle and profight · which have Inow · and to moche ·

Also we have holden and byleved that in the holy sacrament of the Aulter is not the veray flessh and blood of our lord Jesu Cryste · but that it is oonly bredd maad of flour and wyne of the grape ·

Theis Articles Afor rehersed and to us Thomas Seward and Elizabeth by you Reverend Father in Cryste in Jugement severally obiected we confesse that we have holden and byleved The which articles we now undrestond and know to be fals heresies and wrong opinions ayenst the feyth of Cryst and determinacion of holy church · And that the holdyng and bylevyng theym were heretykes · But forasmoch as the lawys of holy church be gounded in mercy · Remembryng that god wyl not the deth of A synner but rather that he be converted and lyve : and also that the church of god here in erth closeth not hir bosom to them that wyl turn ageyn thertoo Ther we the said Thomas and Elizabeth willing to be partyners of the sayd mercy forsake and renounce uttrely alle the said articles wrong opinions and heresies · And Abiure theym and every of theym for evyr more upon theys holy gospels · And not oonly [theym] but also alle other heresies · errors and damned opinions by holy church · Promyttyng by our said oth that from hensforth · we ner non of us shal be wittingly favourer councealer maynteyner ne recyver of any such persones or person pryvyly ner openly · but as sone as we shal have knowlege of any of theym · we shal doo asmoch as shal lye in us to detect and show theym to their ordinaries or to their officers · Submyttyng ourself unto the payn and rigour of the lawe that folkes abiured and fallen ageyn to heresy owen to suffre in such caas · If evyr here after we doo or hold contrary to this our abiuracion or to any part of the same · In wytnes wherof ech of us severally subscribeth with our handys A crosse $+$ $+$ And requir alle cristen people to record and wytnes ayenst us and ech of us If we or eyther of us doo ageyn this our confession and abiuracion from this day forthward · or any part therof ·

335 The above abjuration was made by the said Thomas Seward and Elizabeth his wife before the said bp sitting in judgement in BMV chapel in Ramsbury manor on 8 June 1499, there being present there and then: M. John Pykeryng, canon and prebendary of St Paul's, London; M. Thomas Whitehed, NP; Peter Blount; *et me* Robert Toneys, registrar etc.; and many others. [Fol. 76^v] The bp imposed the following public penance then and there on the said Thomas and Elizabeth, *viz.* that Thomas and Elizabeth, barefoot – and Thomas also bare-headed – both of them bearing a faggot on the shoulder, in the manner of a penitent, are to go before the procession in Faringdon (*Chippyng Faringdon*) parish; and in that procession, after the entry into the ch. before the entrance of the choir, both publicly recite and state, saying after the reading of them by the priest, the above articles and abjuration. Item, that both are to go and do in a like manner on the next Monday [10 June 1499][1] in the market at Faringdon when the greatest multitude of people is there.

336 In the name of god Amen. I John Gray · Myller of the parissh of westhenreth in the County of Berks · of the diocise of Sar' Noted · diffamed · and to you Reverend Father in Cryste John by goddis grace bisshopp of Sar' my Juge and ordinary denounced and detect for a mysbelevyng amn · knowlege and confesse that dyvers tymes and of longe tyme passed I have been drawyng unto certayn mysbelevyng persones that hold and taught fals errours wrong opinions and heresies ayenst the veray fayth and true byleve of holy church · And with thaym I have wittingly kept company and felashipp · beyng present with theym · at the spekyng uttryng and techyng of their fals errours and opinions Not shewyng ner discoveryng theym · but favouryng theym folowyng theym bylevyng them and kepyng their counseyl in the same ·

And thorough their evyl techyng and informacion I have holden and bylevyd that the Images of Cryst , of our blessyd lady and of other sainctys shuld not be wurshipped forsomoch as they be but stokkes and stoones · And by the same reason : non offrynges shuld be maad unto theym · for I have said that to wurchipp theym or to offyr unto them was Idolatrye ·

Also that no man ner woman shuld goo in pilgrimage unto the corps · or reliques or to the Image of any saynct · for I have thought and bylevyd that such pilgrimages be not loefull · and that the money spent in doyng and performyng of theym : is but wasted and lost ·

Theis articles afor rehersed and to me John Gray by you Reverend Father in criste Judicially obiected : I confesse that I have holden and byleved · The which articles I now understond and know to be fals opinions and errours ayenst the determinacion and laudable custome of holy church · But forasmoch as the lawes of the church be grounded in mercy Remembryng that god wyl not the deth of A synnar but rather that he be converted and lyve And that the church of god here in erth closeth not hir bosom to hym that wyl turn ageyn therunto : I therfor wylling to be partyner of the said mercy forsake

---

1   The date on which penance is to be done in the parochial procession is omitted.

and renounce uttrely and also abiure the said articles and ech of
theym upon theis holy gospels · And not oonly theym : but also alle
other opinions and articles contrary to the true feyth of cryste and to
the determinacion of holy church · Promyttyng by my said oth · that
from hensforth I shal nevyr be fevourer · maynteyner · councealer
· ner receyver of any such mysbelevyng or mystechyng persones or
person · But as sone as I shal have undrestondyng or knowledge of
any of theym : I shal endevor me to the best of my power that they
shalbe detected [Fol. 77] and shewed unto their ordinaries or to their
officers · Submyttyng my self unto the payn and sharpnes of the lawe
· that a man abiured and fallen agayn to heresy oweth to suffre in
such caas : If I from this day forthward evyr doo or hold contrary to
this myn abiuracion or to any part of the same · In witnes wherof I
subscribe with myn owen hond makyng A crosse ✝ And require
alle cristen people here present to record and wytnes ayenst me if I
here after doo ayenst my said confession and abiuracion in any poynt ·

337 The present abjuration was made by the said John Gray before
the bp sitting in tribunal in BMV chapel in Ramsbury manor on 10
June 1499, there being present then and there: M. John Bisshopp BTh;
[*blank*], v. of Shrivenham (*Shryvenham*);[1] John Wroughton, gentleman;
et me Robert Toneys, NP, scribe etc.; and many others. The bp then
and there imposed public penance on John Gray in this form, *viz.*
that John Gray is to go, barefoot and bare-headed in the manner of a
penitent, carrying a faggot on his shoulder, before the procession in
West Hendred (*Westhenreth*) parish on the next Sunday[2] [16 June 1499],
and in that procession, after entering the ch. and before the entrance
to the choir, the said John Gray is publicly to recite and state, repeating
after the curate, the said confession and abjuration in the presence and
hearing of the people congregated there. And also that John Gray in
the same manner is to go and do in the next market at Abingdon when
the greatest multitude of people is there.

338 In the name of god · Amen · I John Godson of the paryssh of
Burwardscot alias Burscote in the County of Berks · of the diocise
of Sar' husbondman : Noted · diffamed and to you Reverend Father
in Criste John by goddys grace bisshopp of Sar' denounced and
detected for A mysbelevyng man · knowlege and confesse that I have
been in company and felashipp of dyvers persones mysbelevyng and
techyng that have holden and taught fals errours and heresies ayenst

---

1   According to the list of vicars in Shrivenham ch., John Fawle became v. in 1481
     and was not succeeded until 1522.
2   'on the next Sunday' interlined.

the veray feyth and true byleve of holy church · And with theym I
have wyttyngly been conversaunt receyvyng them in to myn howse
· And was present with theym ther and ellyswher at the uttryng
and techyng of their fals opinions and heresies · Not shewyng ner
discoveryng theym · but favouryng them belevyng them · and kepyng
their counceyll · in the same ·

And by their evyl informacion I have holden and by leved that in the
sacrament of the aulter is not the body of Cryste · but preestys offer
up the said sacrament oonly in the commemoracion of the passion
of cryste ·

Also I have holden and belevyd that Images of Cryste · of our blessyd
lady · and other saynctys : shuld not be wurshipped · Ner no thyng
that is maad or graven with mannys hondys[1]

Also I have said and byleved that the Poop is antecryst : And men
of the church be his disciples · seyng that the poop and the men of
the church be not the veray folowers of petre and Paule which had
but lytle of this worldy substaunce[2] · And more over I thought that
non kept the veray feyth of cryst but such as were of our sect and
opinions ·

[Fol. 77ᵛ] Also I have sayd and bylevyd that A man shuld offer up his
hert to Almyghty god · And kepe his goodys to hym self · affermyng
that such offrynges as been used in the church serve of non other
thyng but to make the preestys ryche and the laye men poore · And
that such offrynges were oonly brought in by the preestys for their
singular profight and covetyse ·

Also I have holden and spoken ayenst pilgrymages to holy saynctes or
to their reliques saying that they profighted not to the doers therof ·
but that the money offred and spent in such use was but wasted and
lost · which myght have been bystowed among pore people that have
great need therof ·

Theis articles afor rehersyd and every of theym · to me John Goodson
by you Reverend Fadre in Cryst Judicially obiected : I confesse that
I have holden and byleved · The which articles Now I understond
and know to be fals opinions and heresies ayenst the feyth of cryste

---

1   'hondys' interlined.
2   Marginal note: in humilite patience and poverte

and the determinacion of holy church · But forasmoch as the lawes
of the church be grounded in mercy Remembryng that god wyl
not the deth of A synner but rather that he be converted and lyve : I
therfor wyllyng to be partyner of the sayd mercy with my free wylle
unconstreyned forsake and abiure alle the said articles and every of
theym upon theis holy gospels · And not oonly theym but also alle
other opinions and articles contrary to the true feyth of cryst and to
determinacion of holy church · Promyttyng by my said oth that from
hensforth I shal nevyr be favourer maynteyner concealer ner receyver
of any mys belevyng as [sic] mystechyng persones or person · but
assone as I shal have knowlege therof any such I shal endevyr to my
power that they shal be denounced and detected unto their ordinaries
or to their officers · Submyttyng my self unto the pain and rigour of
the lawe that is ordeyned in such caas : if ever I doo or hold from
this day forth contrary to this myn abiuracion or any part therof · In
witnes of the which I subscribe with myn own hand · makyng A cros
✝ And require alle cristen people here present : to record and wytnes
ayenst me of this my confession and abiuracion · If I hereafter doo or
hold contrary therunto · or any part of the same ·

339   The present abjuration was read and made by the said John
Goodson before the bp sitting in tribunal in BMV chapel in
Ramsbury manor on 22 June 1499, there being present then and
there: M. Edmund Crome DTh; M. John Foted BTh; Peter Blount;
et me [*name omitted*], NP, scribe, etc.; and many others. Then and
there the bp imposed public penance on John Goodson in this form,
viz. that John, barefoot and bare-headed in the manner of a penitent,
bearing a faggot on the shoulder, is to go in the market at Wantage
next Saturday [29 June 1499] when the greatest multitude of people
are there, and saying after the curate publicly tecite and state his said
confession and abjuration, in the presence of the people congragated
there. And also that that John is to go and do likewise at Buscot
(*Burscote alias Burwardscot*) on the following Sunday [30 June 1499] in
the procession there.

340 [Fol. 78] In the name of god Amen I William Berford otherwyse
called William Carpenter of Cokeswell[1] of the diocise of Sar' ·
Carpenter · byfor you Reverend Fader in cryste John by goddys grace
bisshopp of Sar' my Juge and ordinary knowlege openly And with my
fre wyll confesse here in jugement that byfor this tyme I have holden
and sayd afor dyvers persones that no person beyng of our sect and

1   Great Coxwell or Little Coxwell?

opinions shuld be confessed unto A preest or to any other that were not of our byleve · but oonly to oon of our sect · And that A preest had nomore power in such caas than A good laye man ·

Also I have said and bylevyd that the Images of cryste and of saynctes shuld not be wurshipped Ner offrynges shuld be maad unto theym for they be but stockys and stonys ·

Also I have holden and byleved that the sacrament of the Aulter is not veray body of cryste our savyour but that it is oonly material bredd as other breddys bee ·

Also that no persone is bound to fast or kepe abstinens at any season sayyng that god maad both flessh and fisshe for the sustynaunce of mankynde · And therfor A man may leefully eate alle maner of meetys at alle tymes soo that be eate not ne drynk to moch · and so kepe hymself from glotony[1]

Also I have holden said and bylevyd that Indulgencys graunted by the poop · and other prelatis of the church doo no profight to mannys sowle · sayyng that non may foryeve synne but god aloone ·

Also that goyng of [*sic*] pilgrimages to se the corpsys of sainctys or to their reliques and Imagys is not avaylable to the doers for the sainctys be in hevyn and have no need to our money ·

Theis articles and opinions by you Reverend Fader in Criste to me Judicially obiected And by me confessed in forme afore rehersed with alle other that be contrary to the feyth and determinacion of holy church I forsake and Abiure upon theis holy gospels : And fully promys by the same oth that from hensforth I shal never be favourer receyver concealer ner receyver [*sic*: repeated word] of any person Mystechyng or mysbelevyng to my knowlege · but as sone as I have understondyng of any such I shal detect them or cause them to be detected unto their ordinaries or to their officers · Submyttyng my self unto the payn and rigour of the lawe in such caas provided : If ever from this day forth I doo or hold contrary to this myn abiuracion or any part of the same In wytnes wherof : I subscribe with myn owen hand makyng A crosse ✝ And requyre alle good cristen people here present : to record and wytnes ayenst me of this myn open confession and abiuracion if I here after offend or do contrary to the same in any poynt ·

---

1 'glotony' interlined.

341   The aforesaid abjuration was made by the aforesaid William Berford *alias* Carpenter before the bp sitting in tribunal on 17 July[1] 1499 in the chapel in Ramsbury manor, there being present then and there: M. Edmund Crome DTh; Richard Norton, chaplain; *et me* Robert Toneys, NP, scribe, etc.; and many others. The bp ordered the aforesaid William Berford, on Sunday, 28 July [1499], barefoot and bare-headed in the manner of a penitent, carrying a faggot on the shoulder, to go in the procession at Coxwell (*Cokeswell*); and at Faringdon (*Chyppyng Faryngdon*) on the following Monday [29 July] in the market when the greatest multitude of people are there, reciting after the curate each and every word of his abjuration, in accordance with the schedule made for this purpose, enclosed, and delivered to his curate.

342   In the name of god Amen · I John Gowgh alias Mathews late of Brystoll now of the diocise of Sar' byfor you Reverend Fader in cryst John by goddys grace bisshop of Saresbury my Juge and ordinary knowlege and with my fre wyl here in Jugement confesse openly that byfore this tyme I have holden byleved and sayd · that Images [Fol. 78ᵛ] of the crucifixe · of our blessed lady And of other Saynctys shuld not be wurshipped ner non offrynges shuld be maad unto theym · And that otherwyse to doo was but Idolatrye ·

Also that the poop is anticryst And bishoppes and preestys be his disciples ·

Also that the sacrament of the Aulter is but veray bredd · and not the body of our saviour cryste ·

Also that the cursyng of the poop is not to be dred · And the pardons by him graunted be not profightable to mannys sowle · sayyng that god oonly foryeveth synne and non other ·

Theis articles and every of theym by you reverend fader in cryste to me Judicially obiected and by me confessed In forme afore rehersed I forsake renounce and abiure upon theis holy gospels · And not oonly theym but alle other erroneous opinions and heresies that be contrary to the feyth and determinacion of holy church · Promyttyng by my said oth that from hensforth I shal nevyr be favourer receyver concealer · ner maynteyner[2] of any person mysbelevyng or mystechyng

---

1   'June' in the text, but this would antedate No. 339; and 28 *June* (the designated date for the penance to be done at Coxwell) did not fall on a Sunday in 1499, though 28 *July* did.

2   The order of these nouns follows that of No. 340 which broke with the usual

ayenst the determinacion of holy church · But assone as I shal have knowlege of any such · I shal doo asmoch as in me is that he shal be shewed and detected to his ordinary or to his officers · Submyttyng myself unto the rygour of the lawe in such caas provided : if I from this day forthward offend and doo contrary to this myn abiuracion or any part of the same · In wytnes wherof I subscribe with myn owen hand makyng A crosse · ✝ [*The usual clause* 'And require all Christian people here present...' *is omitted.*]

343   This abjuration was made by the aforesaid John Gowgh *alias* Mathews before the bp in the chapel of Ramsbury manor on 19 July 1499; present: M. Edmund Crome DTh; M. John Pykeryng, cl., canon and prebendary of St Paul's cath., London; *et me* [*name omitted*], NP, scribe, etc.; and others. There and then the bp. ordered that John Gowgh, on the next Sunday [21 July 1499], barefoot and bare-headed, to go publicly in the manner of a penitent, bearing a faggot on his shoulder, in the procession at Faringdon (*Chippyng Faryngdon*), and after the entry into the nave of the ch. before the entrance to the choir, repeating after the curate, to recite each word of his abjuration and confession, following the form in the schedule drawn up for that purpose and sent to the curate.

344   In the name of god Amen · I Joan Martyn late the wyfe of Thomas Martyn of Wantage now deceassed of the diocise of Saresbury · Noted diffamed and to you Reverend Father in criste John by goddys grace bisshopp of Saresbury my Juge and ordinary denounced and detected for a mysbelevyng woman · knowlege and confesse openly and with my free wylle that byfor this tyme I have holden and byleved dyvers opinions and articles contrary to the veray feyth of cryst and to the determinacion of holy church

First that in the sacrament of the Aulter is not the veray body of our savyour but oonly material bred

Also I have holden byleved and sayd that Images of the crucifixe · of our blessed lady and of other saynctys shuld not be wurshipped · ner any offrynges shuld not [Fol. 79] be maad unto theym · And that they which wurshipped theym or offred unto theym dyd Idolatrye ·

---

order 'favourer concealer maynteyner ner receyver' (or 'favourer maynteyner concealer ner receyver' in Nos. 336 and 338); this suggests that Toney's practice was to copy from the last entry in the Register rather than from an independent formulary.

Also I have holden and byleved that men shuld not travail themself ner spend their money in doyng of pilgrymages to holy sainctes or to their reliques · Sayyng that the money spent in such use was but lost and lefte with such as had no nede therof ·

Also I have thought and byleved that every man myght be shryven un to other of their synnes aswele as to a preest · thynkyng that the preest hath no more power ner auctorite in such caas than A lay man ·

Also I have bilevyd and sayd that pardons graunted by the poop and other prelatys of the church be of no strengthe ner doo no profight unto mannys sowle And that such pardons be graunted oonly for gadryng of money and for non other cause ·

Theis articles afor rehersed And to me Joan Martyn by you reverend Fader in cryst iudicially obiected · And by me the said Joan in Jugement of my fre wyl confessed : I now understond and know to be fals errours, wrong opinions and heresies ayenst the feyth of cryste · and the techyng of our mother holy church · And that I holdyng and bylevyng theym was a mysbelevyng woman and an heretyke · But forasmoch as the lawys of holy church be grounded in mercy Remembryng that god wyl not the deth of A synnar but rather that he be converted and lyve : I therfor willing to be partyner of the said mercy forsake renounce uttrely And of my fre wylle unconstreyned abiure and forswere alle the said articles and every of theym upon theis holy gospels · And not only them but also alle other articles and opinions contrary to the true feyth of cryst · and to the determinacion of holy church · Promyttyng by the vertu of my said oth · s [sic] that from hensforth I shal nevyr be favourer maynteyner concealar ner receyver of any heretyk or such mysbelevyng persons to my knowlege openly ner pryvely · But as sone As I shal have understondyng of any of them I shal do my devour that they shal be detected to their ordinaries or to their officers · Submitting my self unto the payn and rigour of the lawe in such caas provided · if evyr from this day forthward I doo or hold contrary to this myne abiuracion or to any parte of the same · In witnes wherof I subscribe with myn owen hond makyng A crosse ✝ And require alle crysten peple her pre sent to record and wytnes ayenst me of this my confession and abiuracion · If I from hensforth doo ageynst the same or any part therof

345 This abjuration was made by the aforesaid Joan Martyn before the bp sitting in tribunal in the chapel in Ramsbury manor on 1 August 1499, there being present then and there: M. Edmund Crome DTh;

Thomas Freman, Robert Pelott, and Richard Wroughton, literates; *et me* Robert Toneys, NP and scribe etc. The bp then and there ordered that that Joan, on the next Saturday [3 August 1499], go barefoot in the manner of a penitent in the public market at Wantage, bearing a faggot on the shoulder and reciting the words of her abjuration after the curate of the parish ch. there says them. Item, she is to go and do likewise on the next Sunday [4 August 1499] in the procession of that parish.

346 [Fol. 79ᵛ] In the name of god Amen · I John Edwardys of Wantage in the County of Berks · of the diocyse of Sar' Carpenter Noted diffamed and to you Reverend fadre in cryste John by goddys grace bisshopp of Saresbury my Juge and ordinary denounced and detect for A mysbelevyng man knowlege and confesse that I have been conversant And kept company with dyvers mysbelevyng and evyl techyng persones the which byleved and taught dyvers articles and opinions contrary to the feith of cryst and to the determinacion of holy church Not shewyng ner discovering the said persones : but favouryng them · bylevyng them · and kepyng their counsell in the same ·

And thorgh their evyl techyng and enformacion I have holden and bylevyd · that Images of Cryst · of our blessyd lady · and of other sayntys shuld not be wurshipped · and that offrynges shuld not be maad unto theym · for they be but stockes and stoonys ·

Also I have holden and bylevyd that men shuld not travayl them self in doyng of pilgrimages Ne spend their money therabout · thynkyng alle the labour and cost doon for such cause but lost and spent in wast ·

Also I have holden And bylevyd that in the sacrament of the Aulter is not the veray body of cryste our savyour but it is oonly bredd · For I have thought that no preest myght have soo great power as to make almyghty god ·

Theis Articles and every of theym afore rehersed · to me John Edwardys by you reverend fader in cryste Iudicially obiected and by me the same John in maner and forme afor rehersed In iugement confessed : I now understond and knowe to be fals errours and heresies · And that I holdyng and bylevyng the same was an heretyke And out of the right feyth and true byleve of holy church · wherfor of my fre wylle unconstreyned I renounce forsake and abiure alle the said articles and every of them upon theis holy gospels · And not only theym but also alle other erroneous articles and opinions that be contrary to the feith of cryste and to the determinacion of holy church · Promytting feythfully by the vertu of my said othe that from hensforth I shal nevyr wittingly be favourer concealar maynteyner ner receyver of any such mysbelevyng of [*sic*] evyl techyng persones or person · openly ner pryvyly · but whan I shal have knowlege of any such I shal shew and discover theym to their ordinaries or to their officers · Submitting myself unto the rigour of the lawe in such caas provided : if I from this day forth offend or doo contrary to this myn abiuracion or to any part of the same · In witnes wherfor [*sic*] I subscribe with myn owen hond makyng a crosse ✝ And require alle cristen people here present to record and wytnes ayenst me of this my confession and abiuracion if I from this day forthward offend in this behalve or doo contrary to the same in any poynt ·

347 This abjuration was made by the aforesaid John Edwardys before the bp in the chapel in Ramsbury manor on 3 August 1499, there being present then and there: M. Edmund Crome DTh; M. John Foted BTh; *et me* Robert Toneys, NP, scribe, etc.; and many others. The bp then and there ordered that that John Edwardys on the next Monday [5 August 1499], barefoot and bare-headed in the manner of a penitent, publicly carrying a faggot on his shoulder, go in the market at Abingdon and there, saying after the priest, recite and state publicly every single word of his abjuration following the form contained in a certain schedule drawn up for that purpose. Item, he is to go and do likewise at Wantage in the market on the following Saturday [10 August 1499]. And similarly on the following Sunday [11 August 1499] in the procession there. And also at Faringdon (*Chipping Faringdon*) on the following Monday [12 August 1499] in the market there.

348 [Fol. 80] Appropriation of Sutton Courtenay (*Courteney, Courtney*) ch. with Appleford (*Appulford*) chapel to Windsor (*Wyndesore*) castle St George royal free chapel: Before the bp in Sonning manor chapel, on 5 October 1495, 14th Indiction, 4 Alexander VI, appeared M. John Pykeryng, cl., proctor for dean and canons Windsor St George, patrons of Sutton Courtenay, and in the presence of M. Robert Toneys BCL, NP by apostolic and imperial authority, bp's registrar and scribe deputed by the bp in this matter, exhibited his proxy:

[1]Letters of the dean and canons of Windsor St George to M. Laurence

---

1   The text runs on without a break for 8 folios.

Cockys DCnL, M. William Cretyng, M. Ralph Hethcoot, M. John Pykeryng BCnL,[1] and Richard Humfreston, literate, appointing them together or singly proctors for appropriating Sutton Courtenay ch. to Windsor [St George] royal free chapel, [Fol. 80ᵛ] dated Windsor chapter house, 1 October 1495.

Before the bp there appeared also M. Laurence Cockys DCnL, canon of Salisbury cath. and proctor for dean and chapter Salisbury cath., and M. Thomas Martyn DCnL, proctor for M. Stephen Berworth, archdn Berks., within whose archdeaconry Sutton Courtenay ch. and Appleford chapel are situated, and exhibited their proxies:

Letters of Edward Cheyne DCn&CL, dean, and chapter of Salisbury cath. to M. Laurence Cockys DCnL appointing him proctor in the matter of the appropriation of Sutton Courtenay ch. to Windsor [St George] royal coll. [*sic*], dated Salisbury chapter house, 29 September 1495.

Letters of Stephen Berworth, [Fol. 81] archdn Berks., to M. Thomas Martyn DCnL appointing him proctor in the matter of the appropriation of Sutton Courtenay ch. with Appleford chapel to Windsor St George free chapel, dated Wallingford (*Walingford*) *in domo habitacionis meae*, 4 October 1495.

[Before the bp] M. John Pykeryng, cl., exhibited a document (*libellum sive articulum*) in the name of the dean and canons of Windsor and, with the express consent of the other proctors, it was read:

The tenor of the document, rehearsing the history of the foundation of Windsor [Fol. 81ᵛ] and its poverty because of the wars and other accidental or unexpected causes; and the recent history of the patronage of Sutton Courtenay ch., *viz.* that John Devoreux, James Baskervile, John Lyngen, Richard Corbet, kts, and William Wykes, gent., feoffees of Walter Devoreaux de Ferrers, kt, lord of the manor and patron of Sutton Courtenay, at the instance of King Edward IV, granted in free alms, with the assent of the said Walter Devoreux of Ferrers, kt, and licence having been obtained from the king, the advowson of Sutton Courtenay ch. with appurtenances to the said dean and canons of Windsor, that it might be appropriated to the said dean and canons of Windsor.

1   *Decretorum Bacall'* – it is unclear whether this refers only to Pykeryng or, as is most likely, to Cretyng and Hethcoot also.

King Edward IV: licence to John Devoreux, James Baskervile, John Lyngen, Richard Corbett, Thomas Cornwayle, kts, Thomas Monyngton, esq., and William Wykes, gent., feoffees of said Walter Devoreux, that they may give or grant the advowson or patronage of said Sutton Courtenay ch. to said dean and canons of Windsor, to be held in free alms of those feoffees; and to said dean and canons of Windsor St George royal free chapel [*sic*] and their successors that they may appropriate Sutton Courtenay ch. and hold it to their use; [Fol. 82] and that by authority of of parliament of King Henry VII at Westminster, said licences and grants are confirmed; power for ordination of perpetual v. in Sutton Courtenay ch. upon the death or cession or resignation of William Paynell, r. there.

M. John Pykeryng produced as witnesses to this document M. William Cretyng and Richard Humfreston whom, at the request of Pykeryng and with the assent of the other proctors, the bp admitted and swore as proctors, and with the assistance of the said scribe the bp examined the document and published the attestations.

[Fol. 82ᵛ] Therefore, with the assent of the dean and chapter of Salisbury cath. and of archdn Berks., the bp decreed the appropriation of Sutton Courtenay ch. etc. Tenor of the bp's decree [repeating all of the above], [Fol. 83] with ordination of v. in Sutton Courtenay, and of compensatory pensions payable annually on the feast of the Annunciation 30s. to the bp, 13s.4d. to the dean and chapter of Salisbury cath., and 10s. to archdn Berks., [Fol. 83ᵛ] and distribution of 10s. alms to the poor of the parish, dated as above, 5 October 1495; witnesses: M. Edmund Crome DTh and M. Ralph Hethcoot BCnL, of Norwich and Salisbury dioceses.

Notarial instrument by Robert Toneys BCL, clerk of Norwich diocese.

349 [Fol. 84] Ordination of v. in Sutton Courtenay ch. with annexed chapel of Appleford (*Appulford*), upon presentation by M. John Morgan DCnL, dean, and canons of Windsor St George royal free chapel, of Reginald Mutt, priest, to be instituted there; and ordination of v's stipend of 28m payable in four portions, at Christmas, Annunciation, Nativity of St John Baptist, and Michelmas. [Fol. 84ᵛ] Sonning, 8 January [1496].

350 [English] The kyng our sovereyn lord well graunteth and provydeth that noen acte made or tobe made in this present parliament extend or be preiudiciall to hys welbeloved in Cryste the dean and Chanons of <u>his fre Chapell</u> of sent george within his Castell of Wyndesor by what so ever name or names the said dean and Chanones be named or called in or of any graunte or grauntes of what soever nature or kynd they be made by any kyng or kyngis reignyng in this realme sithen the first yere of kyng Edward the thirde unto the day of the deth of kyng Edward the iiij[th] nor in or of any acte or actes made for the said deane and Chanons by auctorite of any parliament by any of his progenitours any act or actes made or tobe made in this present parliament to the contrarie notwith standyng.

[Fol. 85 *blank*]

351 [Fol. 85[v]] [List of the bp's temporal and spiritual possessions with valuations for the tenth. Except where noted, the values are identical with those in *Tax. Eccl.*]

Tenth of the temporalities of the bp in Berks. archdeaconry
Abingdon (*Abendon*) deanery: [East] Hendred (*henreth*)   12d.
Newbury deanery: Chieveley (*Chyvele*)   8s.
Reading (*Rading*) deanery: Sonning (*Sonnyng*)   £12.6½d.
[Marginal: Total £12.9s.6½d.]

Tenth of the spiritualities in that archdeaconry
Speen (*Spene*) ch.   40s.
[Marginal: Total 40s.]

Tenth of the temporalities of the bp in Wilts. archdeaconry
Marlborough (*Merleburgh*) deanery: Baydon (*Beydon*)   34s.7d.
Ramsbury (*Remmesbury*)   £6.4s.4d.
Membury (*Mymbury*)   3s.9d.
Avebury deanery: Cannings (*Canyngys*) [Episcopi]   £12.18s.
Cricklade (*Crekelade*) deanery: Bishopstone (*Bysshopeston*)   £6.7s.
[Marginal: Total £27.7s.8d.]

Tenth of the temporalities and spiritualities of the bp in Dorset and Salisbury archdeaconries
Potterne (*Poterne*) deanery: Potterne (*Pottern*) prebend   100s.
Bridport (*Birdport*) deanery: Chardstock (*Cherdstoke*)   73s.6d.
Lyme [Regis]   4¾d.[1]
Langton (*Langdon*) [Herring]   11s.7d.

1   4¼d. in *Taxat. Eccl.*

Shaftesbury deanery: Caundle (*Caundel*) Episcopi	27s.6d.
Sherborne (*Shirborn*) with hamlets	£19.19½d.

[The remaining nine items marginally bracketed]

Salisbury: Salisbury city	£9.4s.4¼d.[1]
Salisbury manor	79s.
Amesbury (*Ambresbury*) deanery: Woodford (*Wodeford*)	67s.
Potterne (*Potern*) deanery: [West] Lavington (*Lavyngton*)	£4.11s.
Potterne (*Potern*)	£9.13s.9d.
Poulshot (*Pollesholt*) pension	2s.
Brixton [Deverill] (*[Bry]teston*) pension	2s.
Prior of [Monk] Sherborne's pension[2] – Winchester dioc.	
in Lavington (*Lavyngton*)	4s.
Keyhaven (*Kyhaven*) and Milford (*Muleford*) [on Sea][3]	10s.

Sum total £103.4s.11d.

352 [Fol. 86][4] Account of the proceedings in the election of a new abbot of Abingdon BMV to succeed John Saunt DTh, who died on 6 January 149[6], having obtained licence from the king,[5] by John Kennyngton, prior and president of the chapter, and by the following monks: Robert Hayles; Richard Norwich, sacrist; Thomas Frysewyth, infirmarer; Miles (*Milo*) Salley, kitchener; Thomas Whightchurch; John Westbury; William Chynnok; John Rowell; Nicholas Indesley, subprior, chamberlain, and gardener; William Benett, treasurer and master of the works; Alexander Shotesbroke, scholar of Oxford; John Bolton; Robert Westwood, precentor; Thomas Comnour, third prior and keeper of Cuddesdon (*Cuttysdon*); Thomas Marcham,[6] subchamberlain; John Clyffe, scholar of Oxford; William Welford; Robert Morton, seneschal; William Fyfyld, almoner; John Cornyssh, subcellarer; Thomas Herford, succentor; Thomas Brystow;

---

1   £9.4s.5d. in *Taxat. Eccl.*
2   The alien priory of Monk Sherborne was suppressed in 1414.
3   In Winchester dioc.
4   A space has been left for the illumination of the 'R' of the first word of this entry
    Reverendo.
5   The petition to the king from John Kenyngton, prior, and the convent of Abingdon
    for licence to elect a new abbot in place of John Sant, who died on 7 [*sic*] January
    [1496], dated Abingdon, 9 January 1496, is in TNA C 82/146/18(117); the bearers
    were Nicholas Inysley, subprior, and Robert Morton, almoner [*sic*], monks; and
    warrant to the Great Seal granting the royal licence to elect, dated Sheen (*Shene*),
    18 March [1496], signed by Purde, is in TNA C 82/146/17(117); it was delivered
    19 March 1496, but was not published in *CPR, Henry VII, 1494-1509.*
6   Occurs as Thomas Westgate on Fol. 88v.

John Sutton; John Brent and Robert Preston, scholar of Oxford.

The prior called a meeting of the chapter for 13 April 1496 to elect a new abbot and summoned William Elworton,[1] professed monk, and each and every absent monk of Abingdon to attend.

Text of the above mandate, directed to William Elworth [sic] etc., [Fol. 86ᵛ] dated 12 April 1496.

On 13 April 1496, after the Mass of the Holy Spirit was solemnly celebrated at the high altar, and the bell for the assembly of the chapter rung, the prior and monks entered the chaper house. There the Word of God was preached in Latin by M. William Harward DTh, the *Veni Creator Spiritus* was sung, and the Holy Spirit invoked. Then John Clyffe, monk, deputed for this purpose, having the original of the above mandate in his hand, certified that he had cited and called at the great north door of the conventual ch., and at the door of the chapter house, those specified in the summons to appear on pain of contumacy; and the prior pronounced the following sentence:

[Fol. 87] Decree of contumacy by John Kennyngton, prior and president of the chapter, against William Elworton, monk, and all others cited who do not appear for the election.

Monition to those having no right in the election to withdraw.

When this monition had been read and all laymen had been excluded, there remained 26 monks and brothers of the said prior in the chapter house;[2] also remaining at the request of the monks: M. John Veysy DCL, to direct and counsel the electors; M. Christopher Myddelton, one of the procurators general of causes at the court of Canterbury, and M. James Souche, Notaries Public and scribes; M. Richard Norton DCn&CL, M. Thomas Hare DCL, and M. George Wood BCnL, witnesses.

Veysy 'our doctor' read the decree *Quia propter* and expounded to the chapter the form and manner of electing. The prior and monks opted for the form of scrutiny and chose Richard Norwich,

---

1   The probably irregular absence of William Elworton must have been already known or his name would not have occurred here but only in the decree of contumacy (below). Elworton was ordained acolyte in 1486 (*Reg. Langton*, 566) but otherwise leaves no trace in the diocesan records.
2   I.e., the prior and 25 other monks.

Thomas Frideswith, and Nicholas Indeslay, monks in priests' orders, as scrutators to take the vote of each and every monk, secretly and individually, in the presence of the notaries and witnesses. [Fol. 87ᵛ] When the votes of all the monks have been taken and faithfully recorded in writing, the scrutators were empowered to make known the result to the monks in the chapter house.

The three scrutators accepted their commission and withdrew to a corner of the chapter house to take the scrutiny, in the presence of the notaries and witnesses, starting with the votes of the three scrutators themselves. Richard Norwich took the oath, in peril of his soul and following God and his conscience, to vote for the most suitable candidate to be abbot and pastor of the said monastery, and he named M. Thomas Rowland BTh, prior of Luffield (*Luffeld*); then Thomas Frideswith, having similarly sworn, named Miles Sauley; then Nicholas Indesley, similarly sworn, named M. Thomas Rowland. Immediately afterwards the three scrutators proceeded to take the scrutiny of the others, secretly and individually. And first I John Kennyngton, prior, called by the three scrutators, and sworn according to the above form, named Nicholas Indesley. And Robert Hayles, John Westbury, William Benett, Alexander Shotesbroke, John Bolton, Robert Morton, Robert Preston, and Thomas Bristow, sworn as above, secretly and individually, named Miles Sauley. And Miles Sauley, Thomas Whightchurch, John Rowell, Robert Westwood, Thomas Comnour, William Chynnok, Thomas Westgate, John Clyff, William Welford, William Fyffyld, John Cornyssh, Thomas Herford, John Brent, and John Sutton, sworn by the said scrutators as above, secretly and individually, named the said M. Thomas Rowland.

All the votes having been taken and recorded as above, and the scrutiny completed, Nicholas Indesley, one of the aforesaid scrutators, [Fol. 88] announced clearly and distinctly the result to the prior and other monks, then and there as follows: In the Name of God Amen. I Nicholas Indesley, one of the scrutators for taking the vote of each and every monk of this chapter having a voice in this election, chosen and deputed for making the result known to you, notify and make known that Richard Norwich, having taken the oath, responded, 'I Richard Norwich name M. Thomas Rowland BTh, prior of Luffield, to be abbot of this monastery.' [Etc. repeating exactly the above account of the voting.]

Consequently we the said John Kennyngton, prior, and the other monks granted to the said Nicholas Indesley power and special mandate to collate the votes cast to determine who received the greater part of the votes of the chapter in the said scrutiny. The same Nicholas Indesley accepted this power and immediately read out the result in these words: In the Name of God Amen. My brothers, in the present election there were twenty-six monks in the chapter house, *viz.* John Kennyngton, prior, Robert Hayles... [Etc. repeating exactly the above attendance list and then the above account of the voting.] [Fol. 88ᵛ] Thus it is clear that the greater part of the whole chapter or convent cast their votes for M. Thomas Rowland to be abbot of this monastery. And thus the said M. Thomas Rowland by reason of numbers is preferred to the others named in this scrutiny.

[There follows an elaborate encomium of Thomas Rowland.]

The same Nicholas Indesley, by virtue of the authority granted to him by the prior and other monks, for himself and in his name and in the name of the prior and other monks, immediately made public the election by majority vote of M. Thomas Rowland to be abbot, solemnly, in this form of words: In the Name of God Amen. Since the monastery of BMV Abingdon, OSB, Salisbury dioc., is vacant by the [Fol. 89] natural death of the well-remembered John Saunct DTh, last abbot, all who ought to have a part by right or custom in the election having been summoned, all entered the chapter house to celebrate the election, and the prior and all other monks were pleased to elect a new abbot by the way of scrutiny. The three scrutators chosen by the prior and convent first took the votes of the scrutators, then those of each and every monk included in this election and present, secretly and individually, in the presence of the notaries and witnesses aforesaid, and recorded them faithfully and collating them following the constitution *Quia Propter*, and the majority of the whole chapter voted for M. Thomas Rowland BTh, prior of Luffield, a discreet man, eminent in learning, virtuous in life and morals, chaste, OSB professed, born legitimately, in priests' orders, of legal age, nothing wanting canonically. Therefore, I Nicholas Indesley, monk of the aforesaid monastery of BM Abingdon, by the authority and power granted to me recorded herein, with the express consent of all the monks having a right and voice in this election, provide the aforesaid M. Thomas Rowland, the grace of the Holy Spirit having been invoked in the Name of the Most Holy and Undivided Trinity and in honour of BMV Abingdon, to this monastery.

The election having been completed, we the prior and each and every one of the monks granted to the distinguished man M. William Warham DCL, keeper or master of the rolls of chancery of our lord king, power and special mandate to publish in English the aforesaid election of M. Thomas Rowland to the clergy and people. Then the psalm [*sic*] *Te Deum Laudamus* was solemnly sung as we approached the high altar of the monastery, and after the psalm was over M. William Warham announced the result of the election in a loud voice in English to the clergy and people congregated there in a great multitude.

Commission to Nicholas Indesley, Richard Norwich, John Clyff, and John Brent [Fol. 89ᵛ] to obtain royal assent to the said election of Rowland, and to present the said Rowland in person or by proxy to the bp of Salisbury for confirmation and blessing. [Fol. 90] 13 April 1496 (Indiction 14; 4 Alexander VI).

353 Notarial instrument by Christopher Middelton, clerk of York dioc., NP, and procurator general of the court of Canterbury.

354 Notarial instrument by James Souche, clerk of Lichfield dioc., NP.

355 Letters patent from the king to the bp signifying the royal assent to the election of M. Thomas Rowland as abbot of Abingdon. [Fol. 90ᵛ] Westminster, 24 April [1496].[1]

356 [Fol. 91] Account of the proceedings in the election of a new abbot of Abbotsbury (*Abbotesburie*) Blessed Peter the Apostle to succeed Hugh (*Hugo*) Dorchestre, who died on 17 May 1496, having obtained licence from the king,[2] by the subprior and convent. John Abbotesbury, prior; Henry Cerne, subprior; William Hampton, seneschal; Thomas Haukechurch, sacrist; Richard Pawley

---

1   Signification of royal assent to the election, 24 April 1496 (*CPR, Henry VII, 1494-1509*, p. 55); mandate for the restitution of temporalities, 12 June 1496 (*ibid.*, p. 56).

2   The petitition to the king from the prior and convent of Abbotsbury for licence to elect a new abbot, dated Abbotsbury, 18 May 1496, is in TNA C 82/149/4(144); the bearer was William Hampton, monk; and warrant to the Great Seal granting the royal licence to elect, dated Sheen (*Shene*), 5 June 1496, signed by Bolman, is in TNA C 82/149/5(144); it was delivered 9 June 1496, but was not published in *CPR, Henry VII, 1494-1509*. The king granted to Geffry Wren, priest, chaplain to the Duke of York, the king's son, the pension which the next abbot of Abbotsbury is bound to give to a clerk at the king's nomination, till he be promoted by the abbot and convent to a competent benefice, dated 3 June 1496; signed by Bolman; delivered 5 September 1496 (TNA C 82/149/2(113); this grant is in English.

(*Pawlegh*), chamberlain; John Shirborn; John Excestre, master of the works (*operarius*); John Portesham, infirmarer (*hospitalarius*); and John Lychett, all priests; and Thomas Bradford, deacon; and John Powrstock (*Powerstock; Powrestock*) and John Coot, in minor orders – constituting the whole monastery, met in full chapter on Wednesday, 15 June 1496, and set the following day, Thursday, 16 June 1496, to hold the election.

On that day, after the monks solemnly celebrated the Mass of the Holy Spirit at the high altar in the choir, and after ringing the bell at the hour of the chapter, each and every one of the monks[1] assembled, [Fol. 91ᵛ] the *Veni Creator Spiritus* was sung, and then the prior ordered all those having no right to participate in the election to withdraw from the chapterhouse [Text of the mandate]; whence John Powrestock and John Coot withdrew; but the following remained by the leave of the chapter: M. Laurence Cockys DCnL, the monks' director of the election; M. Robert Toneys BCL, NP, the monks' scribe and registrar for these proceedings; M. Richard Hatton DCn&CL; and William Ewayn, v. Puncknowle (*Ponkenoll et Bexenton Tollepudell*)[2] and Walter Josepp, r. Puncknowle (*Ponkenoll et Bexenton*), witnesses.

The king's licence was exhibited to the monks and publicly read by M. Robert Toneys, M. Laurence Cockys expounded to the chapter in English the constitution of the general council *Quia propter* and the mode of proceeding contained therein, [Fol. 92] and obtained the agreement to it of all the monks eligible to vote *viz.*, [*the monks are named again*].[3] By the grace of the Holy Spirit, and by unanimous acclaim (himself excepted), John Abbotesbury, the prior, was elected [*the formulaic encomium of the elect follows*]. William Hampton, seneschal, with the authority and special mandate of the whole chapter proclaimed John Abbotesbury's election.

The election proclamation.

The psalm [*sic*] *Te Deum laudamus* was sung as the monks moved from the chapter house to the choir of the monastic church, the bell was rung, and John Abbotesbury was led to the high altar. M.

---

1   They are all listed by name again, in the order given above; variations in the spelling of names are indicated in brackets in the list above.
2   [West] Bexington was united to Puncknowle in 1451.
3   Only the two in minor orders, excluded from the election, are excluded from this list; again, variations in the spelling of names are indicated in brackets in the first list above.

Richard Hatton was deputed by the monks [Fol. 92^v] to publish the election to the clergy and people in English; then they all (except the elect) returned to the chapter house. 'We', Henry Cerne and William Hampton, appointed proctors by the other monks to obtain the assent of John Abbotesbury to his election, found him at 1 p.m. waiting in a small room in the infirmary, and in the presence of the notaries and witnesses aforesaid asked for his assent to his election; he said he wanted to deliberate; later on that day, at 5 p.m., in a lower room which he customarily occupied he gave his assent in the presence of the notaries and witnesses.

Text of formal assent.

Supplication to the bp of Salisbury for confirmation and blessing of the elect, dated Abbotsbury (*Abbotesburie*): chapter house, 13 July 1496.

357 [Fol. 93] Notarial instrument by Robert Toneys BCL, clerk of Norwich dioc., NP by apostolic and imperial authority, recounting above election, which took place on 16 June [1496], Indiction [*omitted*], 4 Alexander VI.

358 Commission by Henry Cerne, subprior of Abbotsbury, and the convent there to William Hampton and Richard Pawley, monks, as proctors to exhibit to the bp of Salisbury whatsoever letters etc. proofs touching the above election of the abbot of Abbotsbury so that it may be confirmed. [Fol. 93^v] Abbotsbury, chapter house, 13 July[1] 1496.

359 Commission to M. Laurence Cockys DCnL and M. William Russell DCnL, canons residentiary of Salisbury cath., to examine and confirm the above election of the abbot of Abbotsbury. Ramsbury, 12 July 1496.

360 Commission to Thomas Russell, literate, to cite all and sundry who wish to oppose the above election of the abbot of Abbotsbury to appear before the bp or his commissary in St Edmund's collegiate ch., Salisbury, on Friday, 15 July 1496, at [Fol. 94] 10 a.m. Ramsbury, 8 July 1496.

361 Account of the examination and confirmation, on 15 July 1496,

---

1   'June' corrected to 'July'.

of the above election of the abbot of Abbotsbury, there being no one to oppose it, by M. Laurence Cockys.

Text of confirmation.

[Fol. 94ᵛ] Text of John Abbotesbury's profession of obedience to the church and bp of Salisbury.

362 Mandate to the archdeacon of Dorset or his official to install John Abbotesbury whose election as abbot of Abbotsbury has been confirmed. Dated etc. [*sic*].

363 Mandate to the subprior and convent of Abbotsbury enjoining obedience to John Abbotesbury, whose election as abbot of Abbotsbury has been confirmed. Dated etc. [*sic*].

364 [Fol. 95] Petition to the king for the restitution of the temporalities of Abbotsbury to John Abbotesbury, whose election as abbot there the bp has confirmed. Dated etc. [*sic*].[1]

365 Account of the election of an abbess of Shaftesbury BMV and St Edward the Martyr, to succeed Alice Gibbes who died 18 December 1496, licence to elect having been obtained from the king,[2] by Thomasina Kemer, prioress and president of the chapter, and the convent there. The prioress and 24 nuns expressly professed

---

1   The original of this petition, dated Corfe (*Corffe*), 25 June 1496, is in TNA C 82/151/5(87), and the warrant to the Great Seal for restitution of temporalities, dated Salisbury, 6 August 1496, and signed by Horwod, is in TNA C 82/151/6. The mandate for the restitution of temporalities is dated 12 August 1496 (*CPR, Henry VII, 1494-1509,* p. 64). The petition by the subprior and convent for the royal assent, dated Abbotsbury (*Abbottesbury*), 16 June 1496, is in TNA C 82/149/28; the bearers were Richard Pawlee and John Portesham, monks; and the warrant to the Great Seal for the royal assent, dated Guildford, 26 June 1496, and signed by Bolman, is in TNA C 82/149/27(75). Signification of royal assent to the election is dated 29 June 1496 (*CPR, Henry VII, 1494-1509,* p. 56).

2   The original petition from the prioress and convent of Shaftesbury for licence to elect a successor to Alicia Gibbes, dated 20 December 1496, is preserved in TNA C 82/157/8a; the bearers of the petition were M. Richard Banter DTh and Morgan Kidwelly, esq. Royal licence to elect, dated 13 December [*sic – rectius* January] (TNA C 82/157/8), delivered 15 January 1497 (*CPR, Henry VII, 1494-1509,* p. 77). See also TNA C 82/157/12: grant to William Pennet, chapl., of the pension which the next abbess of Shaftesbury is bound to give a clerk at the king's nomination, till that clerk be promoted by the Abbess to a competent benefice, dated 27 December 1496, delivered 21 April 1497.

and 11 tacitly professed[1] are named. Those expressly professed: Thomasina Kemer, prioress; Agnes Woodford; Christina Pokeswell; Johanna[2] Walberton; Philippa Bonham; Agnes Prynce; Isolda Grene; Margery Twyneo; Agnes Asshe; Alice Purry; Mary Payn; Agnes Laurence; Jocosa Bulwarden; Elisabeth Shelford; Thomasina Hosy; Margery[3] Saynt John; Emma Roderford; Anna Deynton; Elisabeth Brethyr; Elisabeth Mounpesson; Elisabeth Monmouth; Alice Pevesy; Katherine Thornhylle; Johanna Stokes; Johanna Bulstrod. Those tacitly professed: Margaret Hemmerford; Elianor Pulter; Margaret Payn; Alice Abbot; Elisabeth Souch; Katherine Halle; Johanna Amys; Philippa Catesby; Margaret Coke; Johanna Maunshill; Elisabeth [Fol. 95$^\mathrm{v}$] Godwyn.

On 4 February [1497] the nuns met in the chapter house and fixed the election for Monday, 6 February [1497], at the time of the chapter; however, on that day at the time of the chapter, *viz.* 9 a.m., for good reasons [*not specified*] they prorogued the meeting of the chapter for the election until Thursday, 9 February [1497], at the time of the chapter.

On that day, after the mass of the Holy Spirit had been solemnly sung at the high altar, and the bell had been rung, the prioress and nuns entered the chapter house at the time of the chapter, *viz.* 9 a.m., to hear the Word of God preached by M. Richard Pantere BTh;[4] direction of the election was committed to M. Laurence Cockys DCnL; M. Robert Toneys BCL, cl., NP, remained as scribe; remaining as witnesses were M. Thomas Gilbert DCnL, M. Thomas Martyn DCnL, M. Henry Mounpesson DCnL, M. Walter Stone LicCL, M. Alexander Catour BCnL, and M. Richard Knott, BCnL. Because the king's letters granting the licence to elect could not be found, the chapter was again prorogued to Monday, 13 February

1   Profession was express, when made with the usual ceremonies; tacit, or implied, when the reciprocal engagement between the order and the religious was proved by outward acts; it was sufficient for this purpose to wear the habit of the professed members for some time openly and without objection being made in any one. Pius IX abolished the tacit solemn profession for religious orders (11 June, 1858) and it has fallen into disuse altogether ('Religious Profession' in *The Catholic Encyclopedia*).

2   The spelling of the Christian names of the nuns has been retained without modernisation in some cases because more than one translation is possible – e.g., Johanna may become Joanna, Joan, or Joanne.

3   'Margaret' in subsequent lists.

4   Possibly the same as M. Richard Banter DTh who carried to the king the petition of the nuns to elect a new abbess – see note above.

[1497], at the time of the chapter, 9 a.m. [*Marginal:* with unanimous agreement]

On Saturday, 11 February [1497],[1] the prioress and nuns [Fol. 96] above named, assembled in the chapter house, mindful that the abbey suffered in spiritualities and temporalities from not having an abbess, and willing to proceed to an election with all speed, and all the nuns who ought to have a part in the election being present, they sang the *Veni Creator Spiritus*; after which each and every one of the nuns having been publicly called by name and surname, it was announced that none of the nuns was then absent; Thomasina Kemer, the prioress and president, read in English the monition and protestation, following the form customary in these elections, for all lay persons and those having no right in the election to withdraw from the chapter house, excepting the above M. Laurence Cockys, director; M. Robert Toneys, scribe; M. Thomas Gilbert, M. Thomas Martyn, M. Henry Mounpesson, M. Walter Stoon, and M. Alexander Catour, witnesses; the king's licence to elect was read and explained in English by M. Robert Toneys; the constitution *Quia propter* was expounded by M. Laurence Cockys; 'we' the prioress and nuns discussed the form and manner of the election and decided to proceed by scrutiny; 'we' the prioress and nuns unanimously, except for Christina Pokeswell, Philippa Bonham, and Jocosa Bulwarden, chose as scrutatrices of the proceedings: Christina (*Xpina*) Pokeswell, Philippa Bonham, and Jocosa Bulwarden, our sister nuns OSB, expressly professed, faithful, circumspect, and discreet. [Fol. 96ᵛ] The scrutatrices went into a corner of the chapter house, there, in the presence of the NP and witnesses, to take a secret scrutiny of the votes of the prioress and nuns, *viz.* Philippa Bonham and Jocosa Bulwarden, to whom the third of the scrutatrices, *viz.* Christina (*Xpina*) Pokeswell, having taken the oath to follow God and conscience, gave her vote for Margery Twyneo; then Philippa Bonham did the same and to the other two scrutatrices gave her vote for Margery Twyneo; then Jocosa Bulwarden did the same and to the other two scrutatrices gave her vote for Margery Twyneo. Afterwards, without a pause, the three scrutatricess proceeded to take the scrutiny of all the nuns. First 'I' Thomasina Kemer, prioress, having taken the oath as above, voted for Agnes Asshe. Then Agnes Woodford, Johanna Walberton, Agnes Prynce, Isolda Grene, Mary Payne, Agnes Laurence, Emma Roderford, Anna Deynton, Elisabeth Mounpesson,

---

1   Since this date differs from that immediately above, we may perhaps infer pressure on the nuns by the bp's representatives.

Elisabeth Monmouth, Alice Pevesy, Katherine Thornhill, Margaret Hemmerford, Elianor Pulter, Johanna Bulstrode, Elisabeth Souch, Katherine Halle, Johanna Amys, Philippa Catesby, and Elisabeth Goodwyn, sworn as above, voted for Margery Twyneo. Margery Twyneo, sworn as above, voted for Jocosa Bulwarden. And Agnes Asshe, Alice Pury, Elisabeth Shelford, Thomasina Hosy, Margaret Saynt John, Elisabeth Brethyr, Johanna Stokes, Margaret Payne, Alice Abbot, Margaret Coke, and Johanna Maunshille, sworn as above, voted 'for me' Thomasina Kemer, prioress.

[Fol. 97] Then, 'we' Thomasina Kemer and the other nuns, except Philippa Bonham, gave power to Philippa Bonham to collate the votes and determine the result. 36 nuns tooks part in the election, *viz.* Thomasina Kemer, prioress; [etc.].[1]

Thomasina Kemer voted for Agnes Asshe. Margery Twyneo voted for Jocosa Bulwarden [etc.].[2] Thus it was clear that the greater part of the chapter or convent voted for Margery Twyneo and that Margery Twyneo was elected abbess.

[Fol. 97ᵛ] 'We' the aforesaid Thomasina Kemer, Elisabeth Shelford, Thomasina Hoosy, Elisabeth Brethyr, and Margaret Payne, without guile, fraud, machination, collusion, or any other wickedness, named Margery Twyneo abbess-elect. Then Philippa Bonham was given power by the prioress and other nuns to make public the election of Margery Twyneo.

Formal text of election decree.

'We' prioress and nuns granted power to M. Thomas Gilbert DCnL to publish the election result to clergy and people. 'We' prioress and nuns granted power to Maria Payne and Elisabeth Shelford [Fol. 98] to obtain Margery Twyneo's assent to her election. They then solemnly sang the *Te Deum Laudamus* as they lifted and carried the elect from the chapter house to the conventual church, bells ringing, taking her to the high altar there. M. Thomas Gilbert then announced the election

1   The list of nuns is identical to that immediately above on Fol. 96ᵛ, with the following variant spellings: Agnes Wooford; Christina Pokeswel; Johanna Bulstroode; Johanna Maunshyll.
2   The votes of the nuns are recorded again, with the following variant spelling: Thomasina Hoosey. Jocosa Bulwarden's name is omitted, an understandable error since, as one of the scrutatrices, her name did not occur in the main list (Fol. 96ᵛ) of those who voted for Margery Twyneo.

result in English to the multitude of clergy and people gathered there. On that day, 11 February [1497] in the afternoon, Maria Payne and Elisabeth Shelford went to find Margery Twyneo in a certain upper room in the infirmary to obtain her assent to her election, and Margery replied that she wished to deliberate. On the same day around 4 p.m. they found her a second time in the upper room and asked for her assent to her election. The elect then and there in the presence of the NP and aforesaid witnesses gave her assent.

Formal text of Twyneo's assent to her election.

Petition to the bp for confirmation of the election and blessing of the elect, [Shaftesbury:] chapter house, 18 February [1497].

366 [Fol. 98ᵛ] Royal assent to the above election. Westminster, 27 February [1497].[1]

367 Account of confirmation of the above election by M. Laurence Cockys DCnL, vicar-general in spiritualities, in Donhead St Mary ch. on 13 March [1497]; mandate for installation of the elect directed to the archdeacon of Dorset or his official; commission to Augustine [Church], bp of Lydda to confer blessing on the elect, which he did on 14 March [1497] in Shaftesbury Holy Trinity ch.

Text of Twyneo's profession of obedience; her mark ✝ .

Note that then a petition was sent to the king for the restitution of temporalities.[2]

368 Commission to Augustine [Church], bp. of Lydda, as above. Dated etc. [*sic*]

---

1   TNA C 82/159/22, dated 22 February 1497, delivered 27 February (*CPR Henry VII, 1494-1509*, p. 108). The petition by the prioress and conv. for the royal assent, dated 21 February 1497, is preserved in TNA C 82/159/22a; the bearers were M. David Knollys BCnL and Robert Payn.
2   This petition survives, dated Sonning, 18 March 149[7], in TNA C 82/160/23. Grant of restitution of temporalities to Margery Twyneo, whose fealty was taken by the abbots of Milton and Cerne, M. Edward Cheyne, dean of Salisbury cath., and John Cheyne, king's counsellor and kt *pro corpore*, dated Sheen, 21 March 149[7], signed by Horwod, and delivered 20 April 1497, is TNA C 82/160/23a (*CPR, Henry VII, 1494-1509*, p. 108). TNA C 82/160/23b is the mandate (on paper and in English) to the chancellor to make out the above letters *dedimus potestatem* for taking fealty and homage etc., by the king, dated Sheen, 21 March 149[7].

369 [Fol. 99] Account of the election of a prior of Poughley (*Pougheley*) St Margaret the Virgin (OSA), to succeed Thomas Ware, resigned, licence to elect having been obtained from the prioress and convent Amesbury (*Ambresbury*), order of Fontevrault, patrons. On 6 May 1497, after the Mass of the Holy Spirit had been sung in the conventual ch., the canons met in the chapter house where M. Edmund Crome DTh preached the Word of God to them; the *Veni Creator Spiritus* was sung, the usual protestation[1] was made, the licence to elect was read, and the constitution of the general council *Quia propter* and the form of proceeding was expounded. Then William Woodstok *or* Woodstock, president of the chapter, and all the canons unanimously elected, by the grace of the Holy Spirit, William Mordon, canon of Bradenstoke, OSA, to be prior of Poughley. After the *Te Deum laudamus* had been sung, the election was published to the people in the ch. Later, licence was obtained from Thomas Walsh, prior Bradenstoke, for Mordon to accept his election. After that, on receipt of letters from the patrons, the bp confirmed the election in Sonning manor on 23 May 1497, and wrote to the archdeacon of Berks. or his official for Mordon's installation.

370 Licence to elect a new prior, granted by Alice Fyssher, prioress, and convent Amesbury (*Ambresbury*), order of Fontevrault, to William Woodstok, canon, and the brothers of Poughley priory, on receipt of their letter brought by John Feryby, canon. Amesbury: chapter house, 26 April 1497.

371 [Fol. 99ᵛ] Petition by Alice Fyssher, prioress, and convent Amesbury (*Ambresbury*), to the bp for confirmation of the election of William Moordon to be prior of Poughley, postulated by William Woodstok, Francis Bailour, and John Feryby, professed canons in priests' orders.[2] Amesbury: chapter house, 9 May 1497.

372 Collation of the abbatial dignity of Cerne [BVM &] St Peter the Apostle (OSB), vac. by the death of Roger Bemystre[3] and falling

1 Probably requiring the withdrawal of all persons having no right to take part in the election.

2 These three were probably the only canons of Poughley. In 1525, when Poughley was suppressed for cardinal Wolsey's coll. at Oxford, there were a prior and three canons (Knowles and Hadcock, p. 171).

3 According to the petition to the king by the prior and convent of Cerne for a licence to elect, dated 1 May 1497, Roger Bemystre died 22 April and was buried 24 April 1497 (TNA C 82/162/9a). Licence to elect was granted 11 May 1497, signed by Purde, and delivered 4 July 1497 (TNA C 82/162/9; *CPR, Henry VII, 1494-1509*, p. 106). See also TNA C 82/161/10: grant to John Pediok, one of

to the bp's collation this time by lapse of three months, to Thomas Sam, monk of Cerne. Ramsbury, [*blank*] August 1497. Mandate for installation directed to archdeacon of Dorset or his official; mandate for obedience directed to convent Cerne; petition for royal assent and restitution of temporalities addressed to the king.

373 Text of (above) petition to the king. [Fol. 100] Dated etc. [*sic*].[1]

374 Memo that on 21 September [1497] in Cerne conventual ch. Augustine [Church], bp of Lydda, for and with the authority of bp Blyth, conferred blessing on Thomas Sam, abbot of Cerne; text of Sam's profession of obedience.

375 Collation of the dignity of prioress of Broomhall (*Bromehale*) OSB, vac. by cession or dimission[2] of Alice [*superscript:* Anna] Thomas and falling to the bp's collation this time by lapse of three months,[3] to Elizabeth Leukenor, nun of Broomhall. Ramsbury, 21 August 1498. Mandate for installation directed to archdeacon of Berkshire or his official; mandate for obedience directed to convent Broomhall, etc. in the customary forms.

376 [Fol. 100ᵛ] Certification by Thomas [Bourgchier], archbishop of Canterbury, that on Holy Saturday, 27 April 1484,[4] in Christ Church, Canterbury, Richard Martyn, bp in the universal Church (*in universali ecclesia episcopus*), by special licence celebrated ordinations, at which he ordained to the order of subdeacon James Dyxson, acolyte, Canterbury dioc., to title Osney (*Oseney*) abbey, Lincoln dioc. Dated as above [*sic*], the 30ᵗʰ year of his translation.

---

    the ministers of the king's chapel, of the pension which the next abbot of Cerne is bound to give a clerk at the king's nomination until he be promoted by the abbot to a competent benefice, dated 28 April 1497 [*sic*], signed by Bolman, and delivered 20 April 1497 [*sic*].

1   This is preserved in TNA C 82/165/11a, dated Ramsbury, 9 August 1497. Royal mandate for the restitution of temporalities, dated Woodstock, 17 August 1497, signed by Purde, and delivered 19 August 1497 (TNA C 82/165/11).

2   The use of these terms rather than the more usual 'resignation' may suggest some irregularity.

3   Failure to elect a prioress to succeed Anna Thomas may have resulted from internal dissent among the few remaining nuns. In 1521, when Broomhall was suppressed and its possession subsequently transferred to St John's Coll., Cambridge, there were only the prioress and two other nuns, who 'left the priory as a profane place' (*VCH Berks.*, Vol. 2, pp. 80–81).

4   Holy Saturday fell on 17 April in 1484; the error most probably occurred when the archbp's letter was copied into the register.

377   Letters dimissory from Thomas [Bourgchier], archbishop of Canterbury etc., to James Dyxson to receive orders from any catholic bp. Canterbury: Palace, 31 August 1484, the 31ˢᵗ year of his translation.

378   Certification by Richard Lavender DCnL, vicar-general in spiritualities to John [Russell], bp of Lincoln, that Thomas [Ingilby], bp of Rathlur, on Ember Saturday, 18 September 1484, in Osney (*Oseney*) conventual ch., by authority celebrated ordinations, at which he ordained to the order of deacon James Dyxson, subdeacon, sufficiently dimmised, to title Osney abbey. Dated as above [*sic*].

379   Certification by Thomas [Kempe], bp of London, that James [Wale *or* Wall], bp of Kildare, on Ember Saturday, 18 December 1484, in. St Bartholomew conventual ch. or hosp, Smithfield (*Smythfeld*), London, by authority celebrated ordinations, at which he ordained to the order of priest James Dyxson, deacon, Canterbury dioc., sufficiently dimmised, to title Osney (*Oseney*) abbey. Dated as above [*sic*].

380   Memo that these letters [above 376-379] were exhibited by James Dyxson before the bp at Sonning, 28 January [1498].[1]

381   [Fol. 101] Certification by John [Stanbury], bp of Hereford, that on Ember Saturday, 13 March [1462], in the chapel of St Katherine next to the cloister of Hereford cath., he celebrated ordinations, at which to the order of subdeacon he ordained John Hyde, acolyte, Hereford dioc., to title Polesworth (*Pawlysworth*) nunnery. Dated as above [*sic*].

382   Certification by John [Stanbury], bp of Hereford, that on Holy Saturday, 17 April 1462, in Hereford cath., he celebrated ordinations, at which to the order of deacon he ordained John Hyde, subdeacon, Hereford dioc., to title Polesworth (*Pawlysworth*) abbey, Lichfield dioc. Dated as above [*sic*].

383   Certification by John [Stanbury], bp of Hereford, that on the vigil of Trinity Sunday, 12 June 1462, in Bromyard prebendal ch., he celebrated ordinations, at which to the order of priest he ordained John Hyde, deacon, Hereford dioc., to title Polesworth (*Pawlysworth*) nunnery. Dated as above [*sic*].

---

1   After this entry and **384** Robert Toneys has inscribed his elaborate formal signature.

384 Memo that these letters (above 381-383) were exhibited before the bp at Sonning, 9 March 1498.

[Fol. 101ᵛ *blank*]

ORDINATIONS

385 [Fol. 102] Ordinations celebrated at the altar of BM in Salisbury cath. by Augustine [Church], bp of Lydda, on Holy Saturday, 28 [*sic; rectius* 29] March 1494.

Acolytes

Hugo Foreman OFM of the city of Salisbury
Peter Turnewell
Thomas [*sic; rectius* Robert?] Bulbeck OP
Walter Goff OP

Subdeacons

Richard Pykton, London dioc., dim., t. house or hospital of St John
   by Wilton
Peter Cotell OFM of the city of Salisbury
Walter Crosse OFM of the city of Salisbury
William Gregory, Exeter dioc., dim., t. his choral stall in Salisbury
   cath.
Thomas Clerk, t. his choral stall in Salisbury cath.

Deacons

John Ap Meredith, St Asaph dioc., dim., t. house or monastery of
   Valle Crucis, St Asaph dioc.
Martin *de* Bomia OFM of the city of Salisbury
Stephen Woodlond, monk of Sherborne
John Fyttok, t. his choral stall in Salisbury cath.
Thomas Jacob, t. his choral stall in Salisbury cath.
Thomas Worseley OP

Priests

Robert Walker OFM of the city of Salisbury
Harman Sulbock OFM of the city of Salisbury

John Asshe *alias* Knowdeshyll, t. his choral stall in Salisbury cath.

386 [Fol. 102ᵛ] Ordinations celebrated at the altar of BM in Salisbury cath. by Augustine [Church], bp of Lydda, on Ember Saturday, 20 December 1494.

Acolytes

M. Robert Toneys BCL
Thomas Shirborne, monk of Sherborne
Ralph Pole
John Rawcreame
Thomas Gardyner, monk of Cerne
Thomas Annsyll, canon of the house or priory of Ivychurch
Henry Marshe, canon of the house or priory of Ivychurch
William Rogers
Henry Whitmarsh
John Bevall
Henry Langton
Walter Bawden OP
William Barfoot
William Tussy, choral v. in Salisbury cath.

Subdeacons

John Gerard, t. Sherborne
Robert Chaper, t. Cerne
John Parker, t. Sherborne
Thomas Graunt, York dioc., dim., t. Selby, York dioc.
John Bolton, monk of Abingdon
Thomas Herford, monk of Abingdon
John Brent, monk of Abingdon
Robert Preston, monk of Abingdon
John de Lemosie, Coutances dioc., dim., t. £15 *p.a.* due to him from
    the city of Coutances, with which he says he is content
David Longe, t. Abbotsbury
John Kent, t. house or priory of Stavordale, Bath and Wells dioc.
William Lane, brother of Edington
John Kyngman, brother of Edington
Walter Goffe OP
Robert Bulbeck OP

Deacons

William Gregory, t. his choral stall in Salisbury cath.
Thomas Clerk, t. his stall there
Richard Pykton, London dioc., dim., t. house or hospital of St John
    by Wilton
Roger Mathewe, monk of Cerne
[Fol. 103] William Welford, monk of Abingdon
Thomas Bristow, monk of Abingdon
John Nitton, monk of Abingdon
John Cornyssh, monk of Abingdon
Peter Cotell, OFM of the city of Salisbury
Henry Hammon OP

Priests

Thomas Hygden, t. his choral stall in Salisbury cath.
John Flynt, monk of Sherborne
Nicholas Ton, Exeter dioc., dim., t. Glasney [coll.] ch., Exeter dioc.
Thomas Jacob, t. his choral stall in Salisbury cath.
Pascasius Salesbury, monk of Milton
John Mylton, monk of Milton
John Fawne, t. Cerne
John Mason, t. Ford (*Foord*)

387 Ordinations celebrated in St Helen's parish ch., Abingdon, by
Augustine [Church], bp of Lydda, on Ember Saturday in the first
week of Lent, 14 March [1494].

Exorcists

Elisha Benett
Maurice Hewys
John Huchyns
John Clerk
Edward Mongean
Richard Harper
Henry Johnson
Thomas Chambre
John Caleys
Arthur Lacy BA
Edward John

Antony Cotsale
William Burton
John Purvey
Thomas Hykkes
Richard Davy
Geoffrey Joonys
John Bedall

Acolytes

M. John Byrd BCL, Durham dioc., dim.
Thomas Umfreston, Coventry and Lichfield dioc., dim.
Edward Mungham, Rochester dioc., dim.
Thomas Hykkes
William Agerden OFM
Thomas Denham OFM
M. Richard Denby
John Woodward, London dioc., dim.
M. William Marble MA, London dioc., fellow of All Souls Coll., Oxford, dim. by privilege of the Apostolic See
[Fol. 103ᵛ] M. Thomas Hovenden MA, Canterbury dioc., fellow of the same coll., dim. by the same privilege
M. John Robyns MA, Lincoln dioc., fellow of Magdalen Coll., Oxford, dim. by privilege to that coll.
John Wright, Rochester dioc., dim.
John Welshe OESA of Oxford
John Broun OCist, dim. by privilege to that order from the Apostolic See
Elisha Ruthyne, Bangor dioc., dim.

Subdeacons

Maurice Ap Ieuan Ap Res, St David's dioc., dim., t. house or priory of St John the Evangelist, Carmarthen (*Kernarden*), OSA, St David's dioc.
Robert Coventre, OSA, Lincoln dioc., dim. by John [Morton], Cardinal of St Anastasius, archbp of Canterbury, *sede vacante* Lincoln
Richard Kyrkbystevyn, OCist, Lincoln dioc., dim by privilege to that order
William Allerton, OCist, Lincoln dioc., dim. by privilege to that order
James P[   ], OCist, Lincoln dioc., dim. by privilege to that order

William F[   ], t. New Coll., Oxford

William [   ], Lincoln dioc., fellow of the same coll., dim by apostolic privilege to that coll., t. that coll.

William Wodehoke, London dioc., fellow of Oriel Coll., Oxford, dim., t. same coll.

Nicholas Graunt, canon of Bradenstoke

William Gervys, canon of Bradenstoke

M. Richard Barningham, York dioc., fellow of Balliol (*Bulliol*) Coll., [Oxford,] dim., t. same coll.

Thomas Shirborn, monk of Sherborne

John London, canon of Osney, Lincoln dioc., dim. by privilege from the Apostolic See

John Hoton, York dioc., dim, t. Osney

John Wykley, York dioc., dim., t. St Mary without the Walls, York

William Glovier *alias* Elyott, Exeter dioc., dim., t. house or priory of St Frideswide, Oxford

M. Thomas Mychell MA, Exeter dioc., dim., t. house or priory of St Frideswide, Oxford

Richard Floyde, St Asaph dioc., dim., t. Conway (*Conwey*), St Asaph dioc. [*sic – rectius* Bangor dioc.]

John Harryes, Exeter dioc., dim., t. house or priory of Tywardreath (*Tywardreth*), OSB, Exeter dioc.

Maurice Gwyn, St David's dioc., dim., t. St Dogmells (*Dogmaelis*), OSB [*sic; rectius* OTiron], St David's dioc.

M. Robert Darby, Coventry and Lichfield dioc., dim., t. BVM by Oxford [Rewley]

M. Walter Dudman MA, Exeter dioc., dim., t. Exeter cath.

[Fol. 104] Richard Perott, York dioc., dim., t. Rufford, York dioc.

Roger Irlond, St Asaph dioc., dim., t. Valle Crucis, St Asaph dioc.

Lewis John, Bangor dioc., dim., t. St Seiriol's (*Seriolis*) Penmon, Bangor dioc.

Edward Hale, Coventry and Lichfield dioc., dim., t. Osney, Lincoln dioc.

Thomas Smyth, Durham dioc., dim., t. St Andrew the Apostle, Hexham

John Ocwysnetham, [Down and] Connor (*Coneren'*) dioc., dim., t. Valle Crucis, St Asaph dioc.

John Marchaund, York dioc., dim., t. priory of St Frideswide, Oxford

John Pulker, Lincoln dioc., dim. by John [Morton], archbp. of Canterbury, *sede vacante* Lincoln, t. Osney, Lincoln dioc.

M. Robert Honywood BCL, Canterbury dioc., fellow of All Souls Coll., Oxford, dim. by privilege from the Apostolic See, t. his coll.

M. John Laurence, Exeter dioc., dim., t. house or ch. of St Stephen Launceston, Exeter dioc.

Walter Martyn OFM

Deacons

Thomas Gunthorp, York dioc., dim., t. monastery or priory of BM Newstead (*de Novoloco iuxta Shirewood*)

Walter Banbury, canon of Osney, Lincoln dioc., dim. by privilege from the Apostolic See

John Fitzliones, Dublin dioc., dim., t. his prebend of Howth (*Howght*), Dublin dioc.

William Coort, York dioc., dim., t. his benefice of Upper Clatford (*Up Clatford*), Winchester dioc.

William Hull, Worcester dioc., dim., t. Westwood nunnery, Worcester dioc.

John James, Exeter dioc., dim., t. Rewley by Oxford, Lincoln dioc.

Christopher Wylson, York dioc., dim., t. Blessed Mary Jervaulx (*Jorevallis*), Richmond archdeaconry

Richard Ap Robert, Bangor dioc., dim., t. Conway (*Conwey*) OCist, Bangor dioc.

Morgan Ap Hoel, Bangor dioc., dim., t. Beddgelert (*Beth Kelert*) OSA, Bangor dioc.

Thomas Graunt, York dioc., dim., t. Selby, York dioc.

Philip Jonys, t. Malmesbury

John Smyth, Durham dioc., dim., t. Osney, Lincoln dioc.

M. Thomas Crakenthorp MA, Carlisle dioc., dim., t. Queen's coll., Oxford

[Fol. 104ᵛ] Robert Holyngborn, monk of Christ Ch., Canterbury

John Bockeswell, monk of Christ Ch., Canterbury

Richard Jourdan OFM

Thomas Foord OCist, Exeter dioc., dim. by privilege to his order

Robert Borough OESA of Oxford

John Bolton, monk of Abingdon

Thomas Herford, monk of Abingdon

John Brynt, monk of Abingdon

Robert Preston, monk of Abingdon

Priests

Roger Piers, monk of Sherborne

Robert Newman, Exeter dioc., dim. by privilege to OCist

John Cornysh, monk of Abingdon

Richard Pykton, London dioc., dim., t. house [hospital] of St John by Wilton

John Brown, canon of the house or priory of St Frideswide, Lincoln dioc., dim.

John Englyssh, Dublin dioc., dim., to annuity of 100s. to be paid by Robert Talbot, gent., in the town of Cookstown (*Cokeston*), Co. Dublin

John Ap Meredith, St Asaph dioc., dim.,t. Valle Crucis OCist

Edward Ap John, Bangor dioc., dim., t. St Peter's coll., Ruthin (*Ruthen*), Bangor dioc.

William Pedder, Lincoln dioc., dim., t. Osney, Lincoln dioc.

John Swabee, Lincoln dioc., dim., t. Osney, Lincoln dioc.

388 Ordinations celebrated at the altar of the BVM in Salisbury cath. by Augustine [Church], bp of Lydda, on Sitientes Saturday,[1] 4 April 1495.

Acolytes

Robert Coker, monk of Sherborne
Simon Rommesey, monk of Malmesbury
William Aldey, monk of Malmesbury

[Fol. 105] *Subdeacons*

M. Richard Denby BCL, t. Vaux coll., Salisbury

M. John Lucas BCL, Worcester dioc., dim., t. Kingswood (*Kyngeswood*) OCist, Worcester dioc.

Thomas Malpas, exempt jurisdiction of the Vale of Evesham, dim. by abbot of Evesham OSB, Worcester dioc., t. Whistones (*Wytston*) nunnery OCist by Worcester

Stephen Thomasson, canon of Breamore (*Brynmore*), Winchester dioc., dim.

Robert Scarborgh, canon of Breamore (*Brynmore*), Winchester dioc., dim.

Deacons

Thomas Hervy, Coventry and Lichfield dioc., dim., t. his parish ch. of King's Ripton (*Kyng Rypton*), Lincoln. dioc.

1   The Saturday before Passion Sunday.

William Dokysbury, Coventry and Lichfield dioc., dim., t. Breamore (*Brynmore*), Winchester dioc.

Robert Woleston, monk of Malmesbury

John Pulker, Lincoln dioc., dim. by John [Morton]. Archbp. of Canterbury *sede vacante* Lincoln, t. Osney.

Richard Perott, York dioc., dim., t. Rufford, York dioc.

John Merchaund, York dioc., dim., t. St Frideswide, Oxford

Lewis John, Bangor dioc., dim., t. St Seiriol's (*Seriolis*) Penman, Bangor dioc.

John Kent, t. house or priory Stavordale, Bath and Wells dioc.

William Peers, Exeter dioc., dim., t. St Nectan, Hartland (*Hertlond*), Exeter dioc.

John Gerard, t. Sherborne

John Parker, t. Sherborne

John Okewysnetham, [Down and] Connor (*Coneren'*) dioc., dim., t. Valle Crucis OCist, St Asaph dioc.

Thomas Hewys, Llandaff dioc., dim., t. house or priory of nuns Stamford (*Staunford*) St Michael's, same dioc. [*sic; rectius* Lincoln dioc.]

Priests

Thomas Pauncherdon, monk of Sherborne

Thomas Graunt, York dioc., dim., t. Selby

[Fol. 105ᵛ] William Gregory, t. his choral stall in Salisbury cath.

Philip Jonys, t. Malmesbury

Germanus Dawes, Exeter dioc., dim., t. house or ch. of St Andrew Tywardreath (*Tywardreth*) OSB, Exeter dioc.

Robert Chaper, t. Cerne

Thomas Clerk, Coventry and Lichfield dioc., dim., t. his choral stall in Salisbury cath.

389 Ordinations celebrated at the altar of the BVM in Salisbury cath. by Augustine [Church], bp of Lydda, on Holy Saturday, 18 April 1495.

Acolytes

Thomas Payn

M. Richard Gosmore MA, Bath and Wells dioc., dim.

Subdeacons

Thomas Hyckes, t. St Frideswide, Oxford

John Bo[ne], Worcester dioc., t. St James Stavordale, Bath and Wells dioc.

M. John [Grove] MA, fellow of Magdalen coll., Oxford, t. his coll.

John Cheke, t. Cerne

Deacons

M. John Lucas BCL, Worcester dioc., dim., t. Kingswood (*Kyngeswood*) OCist, Worcester dioc.

M. Richard Denby, t. Vaux Coll.

Thomas Malpas, exempt jurisdiction of the Vale of Evesham, dim. by abbot of Evesham OSB [*sic: not continued overleaf*]

[Fol. 106] John Laurence, Exeter dioc., dim., t. house or ch. St Stephen Launceston, Exeter dioc.

Priests

John Parker, t. Sherborne

William Dokesbury, Coventry and Lichfield dioc., dim., t. house or priory Breamore (*Brynmore*), Winchester dioc.

John Kent, t. house or priory Stavordale, Bath and Wells dioc.

John Okewysnetham, [Down and] Connor dioc., dim., t. Valle Crucis OCist, St Asaph dioc.

William Ayleward, t. Puddletown (*Pydelton*) v.

390 Ordinations celebrated in St Helen's parish ch., Abingdon, by Augustine [Church], bp of Lydda, on Ember Saturday [in the first week of Lent], 26 February [1496].[1]

Exorcists

Thomas Ramsey

Nicholas Stodart

Acolytes

Robert Bedford, monk of Abingdon

Antony Grene, monk of Abingdon

Raynald Lundman, monk of Abingdon

1   *Rectius* 27 February?

Henry Wellys, monk of Abingdon
Stephen Grene

Subdeacons

Robert Kynge, York dioc., dim., t. St Frideswide, Oxford
John Tod, Dunkeld dioc., dim., t. Scottish £10 *p.a.* due to him until
    presented to a more valuable benefice
M. John Goldyn *alias* Wolvedon, Exeter dioc., dim., [Fol. 106ᵛ] t.
    house or priory St Frideswide, Oxford, Lincoln dioc.
John Dyvy, St Asaph dioc., dim., t. Cymmer (*Kymmer*), Bangor dioc.
Maurice Ap David, St Asaph dioc., dim., t. coll. or house St Peter the
    Apostle, Ruthin, Bangor dioc.
M. Edward Grove MA, Chichester dioc., fellow of Magdalen coll.,
    Oxford, dim., t. his coll., with which he says he is content
William Ap Howell, Llandaff dioc., dim., t. Llantarnam (*Lanternam*)
    OCist, Llandaff dioc.
Walter Astell, Lincoln dioc., dim., t. Osney, Lincoln dioc.
Richard Ralegh, Exeter dioc., dim., t. Dunkeswell OCist
Hugo David, Bangor dioc., dim., t. Osney, Lincoln dioc.
M. John Dobbys MA, Lincoln dioc., fellow of New coll., Oxford,
    dim. by privilege from the Apostolic See, t. that coll.
M. John Wyche BCL, Bath and Wells dioc., fellow of New coll.,
    Oxford, dim. by privilege from the Apostolic See, t. that coll.,
    with which he says he is content
Nicholas [Har]den, Durham dioc., dim., t. house of St Bartholomew,
    Newcastle upon Tyne[1]
[Guarnius] Penhaluryk, Exeter dioc., dim. by John [Morton], cardinal
    of St Anastasius, archbishop of Canterbury, *sede vacante* Exeter, t.
    coll. of St Thomas, Glasney (*Grasenheth*) [Penryn], Exeter dioc.
John Goold, scholar of Vaux coll., t. that coll., with which he says
    he is content
Robert Ap Gryffe Ap Dycus, Bangor dioc., dim., t. Beddgelert (*Valle
    Beate Marie de Bethkerlett*), Bangor dioc.
John Kyttes, Bath and Wells dioc., dim., t. St Frideswide, Oxford,
    Lincoln dioc.
Edward Jenyns, Worcester dioc., dim., t. Halesowen OPrem,
    Worcester dioc.
Laurence Greenewood BA, York dioc., dim, t. Osney, Lincoln dioc.
David Floed BCL, fellow of [All] Souls coll., Oxford, dim. by
    privilege from the Apostolic See, t. his coll., with which he says

---

1   The Benedictine nunnery.

he is content.
Edward Smythesby OESA

Deacons

Thomas Wolvercote OSA, of Osney, Lincoln dioc., dim. by privilege
　　from the Apostolic See to that monastery
Henry Hopper OSA, of Osney, Lincoln dioc., dim. by privilege from
　　the Apostolic See to that monastery
John London OSA, of Osney, Lincoln dioc., dim. by privilege from
　　the Apostolic See to that monastery
[Fol. 107] Nicholas Graunt, canon of Bradenstoke OSA
William Gerveys, canon of Bradenstoke OSA
~~William Hoton, Durham dioc.~~ [*sic*][1]
Ralph Eyre, Coventry and Lichfield dioc., dim., t. Bisham (*Bustlesham*)
　　[OSA]
William Morgan, London dioc., t. Osney
William Ketellesden BA, Canterbury dioc., dim., t. St Sepulchre
　　nunnery, Canterbury
John Wright, Rochester dioc., dim., t. house or priory St Andrew
　　the Apostle, Rochester
Edward Moungham, Rochester dioc., dim., t. house or priory St
　　Andrew the Apostle, Rochester
M. William Garrard, Canterbury dioc., dim., t. priory St Gregory
　　without the Walls, Canterbury
John Bigge, t. Montacute, Bath and Wells dioc.

Priests

John Bolton, monk of Abingdon OSB
William Wulford, monk of Abingdon OSB
Thomas Brystow, monk of Abingdon OSB
John Sutton, monk of Abingdon OSB
Thomas Harford, monk of Abingdon OSB
John Brynt, monk of Abingdon OSB
Robert Preston, monk of Abingdon OSB
Thomas Wychurch, monk of Abingdon OSB
William Hoton, Durham dioc., dim., t. Bicester (*Burcestre*), Lincoln
　　dioc.
Edward Ap Res Ap David Pennaunt, St Asaph dioc., dim., t.
　　Basingwerk (*Bassyngwerk*) OCist, St Asaph dioc.

1　See below, under Priests.

M. John Robyns MA, Lincoln dioc., fellow of Magdalen coll., Oxford, dim., t. that coll., with which he says he is content

Richard Ap Robert, Bangor dioc., dim., t. Conway (*Conwey*) OCist, Bangor dioc.

William Ap David, Bangor dioc., r. of Llanelidan (*Lanledad*) parish ch., dim., t. that benefice, with which he says he is content

M. Robert Honywood BCL, fellow of [All] Souls Coll., Oxford, dim. by privilege from the Apostolic see to fellows of that coll., t. said coll., with which he says he is content

391 [Fol. 107ᵛ] Ordinations celebrated in Hungerford prebendal ch. by Augustine [Church], bp of Lydda, on Sitientes Saturday, 19 March 1496.

Acolytes

John Pourstok, monk of Abbotsbury OSB
John Cote, monk of Abbotsbury OSB
John Mylward

Subdeacons

Robert Come, monk of Stanley (*Stanlegh*) OCist
Richard Day, Lincoln dioc., dim., t. Poughley (*Poughlegh*) priory
Thomas Belle, Richmond archdeaconry, dim., t. Marrick (*Marryk*) nunnery, York dioc.
Ancelm Grene, t. house or priory Ivychurch
George Modell, t. priory of St John, Wilton,[1] with which he says he is content
Gruffin Ap David, St David's dioc., dim., t. house or priory St Thomas Martyr, Haverfordwest (*Herford*) [OSA], St David's dioc.
Stephen Grene, t. priory of St John, Wilton,[2] with which he says he is content
John Newe, t. Ivychurch priory

Deacons

M. David Floed BCL, fellow of [All] Souls coll., Oxford, dim. by privilege from the Apostolic See, t. that coll., with which he says

---

1   The hospital of St John the Baptist at Ditchampton.
2   The hospital of St John the Baptist at Ditchampton.

he is content

M. John Goldyn, Exeter dioc., dim., t. house or priory St Frideswide, Oxford

M. Edward Grove, Chichester dioc., fellow of Magdalen coll., Oxford, dim., t. that coll.

Edward Jenyns, Worcester dioc., dim., t. Halesowen OPrem, Worcester dioc.

[Fol. 108] John Kyttes, Bath and Wells dioc., dim., t. St Frideswide priory, Oxford, Lincoln dioc.

Hugo David, Bangor dioc.,dim., t. Osney, Lincoln dioc.

Robert Ap Gryff Ap Dycus, Bangor dioc., dim., t. Beddgelert (*Vallis Beate Marie de Bethkerlett*), Bangor dioc.

Thomas Payn, t. Osney

Maurice Ap David, St Asaph dioc., dim., t. coll. or house St Peter, Ruthin (*Ruthyn*), Bangor dioc.

John Dyvy, St Asaph dioc., dim., t. Cymmer (*Kymner*), Bangor dioc.

William Woodroof BA, Coventry and Lichfield dioc., fellow of Clare hall or coll., Cambridge, dim., t. that coll., with which he says he is content

Thomas Bradford, monk of Abbotsbury OSB

Stephen Thomson, canon of the house or priory of Breamore (*Brymore*), Winchester dioc., dim.

Robert Skarborgh, canon of the house or priory of Breamore (*Brymore*), Winchester dioc., dim.

Priests

William Ketellesden BA, Canterbury dioc., dim., t. St Sepulchre without Canterbury

Robert Wolf BA, Exeter dioc., t. Launceston priory, Exeter dioc.

John Bucklond, monk of Bindon (*Byndon*) OCist

Richard Avenell, monk of Bindon (*Byndon*) OCist

392 Ordinations celebrated at the altar of the BVM in Salisbury cath. by Augustine [Church], bp of Lydda, on Holy Saturday, 2 April 1496.

Acolytes

William Smyth, Exeter dioc., dim.

John Kene of Little Somerford (*Lytle Sommerford*)

William Draycote

[Fol. 108^v] *Subdeacon*

Thomas Durham, vicar-choral of the cath., t. his stall there

Deacons

Ancelm Grene, t. house or priory ch. Ivychurch
Thomas Belle, Richmond archdeaconry, dim., t. Marrick (*Marryk*)
    nunnery, York dioc.
Griffin Ap David, St David's dioc., t. house or priory St Thomas
    Martyr, Haverfordwest (*Herford*) [OSA], St David's dioc., dim.
George Modell, t. priory of St John, Wilton
Stephen Grene, t. priory of St John, Wilton
Robert Combe, monk of Stanley OCist
Walter Gowgh OP city of Salisbury

Priests

Thomas Payn, t. Osney
John Dyer, Worcester dioc., dim., t. Tewkesbury
Peter Guyard OP city of Salisbury

393 Ordinations celebrated in St Peter's parish ch., Marlborough
(*Marleburgh*), by Augustine [Church], bp of Lydda, on Ember Saturday
in the first week of Lent, 18 February [1497].

Acolytes

Robert Hundmanby, York dioc., dim.
M. William Thornhylle, fellow of New coll., Oxford, dim. by
    privilege from the Apostolic See to fellows of that coll.
John Westcot BA
Roger Langman, Exeter dioc., dim.
[Fol. 109] John Crawford
John Olyver, Bath and Wells dioc., dim.

Subdeacons

William Chubbe MA, Exeter dioc., dim., t. Torre OCist [*sic; rectius*
    OPrem], Exeter dioc.
M. Robert Hylle, t. St Frideswide priory, Oxford
Robert Clayton MA, York dioc., dim., t. Newstead priory, York dioc.

Nicholas Ponfold BA, t. Sherborne

William Estwood, York dioc., dim., t. Thame OCist, Lincoln dioc.

John Robynson BA, Durham dioc., fellow of Balliol coll., Oxford, dim., t. that coll.

Richard Baynston OSA of Dorchester, Lincoln. dioc., dim.

John Kene, t. Holy Cross nunnery, Wherwell, Winchester dioc.

John Philipp[ys], Bath and Wells dioc., dim., t. Osney, Lincoln dioc.

John Hawke BA, Exeter dioc., dim., t. Tavistock (*Tavestok*), Exeter dioc.

Thomas Tremayn MA, Exeter dioc., dim., t. Bodmin priory OSA, Exeter dioc.

Richard Roberdys, t. St Frideswide priory, Lincoln dioc.

Henry Turnour, t. St Giles priory by Wilton[1] granted to him for all orders, with which he says he is content

Ralph Wymmeslow OSA of Osney, Lincoln dioc., dim. by privilege from the Apostolic See to that monastery

John Beval, t. house or priory Stavordale, Bath and Wells dioc.

[Fol. 109ᵛ] *Deacons*

William Smyth, Exeter dioc., dim., t. Launceston priory, Exeter dioc.

John Twycros BA, Coventry and Lichfield dioc., t. Osney, Lincoln dioc.

Robert Pynney BA, Bath and Wells dioc., dim., t. Forde, Exeter dioc.

Richard Gosmore MA, Bath and Wells dioc., dim., t. house or priory Stavordale, Bath and Wells dioc.

John Goold, scholar of Vaux Coll., t. that coll.

Roger Chyvals BA, Exeter dioc., dim., t. St Germans priory, Exeter dioc.

Priests

Robert Combe OCist of Stanley (*Stanlegh*)

Walter Banbury OSA of Osney, Lincoln dioc., dim. by privilege from the Apostolic See to that monastery

394 Ordinations celebrated in Salisbury cath. by Augustine [Church], bp of Lydda, on Sitientes Saturday, 11 March [1497].

1   The leper hospital at Fugglestone.

First tonsure

John Feeld

Acolytes

Roger Fowey
Andrew Daberham
Thomas Gylbert
John Hopkyns

[Fol. 110] *Subdeacons*

John Olyver, Bath and Wells dioc., dim., t. Osney, Lincoln dioc., to
    all orders, with which he says he is content
Thomas Blanford, monk of Milton (*Mylton*)
John Shapton, monk of Milton (*Mylton*)
Ralph Haryott, Norwich dioc., dim., t. Osney, Lincoln dioc., to all
    etc. [*sic*]
M. William Thornhylle BCL, fellow of New coll., Oxford, dim. by
    privilege from the Apostolic See to that coll., t. that coll.
Bernard Cornelius OP
John Crawford, scholar of Vaux coll., t. that coll., with which etc.
    [*sic*]
Geoffrey Ap Richard, Llandaff dioc., dim., t. St Mary Neath (*Nethe*)
    OCist, Llandaff dioc.
William Spencer, t. Cerne, to all etc. [*sic*]
Robert Thomas, t. Cerne
Robert Hundmanby, v. choral of Salisbury cath., t. his choral stall
    there
Robert Coker, monk of Sherborne
Thomas Anncel, canon of Ivychurch
Henry Marsshe, canon of Ivychurch

Deacons

Robert Hylle MA, t. house or priory of St Frideswide
Nicholas Ponfold BA, t. Sherborne
Thomas Shirborn, brother of Sherborne
William Lane, brother of the conventual house of Edington
John Kyngman, brother of the conventual house of Edington
[Fol. 110ᵛ] Thomas Tremayne MA, Exeter dioc., dim., t. Bodmin
    priory, Exeter dioc., to all orders etc. [*sic*]

Richard Roberdys, t. house or priory of St Frideswide, Lincoln
    dioc., to all orders etc. [*sic*]
John Kene, t. Holy Cross nunnery, Wherwell, Winchester dioc.
John Philipp[ys], Bath and Wells dioc., dim., t. Osney, Lincoln dioc.
Henry Whelar OFM of Salisbury
Henry Turnour, t. priory of St Giles by Wilton, to all etc. [*sic*]
Hugo Thorp, Coventry and Lichfield dioc., dim., t. Ivychurch, to all
    orders etc. [*sic*]
John Loth, Exeter dioc., dim., t. Montacute priory, Bath and Wells
    dioc.
John Bevall, t. Stavordale priory, Bath and Wells dioc.
John Newe, v. choral of Salisbury cath., t. his stall there

Priests

Richard Ralegh, Exeter dioc., dim., t. Dunkeswell, Chichester dioc.
Nicholas Graunt, canon of Bradenstoke
William Gerveys, canon of Bradenstoke
John Goold, scholar of Vaux Coll., t. that coll., with which he says
    he is content
John Fyttok, v. choral of Salisbury cath., t. his choral stall
William Smyth, Exeter dioc., dim., t. Launceston priory, Exeter dioc.

395 Ordinations celebrated at the altar of the BVM in Salisbury cath.
by Augustine [Church], bp of Lydda, on Holy Saturday, 25 March
1497.

[Fol. 111] *Acolytes*

William Pykenham
Richard Martyn

Subdeacons

Thomas Pepyn, t. Easton (*Eston*) priory
Robert Hodges, Exeter dioc., dim., t. St Mary, Pope St Gregory, and
    St Edmund Frithelstock (*Frythelestoke*) OSA, Exeter dioc.
Thomas Gyllot, t. priory of St John, Wilton

Deacons

John Crawford, scholar of Vaux Coll., t. that coll.

Bernard Cornelius OP of Salisbury

William Spenser, t. Cerne

William Knyght, r. of St Clement's Eastcheap, London, dim., t. his
 benefice

Roger Langman, Exeter dioc., dim., t. Plympton (*Plymton*), Exeter
 dioc.

John Olyver, Bath and Wells dioc., dim., t. Osney, Lincoln dioc.

Thomas Awnsell, canon of Ivychurch

Geoffrey Ap Richard, Llandaff dioc., dim., t. St Mary Neath (*Nethe*)
 OCist, Llandaff dioc.

Robert Hundmanby, v. choral of Salisbury cath., t. his stall there

Priests

Nicholas Ponfold BA, t. Sherborne

Hugo Thorp, Coventry and Lichfield dioc., dim., t. Ivychurch

John Kene, t. Wherwell nunnery, Winchester dioc.

[Fol. 111ᵛ] Thomas Awte, Coventry and Lichfield dioc., dim., t.
 Mottisfont (*Mottesfont*) priory, Winchester dioc.

Thomas Tremayn MA, Exeter dioc., dim., t. house or priory of
 Bodmin, Exeter dioc.

Thomas Tame, r. of Castle Eaton (*Castell Eton*), t. his benefice

Robert Hylle MA, t. St Frideswide, Lincoln dioc.

John Loth, Exeter dioc., dim., t. priory or house of Montacute, Bath
 and Wells dioc.

Henry Turnour, t. priory of St Giles by Wilton for all orders, with
 which he says he is content

396   Ordinations celebrated at the altar of the BVM in Salisbury
cath. by Augustine [Church], bp of Lydda, on Ember Saturday, 23
September 1497.

First tonsure

John Blast

Acolytes

William Crawford, Glasgow dioc., dim.

John Fynche OP

Subdeacon

William Shottow, t. ~~Milton~~ [*sic*] Wilton nunnery for all orders, with
   which he says he is content

Deacons

Thomas Pepyn, t. house or priory of Easton (*Eston*) OTrin
Richard Martyn, fellow of New coll., Oxford, t. that coll.
Hugo Forman OFM
Gerard Merlet OFM
Gilbert Gradus OFM
[Fol. 112] Robert Bulbeck OP of Salisbury
Thomas Gylot, t. house or priory of St John without Wilton

Priests

John Crawford, scholar of Vaux Coll., t. that coll.
John Newe, t. house or priory of Ivychurch
Henry Whelar OFM of Salisbury
Walter Goffe OP of Salisbury

397   Ordinations celebrated in St Peter's parish ch., Marlborough
(*Marleburgh*), by Augustine [Church], bp of Lydda, on Ember Saturday,
10 March [1498].

Acolytes

William Rowle
Thomas Olveston, monk of Malmesbury
John Devenyes, canon of the house or priory of Bradenstoke
John Boxe, canon of the house or priory of Bradenstoke
Thomas Pope, canon of the house or priory of Bradenstoke
Ralph Lagowche
William Horsby
William Frye
John Clynch

Subdeacons

M. Walter Newton BCL, Bath and Wells dioc., dim., t. St Frideswide
   priory, Lincoln dioc.

Gregory Staley BA, Norwich dioc., dim., t. St Frideswide priory

Thomas Horton, Lincoln dioc., dim., t. St Frideswide priory, Lincoln dioc.

[Fol. 112ᵛ] Thomas Conwey, St Asaph dioc., dim., t. Valle Crucis, St Asaph dioc., for all orders etc. [*sic*]

Nicholas Griffeth, St Asaph dioc., dim., t. Osney, Lincoln dioc.

Richard Hewys, Bangor dioc., dim., t. house or priory of Beddgelert (*Bethkelert*) OSA, Bangor fioc.

Robert Peresson, Durham dioc., dim., t. house or hospital of Greatham (*Gretham*), Durham dioc., for all etc. [*sic*]

Oswald Forster, York dioc., dim., t. Osney, Lincoln dioc., for all etc. [*sic*]

William Hanwell, Lincoln dioc., dim., t. Osney, Lincoln dioc., for all etc. [*sic*]

Thomas Perkyn BA, Coventry and Lichfield dioc., dim., t. house or priory of conventual ch. of Maxstoke, Coventry and Lichfield dioc.

Thomas Tovylde BA, Norwich dioc., dim., t. St Frideswide's priory OSA, Lincoln dioc.

M. William Greveson MA, Durham dioc., fellow of Merton Coll., Oxford, dim., t. that coll.

M. Robert Norrys MA, fellow of Oriel Coll., Oxford, t. that coll.

M. John Byrnand MA, York dioc., dim., t. St Frideswide's priory

William Stamp BA, Durham dioc., dim., t. St Frideswide's priory

John Glynne, Bangor dioc., dim., t. Penmon priory OSA, Bangor dioc., for all etc. [*sic*]

John Dean BA, York dioc., dim., t. St Frideswide's priory, Lincoln dioc.

Henry Proctour BA, Coventry and Lichfield dioc., dim., t. St Frideswide's priory

Richard Walter BA, fellow of Magdalen Coll., Oxford, t. that coll.

John Drewett BA, fellow of Magdalen Coll., Oxford, t. that coll.

M. Hugo Thomas MA, Exeter dioc., dim., t. Barnstaple priory OClun, Exeter dioc.

M. William Toker MA, Exeter dioc., dim., t. St John's priory,[1] Exeter dioc., for all etc. [*sic*]

James Herryngton, York dioc., r. of Badsworth (*Baddesworte*), York dioc., dim., t. his ch.

M. Thomas Hovynden MA, Canterbury dioc., fellow of [All] Souls Coll., Oxford, dim. by privilege of the Apostolic See to fellows of that coll., t. said coll.

---

1   Probably the hospital or priory of St John the Baptist in Exeter.

Thomas Tewkesbury, monk of Malmesbury

Thomas Penne, canon of the house or priory of Bradenstoke OSA

Richard Bedford, canon of the house or priory of Bradenstoke OSA

[Fol. 113] M. John John [*sic*] Newman BCL, fellow of New Coll., Oxford, t. that coll.

Richard Danyell, brother [*sic*] of Bindon OCist

Nicholas Ap Mered[ith], St Asaph dioc., dim., t. Chester nunnery, Coventry and Lichfield dioc.

Robert Rawlyns, t. St Frideside's priory

Nicholas Stodard, Bangor dioc., dim., t. Cymmer (*Kymner*), Bangor dioc.

Robert Dikson, brother of the house or priory of Easton (*Eston*) OTrin

John Hopkyns, t. Milton (*Mylton alias Mydelton*) OSB for all orders, with which he says he is content.

Deacons

M. John Adams MA, Bath and Wells dioc., fellow of Merton Coll., Oxford, dim., t. said coll.

M. Thomas Farne BCL, Durham dioc., dim., t. Newcastle-upon-Tyne nunnery

Edmund Forest, canon of the house or priory of Llanthony (*Lanthony*) by Gloucester, Worcester dioc., dim.

William Aldey, Malmesbury OSB [*sic*]

Simon Romsey, Malmesbury OSB [*sic*]

William Launcysse, Exeter dioc., dim., t. Barnstaple priory

Priests

M. Thomas Wolsey, MA, Norwich dioc., fellow of Magdalen Coll., Oxford, dim., t. that coll.

John Bevall, t. Stavordale priory, Bath and Wells dioc., for all etc. [*sic*]

William Lane, brother of the conventual house of Edington

John Kyngman, brother of the conventual house of Edington

398 Ordinations celebrated in Sonning (*Sonnyngys*) parish ch. by the bp on Sitientes Saturday, 31 March 1498.

Exorcist

John Dean

Acolyte

John Haddon

[Fol. 113ᵛ] *Subdeacons*

Richard Whykhoop OFM of Oxford
Ralph Lagowch, t. Cerne
John Lemynstre, monk of Reading
Thomas Wyrcestre, monk of Reading
Thomas Lokyngton, canon of Bisham (*Bustlesham*)

Deacons

M. Robert Norreys MA, fellow of Oriel Coll., Oxford, t. that coll.
Thomas Tovyld, Norwich dioc., dim., t. St Frideswide's priory
Richard Ward, canon of the house or priory of Bisham (*Bustlesham
     Montagu*)
John Southwerk, canon of the house or priory of Bisham (*Bustlesham
     Montagu*)
Richard Walter BA, fellow of Magdalen Coll., Oxford, t. that coll.
John Drewett BA, fellow of Magdalen Coll., Oxford, t. that coll.
Robert Dykson, brother of the house or priory of Easton (*Eston*)
     OTrin
Robert Rawlyns, t. St Frideswide's priory
Richard Herford, monk of Reading
Henry Hawe, monk of Reading
Richard Ludlow, monk of Reading

Priests

Henry Osborn, Bath and Wells dioc., dim., t. St Saviour Bermondsey
     (*Barmondesay*) OClun, Winchester dioc., for all orders, with which
     he says he is content
John Platfote OFM of Oxford

399 Ordinations celebrated in the conventual and prebendal ch. of
Sherborne by the bp on the vigil of Trinity, 9 June 1498.

[Fol. 114] *Exorcists*

William Hallesey

Richard Philipp'
Thomas Blower
Thomas Holme
John Andrewe
John Poskyn

Acolytes

Robert Peres
John Benett
Richard Dawe
John Woodcocke
Robert Brace
Robert Popyll

Subdeacons

John At Mylle, t. Abbotsbury
William Fynyng, Bath and Wells dioc., t. Bruton priory, Bath and
    Wells dioc.
John Rawcrayn, t. Abbotsbury
Robert Westbury, monk of Cerne
Thomas Gardyner, monk of Cerne
William Mylton, monk of Cerne

Deacons

Richard Danyell, brother [*sic*] of Bindon (*Bendon*)
John Combe, brother and monk of Montacute priory OClun, Bath
    and Wells dioc., dim. by privilege from the Apostolic See to that
    order
Richard Pytmyster, brother and monk of Montacute priory OClun,
    Bath and Wells dioc., dim. by privilege from the Apostolic See to
    that order
John Pourstock, monk of Abbotsbury
John Coot, monk of Abbotsbury
Thomas Blanford, monk of Milton
John Shapton, monk of Milton
John Hopkyns, t. Milton
John Townesend, Bath and Wells dioc., dim., t. BM Newenham
    (*Newham*), Exeter dioc.

Priests

Roger Mathew, monk of Cerne

Robert Dykson, brother of the house or priory of Easton (*Eston*) OTrin

Thomas Gylot, t. priory of St John without Wilton

Thomas Pepyn, t. house or priory of Easton (*Eston*)

John Mylward, t. Abbotsbury

William Amys, Bath and Wells dioc., dim., t. house or priory of Stavordale, Bath and Wells dioc.

Roger Fowey, fellow of [All] Souls Coll., Oxford, t. that coll.

[Fol. 114ᵛ] M. Robert Noreys MA, fellow of Oriel Coll., Oxford, t. that coll.

Richard Waltere BA, fellow of Magdalen Coll., Oxford, t. that coll.

John Drewett BA, fellow of Magdalen Coll., Oxford, t. that coll.

Robert Rawlyns, t. St Frideswide's priory, Lincoln dioc.

Ralph Lagowch, t. Cerne

400 Ordinations celebrated in St Nicholas's parish ch., Abingdon, by Augustine [Church], bp of Lydda, on Ember Saturday, 22 September 1498.

Acolytes

M. Arthur Coo BCL, Norwich dioc., dim.

M. Thomas Hylle

Robert Adams BA, Bath and Wells dioc., dim.

Nicholas Stream, Coutances dioc., dim.

Thomas Karvell OSA

Thomas Coutlen OSA

Henry Carre OSA

William Aldam OSA

Richard Cosyn

Subdeacons

M. Robert Woodward, fellow of All Souls Coll., Oxford, t. that coll., with which he says he is content

Richard Rathbon, Coventry and Lichfield dioc., dim., t. St Mary Chester nunnery

M. William Horsey BCn&CL, t. his free chapel of Clifton,[1] with which he says he is content

John Cobbe BA, Norwich dioc., dim., t. Mettingham (*Metyngham*) coll., Norwich dioc.

William Symson, York dioc., dim., t. Marrick (*Marryk*) nunnery OSA, York dioc.

Robert Glest OFM of Oxford

[Fol. 115] John [   ], Durham dioc., dim., t. priory of St Andrew the Apostle, Hexham (*Hextyldesham*), York dioc., for all etc. [*sic*]

John Huddisfeld, t. monastery or priory of Plympton, Exeter dioc., for all etc. [*sic*]

Thomas Wolveston, monk of Malmesbury

Robert Bedford, monk of Abingdon

Antony Grene, monk of Abingdon

Reginald London, monk of Abingdon

Henry Wellys, monk of Abingdon

John Cornforth, monk of Abingdon

William Hutton, monk of Abingdon

Deacons

William Fynyng, Bath and Wells dioc., dim., t. Bruton priory OSA, Bath and Wells dioc.

Thomas Tewkesbury, monk of Malmesbury

Thomas Glest OFM of Oxford

Roger Spernell OFM of Oxford

Priests

M. Thomas Cause MA, fellow of Queen's coll., Oxford, Lincoln dioc., dim., t. that coll.

Richard Stere, t. Christchurch Twynham OSA, Winchester dioc., for all orders etc. [*sic*]

Richard Danyel, monk of Bindon (*Byndon*) OCist

Richard Hewys, Bangor dioc., dim., t. Beddgelert (*Bethkerlet*) priory, Bangor dioc., for all orders etc. [*sic*]

Richard Bensyndon OSA of Dorchester, Lincoln dioc., dim.

Nicholas Griffeth, St Asaph dioc., dim., t. Osney, Lincoln dioc.

Thomas Perkyns, Coventry and Lichfield dioc., dim., t. conventual ch. of Maxstoke, Coventry and Lichfield dioc.

John Glynne, Bangor dioc., dim., t. Penmon, Bangor dioc.

---

1   Probably Clifton in Ashbourn, Derbyshire.

William Aldey, monk of Malmesbury
Simon Rumsey, monk of Malmesbury

401 [Fol. 115^v] Ordinations celebrated in St Peter's parish ch., Marlborough (*Marleburgh*), by Augustine [Church], bp of Lydda, on 23 February [1499].

Exorcists

M. Thomas Yonge BCL
Leonell Walton, monk of Stanley (*Stanlegh*)
Nicholas Saundres
John Heryng

Acolytes

M. Thomas Halsey BCL, Lincoln dioc., fellow of [All] Souls coll., Oxford, dim. by privilege from the Apostolic See to fellows of that coll.
M. Thomas Yonge BCL
Richard Herberd, fellow of New coll., Oxford
William Buttermer
Robert Malmesbury, monk of Stanley (*Stanlegh*)
Leonell Walton, monk of Stanley (*Stanlegh*)
Nicholas Saundres
John Heryng

Subdeacons

M. Maurice Syw alias Johns, St David's dioc., BCn&CL, dim., t. Osney, Lincoln dioc.
M. Griffin Padarn alias Lloyd, BCL, St David's dioc., dim., t. Vale Royal, Coventry and Lichfield dioc.[1]
John Ap Thoma, St Asaph dioc., dim., t. Osney, Lincoln dioc.
John Glover, BA, Worcester dioc., fellow of [All] Souls coll., Oxford, dim. by privilege from the Apostolic See to that coll., t. that coll.
James Fraunces, Bath and Wells dioc., dim., t. his patrimony of the value 10 marks *p.a.*, with which he says he is content
Humphrey Berret, Coventry and Lichfield dioc., t. collegiate ch. of Tong, Coventry and Lichfield dioc.

1   Emden, *A Biographical Register of the University of Oxford*, incorrectly reads t. *Rewley*.

William Croppe BA, Exeter dioc., dim., t. Sherborne

Walter Can BA, Exeter dioc., dim., t. Buckfast (*Bukfast*) OCist, Exeter dioc.

M. John Kenwood BCL, Exeter dioc., dim., t. Osney

[Fol. 116] M. John Middelton BCL, York dioc., dim., t. Welbeck (*Welbek*) OPrem, York dioc.

[Richard] Harries BA, Coventry and Lichfield dioc., dim., t. Lilleshall (*Lulleshull*), Coventry and Lichfield dioc.

[William] Goodrych BA, Worcester dioc., dim., t. hospital of St Bartholomew, Gloucester, Worcester dioc.

Thomas Samper BA, York dioc., dim., t. St Frideswide's priory, Oxford, Lincoln dioc.

John Dove, Lincoln dioc., dim., t. Rewley, Lincoln dioc.

William Witham, York dioc., dim., t. Marrick (*Marryk*) nunnery, York dioc.

Gruff' Ap Holl, St Asaph dioc., dim., t. BVM Cymmer (*Kemer*) OCist, Bangor dioc.

William Rawson, York dioc., dim., t. his benefice, Folkington (*Fekyngton*) parish ch., Chichester dioc.

Thomas Upcote, t. Cerne

Edmund Symson, York dioc., dim., t. BM Coverham, York dioc.

Richard Taylour, Carlisle dioc., dim., t. Jervaulx (*Jorevall*) OCist, York dioc.

M. Thomas Hunt BCL, Exeter dioc., dim., t. Barnstaple priory, Exeter dioc.

John Watson, Durham dioc., dim., t. hospital of BM Greatham (*Gretham*), Durham dioc.

M. James Horton BCL, fellow of New coll., Oxford, t. his coll.

M. Thomas Makeyt BCL, Winchester dioc., fellow of the same coll., dim. by privilege from the Apostolic See to fellows of that coll., t. said coll.

Laurence Hwys, Bangor dioc., dim., t. Beddgelert (*Bethkelert*) priory, Bangor dioc.

Richard Wood, York dioc., dim., t. Osney

Richard Dawe, t. Bindon (*Bendon*) OCist

Thomas Pope, canon of Bradenstoke (*Bradnestok*) priory

Richard Blake, Norwich dioc., dim., t. St Frideswide's priory

John Batwell, Bath and Wells dioc., dim., t. Muchelney, Bath and Wells dioc.

William Rewys, Canterbury dioc., v. choral of Salisbury cath., dim., t. his stall

[Fol. 116ᵛ] *Deacons*

Nicholas Streme, Coutances dioc., dim., t. £15 from the land of
Mathew Baker, esq., Coutances dioc., with which he says he is
content

M. William Horsey BCn&CL, t. his free chapel of Clifton (*Clyfton*)

Richard Rathbown, Coventry and Lichfield dioc., dim., t. Chester
nunnery

Laurence Westcote, Bath and Wells dioc., dim., t. St Frideswide's priory

Roger Cowper, Coventry and Lichfield dioc., dim., t. Norton,
Coventry and Lichfield dioc.

Arthur Coo, Norwich dioc., dim., t. Osney

William Shottow, t. Wilton nunnery

John Huddisfeld, t. Plympton, Exeter dioc.

Thomas Penne, canon of the house or priory of Bradenstoke
(*Bradnestok*)

Thomas Olveston, monk of Malmesbury

Priests

Thomas Tovyld, Norwich dioc., dim., t. St Frideswide's priory

William Pympyll, Bath and Wells dioc., dim., t. Montacute, Bath and
Wells dioc.

William Fynnyng, Bath and Wells dioc., dim., t. Bruton priory OSA,
Bath and Wells dioc.

Ralph Wymmesley, canon of Osney, Lincoln dioc., dim. by privilege
from the Apostolic See to that monastery

Robert Wulasston, monk of Malmesbury

402 Ordinations celebrated in Salisbury cath. by Augustine [Church],
bp of Lydda, on Holy Saturday, 30 March 1499.

[Fol. 117] *Acolytes*

John Blast
John Philips
Richard Grene, Winchester dioc.

Subdeacons

Robert Malmesbury, monk of Stanley
William Botermere, t. priory of Blessed Margaret by Marlborough
(*Marleburgh*)

Deacons

Humphrey Barett, Coventry and Lichfield dioc., dim., t. Tong coll.,
    Coventry and Lichfield dioc.
John Bottewele, Bath and Wells dioc., dim., t. Muchelney (*Mochelney*),
    Bath and Wells dioc.
Richard Dawe, t. Bindon (*Byndon*) OCist
William Rewys, Canterbury dioc., dim., t. his choral stall in Salisbury
    cath.
John Rawrayn, t. Abbotsbury OSB
Henry Marssh, canon of the house or priory of Ivychurch

Priests

Roger Cowper, Coventry and Lichfield dioc., dim., t. Norton
John Huddysfeld, t. monastery or priory of Plympton, Exeter dioc.

INDEX OF PERSONS AND PLACES

Place names occurring in dating clauses are indexed in the bishop's itinerary (pp xvii–xxiii) and not where they appear in the text. Common inductors (the four archdeacons and the dean of Salisbury cath.) are not indexed; all other inductors *are* indexed.

F, E, A, S, D, P appended to serial numbers identify orders conferred in the ordination lists as first tonsure, exorcist, acolyte, subdeacon, deacon, and priest respectively. Where ordinands are from Salisbury dioc., this is not recorded in the index; the origin of all other ordinands is recorded.

References in arabic figures are to entry numbers, those in roman figures to the introduction.

prebendal ch., 391

vicarage, 236

Hungerford, Robert, lord, founder of Hungerford chantry in Salisbury cath., 267

Hungerford, Walter, kt, patron, 4, 91, 138, 154, 231

Hunt, Robert, cantarist Lord Beauchamp's chantry in Salisbury cath., 206

Hunt, M. Thomas BCL, Exeter dioc., 401S

Huntingdon, archdeaconry, ix

Huntrode, William, chapl., r. North Tidworth, 227

Huntyngdon, John, r. Pangbourne, 164

Hurley (*Hurle, Hurlegh*) priory (OSB),

prior *see* John Hilston

prior and convent,

collectors of the great subsidy (1497), 295, 298, 300, 302

patrons, 73

Hurst, Berks. *see* St Nicholas Hurst

Husee, Thomas, esq., patron, 38

Husse, Robert, prebendary of Lyme and Halstock in Salisbury cath., 156

Hutton, William, OSB, monk of Abingdon, 400S

Hwys, Laurence, Bangor dioc., 401S

Hyde, James, witness, 261a

Hyde, M. John, chapl., v. Sonning, 320, 322

v. Tilehurst, 74

inductor, 115

Hyde, John, 381S, 382D, 383P, 384

Hyde by Winchester St Peter's abbey (OSB), abbot and convent, patrons, 101, 103, 232

Hygden, Thomas, choral vicar of Salisbury cath., 386P

Hygons, William, chapl., v. Sherston, 223

Hykkes *or* Hyckes, Thomas, 387E, 387A, 389S

Hylle, Christopher, priest, v. West Hendred St Mary, 145

Hylle, John, chapl., v. Longbridge Deverill, 136

Hylle, M. Robert MA, 393S, 394D, 395P

Hylle, M. Thomas, 400A

Hylle, M. Walter, r. Semley, 78

Hyslyngton, M. John DTh, r. Shaftesbury St Rumbold, 177

Idmiston (*Idmoston*),

free chapel of St Nicholas de Burglen, Porton, 32

vicarage, exempt from clerical tenth (1495), 284

Ilsley – *see* West Ilsley

Imber (*Ymmer*) ch. or chapel, not assessed but liable for clerical tenth (1495), 286

Indeslay *or* Indesley *or* Inysley, Nicholas, OSB, subprior, chamberlain, and gardener Abingdon, 352, 352n

Ingilby, Thomas, bp of Rathlur, suffragan in Canterbury dioc., 378

Inglesent, Nicholas ALibM, r. Poulshot, 229

Inglesham vicarage, exempt from clerical tenth (1495), 284

Inkpen (*Ynkepenne*) ch., exempt from clerical tenth (1495), 284

Innocent VIII, pope, xii, 306, 308

Irelond, William MA, r. Besselsleigh, 191

Irlond, Roger, St Asaph dioc., 387S

Ivychurch (*Ederose Ivechurch*) priory (OSA), 279a

orders conferred on canons, 386, 394, 395, 402

orders conferred to t., 391, 392, 394, 395, 396

prior *see* Richard Page

prior and conv., patrons, 39, 112

Iwerne Courtney (*Ewern Courtenay*) ch., 1n

Jackson, Thomas, chapl., r. Besselsleigh, 191

Jacob, Thomas, vicar-choral of Salisbury cath., 385D, 386P

James, John, Exeter dioc., 387D

Jane, M. Thomas DCnL,

patron, 10

prebendary of Fordington and Writhlington in Salisbury cath., 176

Jane, M. William, v. Marcham, 66

Jekyll, Richard, priest, v. Winterborne (*Wynterborn*) St Martin vicarage, 119

Jenyns, Edward, Worcester dioc., 390S, 391D

Jersey, x

Jerusalem pilgrimage, 266

Jervaulx (*Jorevall, Jorevallis*) BM abbey (OCist), Richmond archdeaconry, orders conferred to t., 387, 401

John [ ], Durham dioc., 400S

John, Edward, 387E

John, Lewis, Bangor dioc., 387S, 388D

Johns alias Syw, M. Maurice BCn&CL, St David's dioc., 401S

Johnson, Henry, 387E

Jokyns, William, r. Ludgershall, 205

Joly, Laurence, chapl., v. Aldworth, 163

Jolyf, M. John MA, r. Belchalwell, 137

Jonys, David, v. Sutton Benger, 169

Jonys, Philip, 387D, 388P

Jonys, M. William BCnL,

close, Leadenhall (*Ledenhalle*), 269
dean and chapter, xvii, 248, 271, 279a,
  289, 289a, 348
  patrons, 200, 267
  pension, 348
dean, jurisdiction, 236
  and see Edward Cheyne
Hungerford chantry, 267
Lord Beauchamp's chantry, 206
master (*custos*) of the choristers, patron,
  192, 202
prebends or prebendaries,
  Alton Australis, 318n
  Alton Borealis (*Aulton Borialis*), 114
  Axford, x, 84, 243
    valuation for great subsidy (1497), 297
  Beminster (*Bemystre*) Secunda, x, 149,
    242
  Bishopstone (*Bisshoppeston*), 181, 269
  Bitton (*Bytton*), 209
  Calne, 81, 95, 98
  Chisenbury (*Chesingbury* or
    Chesyngbury, Chute et Chesingbury) and
    Chute 98, 188, 219, 252n
  Fordington and Writhlington (*ffordyng-
    ton et Wrythelyngton, Fordington et
    Wrythelington*), 176
  Gillingham, 1
  Lyme [and Halstock] in Salisbury cath.,
    156
  Ramsbury, 252n
  Ratfyn (*Rotfen*). 210
  Stratton, x, 241
  Torleton, 55
  Warminster (*Warmynstre, Warmynster
    alias Warmystre Netherbury, Warmystre
    alias Warmynystre in laico feudo*), 67, 79,
    123, 155
  Wilsford and Woodford (*Woodford alias
    Wyvelesford*), 27, 160
  Yatesbury, 89, 252n
  Yetminster (*Yatemystre*) Prima, 166
seal, 271
subdean, 99
succentor, 217
tomb of bp Blyth, xxiii
treasurer, 81, 95, 98
vicars choral *see* John Asshe, John Kent,
  John Nytyngale, John Tanner, William
  Tussey
city, valuation, 351
Close, xviii
diocese,
  assessment for great subsidy (1497), 294,
    302

sede vacante administration, xi, xiv
earldom, 227
episcopal palace, xx, xxi, 270
  keeper *see* John Alston
friary OFM, orders conferred on friars, 385,
  386, 394, 396
friary OP, orders conferred on friars, 392,
  395, 396
gaol, keeper or governor *see* Robert Balgey
manor, valuation, 351
St Edmund collegiate ch., 360
St Nicholas hospital, 23, 99, 201
St Thomas the Martyr ch.,
  desecration and reconciliation of
    churchyard, 249
  Robert Godmanston's chantry, 200
  Vaux coll., orders conferred to t., 388, 389,
    390, 393, 394, 395, 396
Salley *or* Sauley, Miles, OSB, kitchener
  Abingdon, 352
Salmon, Hervey, cl., r. Frome Vauchurch, 117
Salvan, Ralph, esq., patron, 239
Salwey, John, cantarist of the BVM in
  Chippenham St Andrew ch., 91
Sam, Thomas, OSB, abbot Cerne, 372-374
Samper, Thomas BA, York dioc., 401S
Sampson, John, priest, v. Sutton Benger, 169,
  197
Samuel, Elizabeth, OSB, prioress, Studley
  BVM, Lincoln dioc., 127
Samuell, Walter, cl., v. or keeper of Seacourt
  (*Sekworth*) free chapel, 127
Sandes, William, gentleman, bailiff of the
  lordship of Godalming (*Godalmyng*),
  Surrey, 257
Sant *or* Saunt *or* Saunct, John DTh, OSB,
  abbot of Abingdon, 352, 352n
  convocation proctor, 279a
Saundres, Nicholas, 401E, 401A
Savage, John, esq., patron, 162
Savage, Thomas, bp of London, 287, 288,
  288a, 289, 289a, 291, 299, 306, 311
Savery, Robert, v. Marlborough, 108
Saxella, M. Francisco DTh, 305
Saye, M. Thomas BCL, r. Tidpit, 204
Saynt John, John, Bonhomme, priest, dean *or*
  r. Edington, 62
  convocation proctor, 279a, 290
Saynt John, Margaret *or* Margery, OSB of
  Shaftesbury, 365
Scarborgh *or* Skarborgh, Robert, OSA,
  canon of Breamore, 388S, 391D
Scochyn, Agnes *or* Annes, wife of Thomas
  Scochyn, abjuration of heresy, 323, 324
Scochyn *or* Sochyn, Thomas, tailor, 323

abjuration of heresy, 319, 320

Scott, Edward, cl., bp's proctor for visiting Rome, 272

Seacourt (*Sekworth*) free chapel, 127

Seffton, Henry, chapl., r. Teffont Evias, 231

Selby abbey (OSB), York dioc., orders conferred to t., 386, 387, 388

Semley (*Semele*) ch., 78

Seward, Elizabeth, wife of Thomas Seward, abjuration of heresy, 334, 335

Seward, Thomas, husbandman, abjuration of heresy, 334, 335

Sewy, Richard, OSA, prior Bisham, convocation proctor, 279a

Shaftesbury,
  abbey (OSB nuns), xi, xviii, xxi
    abbess *see* Alice Gibbes, Margery Twyneo
    abbess and conv., 263
      election of abbess, xiii, 365-368
      patrons, 16, 21, 25, 28, 75. 97, 177, 179, 186, 221
    prioress *see* Thomasina Kemer
  deanery, 351
    benefices not assessed but liable for clerical tenth (1495), 286
    cures or benefices exempt from clerical tenth (1495), 284, 285
  Holy Trinity ch., 367
  St James ch., exempt from clerical tenth (1495), 284
  St Laurence ch., 186
    not assessed but liable for clerical tenth (1495), 286
  St Martin ch., 75
  St Martin parish, hospital of St John the Baptist, 179
  St Rumbold (*S. Rowald, S. Rumwald juxta Shafton'*) ch., 177
    exempt from clerical tenth (1495), 284
    valuation for great subsidy (1497), 297

Shapton, John, OSB, monk of Milton, 394S, 399D

Sheen Charterhouse of Jesus of Bethlehem (OCarth), Winchester dioc.,
  exempt from clerical tenth (1495), 280
  prior and conv., patrons, 146, 147

Shefford *see* Great Shefford *or* Little Shefford

Shelford, Elisabeth, OSB of Shaftesbury, 365

Shepherd, William, chapl., r. Poole Keynes,196

Shephey, John,
  chapl. of the free chapel of Worplesdon, Lincoln dioc., 2
  r. Stockton 2

Shepperd, John, r. West Chelborough, 45

Shepton, John, r. Up Cerne, 7

Sherborne (*Shirborn*),
  abbey (OSB), 399, xi, xxi
    abbot *see* Peter Rampsham
    abbot and conv., patrons, 76
    orders conferred on monks, 385, 386, 387, 388, 394
    orders conferred to t., 386, 388, 389, 393, 394, 395, 401
  castle, xviii, xxi
    constable *see* Giles Daubeney
  ch. with hamlets, valuation, 351

Sherborne *or* Shirborn, M. Robert,
  prebendary of Warminster in Salisbury cath., 67, 79
  r. Childrey ch., 131

Sherrington (*Sheryngton alias Sherston*) ch., exempt from clerical tenth (1495), 284

Sherston vicarage, 223

Shirborn – see Sherborne

Shirborn, John, OSB of Abbotsbury, priest, 356

Shirborne, Thomas, OSB, monk of Sherborne, 386A, 387S, 394D

Shirwood, M. William, v. Malmesbury St Paul, 184

Shoreham ch., exempt from clerical tenth (1495), 280

Short, Hugh, priest, r. Stanbridge, 18

Shotesbroke, Alexander, OSB of Abingdon, scholar of Oxford, 352

Shottesbrooke (*Shotesbroke*) coll. ch., 121
  valuation for great subsidy (1497), 297

Shottow, William, 396S, 401D

Shrivenham (*Shryvenham*) ch., 318, 318n
  v., 318, 318n, 337

Skakylthorp, Thomas, chapl., v. Bishopstone prebendal ch., 181

Skynner, John, v. Thatcham, 195

Skynner, M. William MA, priest, v. Buckland, 129

Skypton, M. Richard, a senior chancery cl., 294, 294n

Sloughter, M. William, r. Christian Malford, 96

Smithfield (*Smythfeld*), London, St Bartholomew conventual ch. or hosp, 379

Smyth, John, chapl., proctor for Henry Sutton, 106

Smyth, John, Durham dioc., 387D

Smyth, Philip, v. Fisherton Delamere, 13

Smyth, Thomas, Durham dioc., 387S

Smyth, William, Exeter dioc., 392A, 393D, 394P

INDEX OF SUBJECTS

References in arabic figures are to entry numbers, those in roman figures to the introduction.

WILTSHIRE RECORD SOCIETY
(AS AT MAY 2015)

President: DR NEGLEY HARTE
Honorary Treasurer: IVOR M. SLOCOMBE
Honorary Secretary: MISS HELEN TAYLOR
General Editor: S.D. HOBBS

Committee:
DR V. BAINBRIDGE
D. CHALMERS
DR A. CRAVEN
DR D.A. CROWLEY
MRS S. THOMSON
K.H. ROGERS

Honorary Independent Examiner: C.C. DALE
Correspondent for the U.S.A.: SENIOR JUDGE R.W. OGBURN

PRIVATE MEMBERS

ADAMS, MS S, 23 Rockcliffe Avenue, Bathwick, Bath BA2 6QP

ANDERSON, MR D M, 6 Keepers Mews, Munster Road, Teddington, Middlesex TW11 9NB

BADENI, COUNTESS JUNE, Garden Cottage, Norton, Malmesbury SN16 0JX

BAINBRIDGE, DR V, 60 Gloucester Road, Lower Swainswick, Bath BA1 7BN

BANKS, MR B H, 16 Velley Hill, Gastard, Corsham, SN13 9PU

BARNETT, MR B A, 3 The Orangery, Academy Drive, Corsham, SN13 0SF

BATHE, MR G, Byeley in Densome, Woodgreen, Fordingbridge, Hants SP6 2QU

BAYLIFFE, MR B G, 3 Green Street, Brockworth, Gloucester GL3 4LT

BENNETT, DR N, Hawthorn House, Main Street, Nocton, Lincoln LN4 2BH

BERRETT, MR A M, 10 Primrose Hill Road, London NW3 3AD

BERRY, MR C, 17 Fore Street, Hayle, Cornwall TR27 4DX

BLAKE, MR P A, 18 Rosevine Road, London SW20 8RB

BOX, MR S D, 73 Silverdale Road, Earley, Reading RG6 2NF

BRAND, DR P A, 155 Kennington Road, London SE11 6SF

BROWN, MR D A, 36 Empire Road, Salisbury SP2 9DF

BROWN, MR G R, 6 Canbury Close, Amesbury, Salisbury SP4 7QF

BROWNING, MR E, 58 Stratton Road, Swindon SN1 2PR

BRYSON, DR A, Humanities Research Institute, 34 Gell Street, Sheffield S3 7QW

CARRIER, MR S, 9 Highfield Road, Bradford on Avon BA15 1AS

CARTER, MR D, Docton Court, 2 Myrtle Street, Appledore, Bideford EX39 1PH

CAWTHORNE, MRS N, 45 London Road,

Camberley, Surrey GU15 3UG

CHALMERS, MR D, Bay House West, Bay Hill, Ilminster, Somerset TA19 0AT

CHANDLER, DR J H, 8 Lock Warehouse, Severn Road, Gloucester GL1 2GA

CHURCH, MR T S, 12 Cathedral View, Winchester SO23 0PR

CLARK, MR G A, Highlands, 51a Brook Drive, Corsham SN13 9AX

CLARK, MRS V, 29 The Green, Marlborough SN8 1AW

COLCOMB, MR D M, 38 Roundway Park, Devizes SN10 2EO

COLES, MR H, Ebony House, 23 Lords Hill, Coleford, Glos GL16 8BG

COLLINS, MR A, 22 Innox Mill Close, Trowbridge BA14 9BA

COLLINS, MR A T, 36 Wasdale Close, Horndean, Waterlooville PO8 0DU

CONGLETON, LORD, West End Lodge, Ebbesbourne Wake, Salisbury SP5 5JW

COOMBES-LEWIS, MR R J, 45 Oakwood Park Road, Southgate, London N14 6QP

COOPER, MR S, 12 Victory Row, Royal Wootton Bassett, Swindon SN4 7BE

CRAVEN, DR A, 17 Steamship House, Gasferry Road, Bristol BS1 1GL

CROOK, MR P H, Bradavon, 45 The Dales, Cottingham, E Yorks HU16 5JS

CROUCH, MR J W, 25 Biddesden Lane, Ludgershall, Andover SP11 5PJ

CROWLEY, DR D A, 7 Eversley Court, Wymering Road, Southwold IP18 6BF

CUNNINGTON, MS J, 2766 Folkway Drive, Unit 40, Mississauga, Ont. L5L 3M3, Canada

DAKERS, PROF C, Ferneley Cottage, Water Street, Berwick St John, Shaftesbury SP7 0HS

D'ARCY, MR J N, The Old Vicarage, Edington, Westbury BA13 4QF

DAVIES, MRS A M, Barnside, Squires Lane, Old Clipstone, Mansfield NG21 9BP

DUNFORD, MRS J, 2 Greenditch House, Parsonage Lane, Chilcompton, Radstock Som BA3 4JU

DYSON, MRS L, 1 Dauntsey Ct, Duck St, West Lavington, Devizes SN10 4LR

EDE, DR M E, 12 Springfield Place, Lansdown, Bath BA1 5RA

EDWARDS, MR P C, 33 Longcroft Road, Devizes SN10 3AT

FIRMAGER, MRS G M, 72b High Street, Semington, Trowbridge BA14 6JR

FOSTER, MR R E, Cothelstone, 24 Francis Way, Salisbury, SP2 8EF

FOWLER, MRS C, 10 Ullswater Road, Wimborne, Dorset, BH21 1QT

FROST, MR B C, Red Tiles, Cadley, Collingbourne Ducis, Marlborough SN8 3EA

GAISFORD, MR J, 8 Dudley Road, London NW6 6JX

GALE, MRS J, PO Box 1015, Spit Junction, NSW 2088, Australia

GHEY, MR J G, Little Shute, Walditch, Bridport DT6 4LQ

GODDARD, MR R G H, Sinton Meadow, Stokes Lane, Leigh Sinton, Malvern, Worcs WR13 5DY

GOSLING, REV DR J, 1 Wiley Terrace, Wilton, Salisbury SP2 0HN

GOUGH, MISS P M, 39 Whitford Road, Bromsgrove, Worcs B61 7ED

GRIFFIN, D, C J, School of Geography, Queen's University, Belfast BT7 1NW

GRIST, MR M, 38 Springfield, Bradford on Avon BA15 1BB

HARDEN, MRS J O, The Croft, Tisbury Road, Fovant, Salisbury SP3 5JU

HARE, DR J N, 7 Owens Road, Winchester, Hants SO22 6RU

HARTE, DR N, St Aldhelm's Cottage, 5 Stokes Road, Corsham SN13 9AA

HEATON, MR R J, 60 Roberts Ride, Hazlemere, High Wycombe HP15 7AF

HELMHOLZ, PROF R W, Law School, 1111 East 60th Street, Chicago, Illinois 60637 USA

HERRON, MRS Pamela M, 25 Anvil Crescent, Broadstone, Dorset BH18 9DY

HICKMAN, MR M R, 184 Surrenden

Road, Brighton BN1 6NN

HICKS, MR I, 153 Cornbrash Rise, Trowbridge BA14 7TU

HICKS, PROF M A, Department of History, University of Winchester SO22 4NR

HILLMAN, MR R B, 20 West Ashton Road, Trowbridge BA14 7BQ

HOBBS, MR S, 63 West End, Westbury BA13 3JQ

HORNBY, MISS E, 70 Archers Court, Castle Street, Salisbury SP1 3WE

HOWELLS, DR Jane, 7 St Mark's Rd, Salisbury SP1 3AY

HUMPHRIES, MR A G, Rustics, Blacksmith's Lane, Harmston, Lincoln LN5 9SW

INGRAM, DR M J, Brasenose College, Oxford OX1 4AJ

JAMES, MR & MRS C, 20 The Willows, Yate, Bristol, BS37 5XL

JEACOCK, MR D, 16 Church Street, Wootton Bassett, Swindon SN4 7BQ

JOHNSTON, MRS J M, Greystone House, 3 Trowbridge Road, Bradford on Avon BA15 1EE

KEEN, MR A.G. 38 Rawson Street, Bilton, Harrogate HG1 4NU

KENT, MR T A, Rose Cottage, Isington, Alton, Hants GU34 4PN

KITE, MR P J, 13 Chestnut Avenue, Farnham GU9 8UL

KNEEBONE, MR W J R, 12 Hollis Way, Southwick, Trowbridge BA14 9PH

KNOWLES, MRS V A, New Woodland Cottage, Stanton St Bernard, Marlborough SN8 4LP

LANSDOWNE, MARQUIS OF, Bowood House, Calne SN11 0LZ

LAWES, MRS G, 48 Windsor Avenue, Leighton Buzzard LU7 1AP

LEE, DR J, 66 Kingshill Road, Bristol, BS4 2SN

LUSH, DR G J, 5 Braeside Road, West Moors, Ferndown, Dorset BH22 0JS

MARSH, REV R, 67 Hythe Crescent, Seaford, East Sussex BN25 3TZ

MARSHMAN, MR M J, 13 Regents Place, Bradford on Avon BA15 1ED

MARTIN, MS J, 21 Ashfield Road, Chippenham SN15 1QQ

MASLEN, MR A, 27 Fell Road, Westbury BA13 2GG

MATHEWS, MR R, 57, Anthony Road, Denistone, NSW 2114, Australia

MOLES, MRS M I, 40 Wyke Road, Trowbridge BA14 7NP

MONTAGUE, MR M D, 115 Stuarts Road, Katoomba, NSW 2780, Australia

MORIOKA, PROF K, 3-12, 4-chome, Sanno, Ota-ku, Tokyo, Japan

MORLAND, MRS N, 33 Shaftesbury Road, Wilton, Salisbury SP2 0DU

NAPPER, MR L R, 9 The Railway Terrace, Kemble, Cirencester GL7 6AU

NEWBURY, MR C COLES, 6 Leighton Green, Westbury BA13 3PN

NEWMAN, MRS R, Tanglewood, Laverstock Park, Salisbury SP1 1QJ

NICOLSON, MR A, Sissinghurst Castle, Cranbrook, Kent TN17 2AB

NOKES, MR P M A, c/o Parnella House, 23 Market Place, Devizes SN10 1JQ

OGBOURNE, MR J M V, 4 Aster Drive, Stafford ST16 1FH

OGBURN, MR D A, 110 Libby Lane, Galena, Missouri 65656, USA

OGBURN, SENIOR JUDGE R W, 303 West Hahn's Peak Avenue, Pueblo West, Colorado, 81007, USA

PARKER, DR P F, 45 Chitterne Road, Codford St Mary, Warminster BA12 0PG

PATIENCE, MR D C, 29 Priory Gardens, Stamford, Lincs PE9 2EG

PERRY, MR W A, 11 Buttercup Close, Salisbury SP2 8FA

POWELL, MRS N, 4 Verwood Drive, Bitton, Bristol BS15 6JP

PRICE, MR A J R, Littleton Mill, Littleton Pannell, Devizes SN10 4EP

PRIDGEON, DR E, 85 Kings Chase, Brentwood, Essex CM14 4LD

RAYBOULD, MISS F, 20 Radnor Road, Salisbury SP1 3PL

RAYMOND, MR S, 38 Princess Gardens, Trowbridge BA14 7PT

ROBERTS, MS M, 45 Spratts Barn, Royal Wootton Bassett, Swindon SN4 7JR

ROGERS, MR K H, Silverthorne House, East Town, West Ashton, Trowbridge BA14 6BE

ROLFE, MR R C, 4 The Slade, Newton Longville, Milton Keynes MK17 0DR

SAUNT, MRS B A, The Retreat, Corton, Warminster, BA12 0SL

SHARMAN-CRAWFORD, MR T, One Mapledurham View, Tilehurst, Reading RG31 6LF

SHELDRAKE, MR B, The Coach House, 4 Palmer Row, Weston super Mare, BS23 1RY

SHEWRING, MR P, 73 Woodland Road, Beddau, Pontypridd, Mid-Glamorgan CF38 2SE

SINGER, MR J, 49 Bradwall Road, Sandbach, Cheshire CW11 1GH

SLOCOMBE, MR I, 11 Belcombe Place, Bradford on Avon BA15 1NA

SMITH, MR P J, 6 Nuthatch, Longfield, Kent DA3 7NS

SNEYD, MR R H, Court Farm House, 22 Court Lane, Bratton, Westbury BA13 4RR

SPAETH, DR D A, School of History and Archaeology, 1 University Gardens, University of Glasgow G12 8QQ

STEVENAGE, MR M, 49 Centre Drive, Epping, Essex CM16 4JF

STONE, MR M J, 26 Awdry Close, Chippenham SN14 0TQ

SUTER, MRS C, 16 Swindon Road, Highworth, Swindon, SN6 7SL

SUTTON, MR A E, 22 Gravel Hill, Wimborne BH21 1RR

TATTON-BROWN, MR T, Fisherton Mill House, Mill Road, Salisbury, SP2 7RZ

TAYLOR, MR C C, 11 High Street, Pampisford, Cambridge CB2 4ES

TAYLOR, MISS H, 14 Pampas Court, Warminster BA12 8RS

THOMPSON, MR & MRS J B, 1 Bedwyn Common, Great Bedwyn, Marlborough SN8 3HZ

THOMSON, MRS S M, Home Close, High St, Codford, Warminster BA12 0NB

VINE, MR R E, 11 Brocks Mount, Stoke sub Hamdon, Somerset, TA14 6PJ

WAITE, MR R E, 18a Lower Road, Chinnor, Oxford OX9 4DT

WARREN, MR P, 6 The Meadows, Milford Mill Road, Salisbury SP1 2SS

WILLIAMSON, B, 40 Florence Park, Bristol BS6 7LR

WILTSHIRE, MR J, Cold Kitchen Cottage, Kingston Deverill, Warminster BA12 7HE

WILTSHIRE, MRS P E, 23 Little Parks, Holt, Trowbridge BA14 6QR

WOODWARD, A S, 35 West Ridge Drive, Stittsville, Ontario K2S 1S4, Canada

WRIGHT, MR D P, Gerrans, Coast Road, Cley-next-the-Sea, Holt NR25 7RZ

YOUNGER, MR C, The Old Chapel, Burbage, Marlborough SN8 3AA

UNITED KINGDOM INSTITUTIONS

Aberystwyth
  National Library of Wales
  University College of Wales
Bath. Reference Library
Birmingham. University Library
Bristol
  University of Bristol Library
Cambridge. University Library
Cheltenham. Bristol and Gloucestershire Archaeological Society
Chippenham
  Museum & Heritage Centre
  Wiltshire and Swindon History Centre
Coventry. University of Warwick Library
Devizes
  Wiltshire Archaeological & Natural History Society
  Wiltshire Family History Society
Durham. University Library
Edinburgh
  National Library of Scotland
  University Library
Exeter. University Library
Glasgow. University Library

Leeds. University Library
Leicester. University Library
Liverpool. University Library
London
　British Library
　College of Arms
　Guildhall Library
　Inner Temple Library
　Institute of Historical Research
　London Library
　The National Archives
　Royal Historical Society
　Society of Antiquaries
　Society of Genealogists
Manchester. John Rylands Library
Marlborough
　Memorial Library, Marlborough
　　College
　Merchant's House Trust
　Savernake Estate Office
Norwich. University of East Anglia

Library
Nottingham. University Library
Oxford
　Bodleian Library
　Exeter College Library
Reading. University Library
St Andrews. University Library
Salisbury
　Bourne Valley Historical Society
　Cathedral Library
　Salisbury and South Wilts Museum
Southampton. University Library
Swansea. University College Library
Swindon
　English Heritage
　Swindon Borough Council
Taunton. Somerset Archaeological and
　Natural History Society
Wetherby. British Library Document
　Supply Centre
York. University Library

INSTITUTIONS OVERSEAS

AUSTRALIA
Adelaide. University Library
Crawley. Reid Library, University of
　Western Australia
Melbourne. Victoria State Library

CANADA
Halifax. Killam Library, Dalhousie
　University
Toronto, Ont
　Pontifical Inst of Medieval Studies
　University of Toronto Library
Victoria, B.C. McPherson Library,
　University of Victoria

EIRE
Dublin. Trinity College Library

GERMANY
Gottingen. University Library

JAPAN
Sendai. Institute of Economic History,
　Tohoku University
Tokyo. Waseda University Library

NEW ZEALAND
Wellington. National Library of New
　Zealand

UNITED STATES OF AMERICA
Ann Arbor, Mich. Hatcher Library,
　University of Michigan
Athens, Ga. University of Georgia
　Libraries
Atlanta, Ga. The Robert W Woodruff
　Library, Emory University
Bloomington, Ind. Indiana University
　Library
Boston, Mass. New England Historic
　and Genealogical Society
Boulder, Colo. University of Colorado
　Library
Cambridge, Mass.
　Harvard College Library
　Harvard Law School Library
Charlottesville, Va. Alderman Library,
　University of Virginia
Chicago
　Newberry Library
　University of Chicago Library
Dallas, Texas. Public Library
Davis, Calif. University Library
East Lansing, Mich. Michigan State
　University Library
Evanston, Ill. United Libraries, Garrett/
　Evangelical, Seabury
Fort Wayne, Ind. Allen County Public
　Library

Houston, Texas. M.D. Anderson Library, University of Houston

Iowa City, Iowa. University of Iowa Libraries

Ithaca, NY. Cornell University Library

Los Angeles
Public Library
Young Research Library, University of California

Minneapolis, Minn. Wilson Library, University of Minnesota

New York
Columbia University of the City of New York

Princeton, N.J. Princeton University Libraries

Salt Lake City, Utah. Family History Library

San Marino, Calif. Henry E. Huntington Library

Santa Barbara, Calif. University of California Library

South Hadley, Mass. Williston Memorial Library, Mount Holyoke College

Urbana, Ill. University of Illinois Library

Washington. The Folger Shakespeare Library

Winston-Salem, N.C. Z.Smith Reynolds Library, Wake Forest University

LIST OF PUBLICATIONS

The Wiltshire Record Society was founded in 1937, as the Records Branch of the Wiltshire Archaeological and Natural History Society, to promote the publication of the documentary sources for the history of Wiltshire. The annual subscription is £15 for private and institutional members. In return, a member receives a volume each year. Prospective members should apply to the Hon. Secretary, c/o Wiltshire and Swindon History Centre, Cocklebury Road, Chippenham SN15 3QN. Many more members are needed.

The following volumes have been published. Price to members £15, and to non-members £20, postage extra. Most volumes up to 51 are still available from the Wiltshire and Swindon History Centre, Cocklebury Road, Chippenham SN15 3QN. Volumes 52-66 are available from Hobnob Press, c/o 8 Lock Warehouse, Severn Road, Gloucester GL1 2GA

1. *Abstracts of feet of fines relating to Wiltshire for the reigns of Edward I and Edward II*, ed. R.B. Pugh, 1939
2. *Accounts of the parliamentary garrisons of Great Chalfield and Malmesbury, 1645–1646*, ed. J.H.P. Pafford, 1940
3. *Calendar of Antrobus deeds before 1625*, ed. R.B. Pugh, 1947
4. *Wiltshire county records: minutes of proceedings in sessions, 1563 and 1574 to 1592*, ed. H.C. Johnson, 1949
5. *List of Wiltshire boroughs records earlier in date than 1836*, ed. M.G. Rathbone, 1951
6. *The Trowbridge woollen industry as illustrated by the stock books of John and Thomas Clark, 1804–1824*, ed. R.P. Beckinsale, 1951
7. *Guild stewards' book of the borough of Calne, 1561–1688*, ed. A.W. Mabbs, 1953
8. *Andrews' and Dury's map of Wiltshire, 1773: a reduced facsimile*, ed. Elizabeth Crittall, 1952
9. *Surveys of the manors of Philip, earl of Pembroke and Montgomery, 1631–2*, ed. E. Kerridge, 1953
10. *Two sixteenth century taxations lists, 1545 and 1576*, ed. G.D. Ramsay, 1954
11. *Wiltshire quarter sessions and assizes, 1736*, ed. J.P.M. Fowle, 1955
12. *Collectanea*, ed. N.J. Williams, 1956
13. *Progress notes of Warden Woodward for the Wiltshire estates of New College, Oxford, 1659–1675*, ed. R.L. Rickard, 1957
14. *Accounts and surveys of the Wiltshire lands of Adam de Stratton*, ed. M.W. Farr, 1959
15. *Tradesmen in early-Stuart Wiltshire: a miscellany*, ed. N.J. Williams, 1960
16. *Crown pleas of the Wiltshire eyre, 1249*, ed. C.A.F. Meekings, 1961
17. *Wiltshire apprentices and their masters, 1710–1760*, ed. Christabel Dale, 1961
18. *Hemingby's register*, ed. Helena M. Chew, 1963
19. *Documents illustrating the Wiltshire textile trades in the eighteenth century*, ed. Julia de L. Mann, 1964
20. *The diary of Thomas Naish*, ed. Doreen Slatter, 1965
21–2. *The rolls of Highworth hundred, 1275–1287*, 2 parts, ed. Brenda Farr, 1966, 1968
23. *The earl of Hertford's lieutenancy papers, 1603–1612*, ed. W.P.D. Murphy, 1969
24. *Court rolls of the Wiltshire manors of Adam de Stratton*, ed. R.B. Pugh, 1970
25. *Abstracts of Wiltshire inclosure awards and agreements*, ed. R.E. Sandell, 1971
26. *Civil pleas of the Wiltshire eyre, 1249*, ed. M.T. Clanchy, 1971
27. *Wiltshire returns to the bishop's visitation queries, 1783*, ed. Mary Ransome, 1972
28. *Wiltshire extents for debts, Edward I – Elizabeth I*, ed. Angela Conyers, 1973
29. *Abstracts of feet of fines relating to Wiltshire for the reign of Edward III*, ed. C.R. Elrington, 1974
30. *Abstracts of Wiltshire tithe apportionments*, ed. R.E. Sandell, 1975

31. *Poverty in early-Stuart Salisbury,* ed. Paul Slack, 1975
32. *The subscription book of Bishops Tounson and Davenant, 1620–40,* ed. B. Williams, 1977
33. *Wiltshire gaol delivery and trailbaston trials, 1275–1306,* ed. R.B. Pugh, 1978
34. *Lacock abbey charters,* ed. K.H. Rogers, 1979
35. *The cartulary of Bradenstoke priory,* ed. Vera C.M. London, 1979
36. *Wiltshire coroners' bills, 1752–1796,* ed. R.F. Hunnisett, 1981
37. *The justicing notebook of William Hunt, 1744–1749,* ed. Elizabeth Crittall, 1982
38. *Two Elizabethan women: correspondence of Joan and Maria Thynne, 1575–1611,* ed. Alison D. Wall, 1983
39. *The register of John Chandler, dean of Salisbury, 1404–17,* ed. T.C.B. Timmins, 1984
40. *Wiltshire dissenters' meeting house certificates and registrations, 1689–1852,* ed. J.H. Chandler, 1985
41. *Abstracts of feet of fines relating to Wiltshire, 1377–1509,* ed. J.L. Kirby, 1986
42. *The Edington cartulary,* ed. Janet H. Stevenson, 1987
43. *The commonplace book of Sir Edward Bayntun of Bromham,* ed. Jane Freeman, 1988
44. *The diaries of Jeffery Whitaker, schoolmaster of Bratton, 1739–1741,* ed. Marjorie Reeves and Jean Morrison, 1989
45. *The Wiltshire tax list of 1332,* ed. D.A. Crowley, 1989
46. *Calendar of Bradford-on-Avon settlement examinations and removal orders, 1725–98,* ed. Phyllis Hembry, 1990
47. *Early trade directories of Wiltshire,* ed. K.H. Rogers and indexed by J.H. Chandler, 1992
48. *Star chamber suits of John and Thomas Warneford,* ed. F.E. Warneford, 1993
49. *The Hungerford Cartulary: a calendar of the earl of Radnor's cartulary of the Hungerford family,* ed. J.L. Kirby, 1994
50. *The Letters of John Peniston, Salisbury architect, Catholic, and Yeomanry Officer, 1823–1830,* ed. M. Cowan, 1996
51. *The Apprentice Registers of the Wiltshire Society, 1817–1922,* ed. H. R. Henly, 1997
52. *Printed Maps of Wiltshire 1787–1844: a selection of topographical, road and canal maps in facsimile,* ed. John Chandler, 1998
53. *Monumental Inscriptions of Wiltshire: an edition, in facsimile, of Monumental Inscriptions in the County of Wilton, by Sir Thomas Phillipps,* ed. Peter Sherlock, 2000
54. *The First General Entry Book of the City of Salisbury, 1387–1452,* ed. David R. Carr, 2001
55. *Devizes Division income tax assessments, 1842–1860,* ed. Robert Colley, 2002
56. *Wiltshire Glebe Terriers, 1588–1827,* ed. Steven Hobbs, 2003
57. *Wiltshire Farming in the Seventeenth Century,* ed. Joseph Bettey, 2005
58. *Early Motor Vehicle Registration in Wiltshire, 1903–1914,* ed. Ian Hicks, 2006
59. *Marlborough Probate Inventories, 1591–1775,* ed. Lorelei Williams and Sally Thomson, 2007
60. *The Hungerford Cartulary, part 2: a calendar of the Hobhouse cartulary of the Hungerford family,* ed. J.L. Kirby, 2007
61. *The Court Records of Brinkworth and Charlton,* ed. Douglas Crowley, 2009
62. *The Diary of William Henry Tucker, 1825–1850,* ed. Helen Rogers, 2009
63. *Gleanings from Wiltshire Parish Registers,* ed. Steven Hobbs, 2010
64. *William Small's Cherished Memories and Associations,* ed. Jane Howells and Ruth Newman, 2011
65. *Crown Pleas of the Wiltshire Eyre, 1268,* ed. Brenda Farr and Christopher Elrington, rev. Henry Summerson, 2012
66. *The Minute Books of Froxfield Almshouse, 1714–1866,* ed. Douglas Crowley, 2013
67. *Wiltshire Quarter Sessions Order Book, 1642-1654,* ed. Ivor Slocombe, 2014

VOLUMES IN PREPARATION

The Churchwardens' accounts of St. Mary's, Devizes, 1600–1700, edited by Alex Craven; *The Arundells in the late 18th century*, edited by Barry Williamson; *Public health in 19th-century Wiltshire*, edited by Negley Harte; *Braydon Forest explained, 1086-1640*, edited by Douglas Crowley; *The parish registers of Thomas Crockford, 1613–29*, edited by C.C. Newbury. The volumes will not necessarily appear in this order.

A leaflet giving full details may be obtained from the Hon. Secretary, c/o Wiltshire and Swindon History Centre, Cocklebury Road, Chippenham, Wilts. SN15 3QN.